Can Themba

Can Themba

The Making and Breaking of the Intellectual Tsotsi

A BIOGRAPHY

Siphiwo Mahala

WITS UNIVERSITY PRESS

Published in South Africa by:
Wits University Press
1 Jan Smuts Avenue
Johannesburg 2001

www.witspress.co.za

First published 2022

http://dx.doi.org.10.18772/12022037311

978-1-77614-731-1 (Paperback)
978-1-77614-732-8 (Hardback)
978-1-77614-733-5 (Web PDF)
978-1-77614-734-2 (EPUB)

This work is based on research supported by the National Institute for the Humanities and Social Sciences. Opinions expressed are those of the author and are not necessarily to be attributed to the NIHSS.

Project manager: Alison Paulin
Editor: Helen Moffett
Copyeditor: Sally Hines
Proofreader: Lisa Compton
Indexer: Elaine Williams
Cover design: Hybrid Creative
Cover image: © Jürgen Schadeberg; permission to use granted by Claudia Schadeberg.
Typeset in 10.5 point Plantin

In memory of Professor Mbulelo Mzamane,
whose light still shines my path

Can Themba was what he was and not what he could have been because his country is what it is.

Harry Mashabela — *The Classic* (1968), 10

Contents

List of Illustrations

Acknowledgements

This book is based on my thesis 'Inside the House of Truth: The Construction, Destruction and Reconstruction of Can Themba', which was submitted for the fulfilment of my doctoral degree at the University of South Africa (UNISA) in 2017. I am indebted to the Department of English Studies at UNISA for accepting my proposal and affording me an opportunity to pursue doctoral studies on the life of Can Themba. I am particularly grateful to Professor Michael Kgomotso Masemola, who guided me through the process. The book was written under the auspices of the Johannesburg Institute for Advanced Study at the University of Johannesburg and supported by the National Institute for the Humanities and Social Sciences.

The following individuals graciously made time to talk about Can Themba during the research stage of this project between the years 2013 and 2020: Njabulo S. Ndebele, Keorapetse Kgositsile, Pitika Ntuli, Nadine Gordimer, Don Mattera, Mothobi Mutloatse, Jürgen Schadeberg, Joe Thloloe, Anne Themba, Juby Mayet, Lucas Ledwaba, Muxe Nkondo, Mbulelo Mzamane, Peter Magubane, Mangosuthu Buthelezi, Sol Rachilo, Ahmed Kathrada, Parks Mangena, Simon Maziya, Malcolm Hart, Lindiwe Mabuza and Abdul Bham. Some of the interviewees, including Mbulelo Mzamane, Nadine Gordimer, Anne Themba, Ahmed Kathrada, Keorapetse Kgositsile, Jürgen Schadeberg, Juby Mayet, Parks Mangena, Lindiwe Mabuza and Malcolm Hart, have since passed on. In addition to these formal interviews, I had casual musings with a number of people who shared insights and perspectives on Can Themba and his generation. Among others, I can make mention of Ngũgĩ wa Thiong'o and the late Lewis Nkosi, whose formidable insights were most edifying.

I thank my editor, Helen Moffett, who once again demonstrated the utmost patience, mental dexterity and erudition as we walked the precarious journey towards delivering our fourth baby together.

I unreservedly acknowledge legendary writer-turned-filmmaker Mtutuzeli Matshoba, who assisted with the recording of my conversations with some of the people who knew Themba. Matshoba brought on board a distinguished film crew, including Wiseman Mabusela, Lawrence Lerato Lichaba, Mpho Ramathuthu, Michael Moagi Matsie and Paul Zisiwe. Special thanks to my research assistant, Uviwe Mshumpela, who has been my reliable companion on this journey.

This book would not have been possible without the support of Can Themba's daughters, Morongwa and Yvonne Themba, who graciously gave me access to family documents. They also granted me permission to peruse their father's student records at the University of Fort Hare. I would like to extend a special word of gratitude to the Amazwi South African Museum of Literature for their assistance during the research stage of this project.

I thank my family for their unyielding support and patience while I was pursuing this project. I could not be the husband that I wanted to be to my wife, Miliswa, nor was I able to be the father that I ought to have been to our three daughters, Mihlali, Qhama and Kuhle; they nevertheless remained supportive of my endeavours throughout this period.

Lastly, I am grateful for the phenomenal life of Can Themba. Although he died more than fifty years ago, he continues to inspire writers and readers with the timelessness of his works. This book will hopefully make a significant contribution to the long journey towards rediscovering and immortalising Can Themba.

Introduction

> *He [Can Themba] lent to his thoughts the same vivid imagery, sharp staccato rhythm of the township language of the urban tsotsi, because he himself was the supreme intellectual tsotsi of them all.*
>
> Lewis Nkosi — *Writing Home* (2016), 208

Lewis Nkosi's words have become so familiar to readers and scholars of Can Themba that we have forgotten how startling they are, given that tsotsis were (and are) feared criminals, while Themba was the quintessential black urban intellectual of his times. But they plunge us into the heart of the myth of who Themba really was, reflecting his status as a writer who straddled fault lines, epitomised paradoxes, and about whom both too much and too little is known (or assumed).

One of these paradoxes is that when Themba died in 1967, at the tender age of 43, he did not have a book to his name – and yet he remains one of the most influential minds in the history of literature and journalism in South Africa. More than half a century later, his name is still part of public discourse and creative flow. This bears testament to the resilience of his voice, which continues to reverberate from beyond the grave.

Themba's short story 'The Suit' remains his most famous work and arguably the most successful short story by a South African writer. First published in the inaugural issue of Nat Nakasa's literary journal *The Classic* in 1963, it remains the pinnacle of his creative output.[1] Aggrey Klaaste rightfully describes 'The Suit' as a story that has 'all the elements of a classic'.[2] Over a period of nearly six decades, it has been translated, republished and adapted numerous times into different genres, ranging from graphics to theatre and film. The overwhelming success of 'The Suit' has unfortunately overshadowed many of Themba's other works, some of which have equally great potential.

The critical work published on Themba thus far mostly covers his journalistic and literary productions. Where his biographical background surfaces, it is primarily with regard to the period when he worked for *Drum* magazine, and very little about his life pre- and post-*Drum* has been documented. David Rabkin argues that a lot more has been written about Themba than he had himself written.[3] Yet, the converse is also true: Themba wrote a great deal, but because of the difficulties of collating his work (see Chapter 16), some of it has received little critical attention.

This leaves a significant void in our critical evaluation and understanding of his works, as well as what made him and what broke him in the end.

Despite the fact that Themba features in almost every historic study pertaining to *Drum* magazine and Sophiatown, and that his peers have written extensively about him, there is no study that comprehensively explores his human experience. This book endeavours to consolidate the dispersed fragments necessary in re-membering the vital elements in reconstructing Themba's life and literary legacy.

Themba was as fun and exciting in person as he was as a writer. His intellectual acumen, artistic flair, scholarly aptitude, expansive sense of irony, and abundant wit and humour are some of his characteristics most distinctly remembered by those who interacted with him either in person or through his works. Ursula A. Barnett, literary critic, described Themba as 'the most interesting personality and perhaps the most talented of the writers of the late fifties and early sixties'.[4]

Nkosi was probably the most distinguished chronicler (and also the fiercest critic) of the 1950s' *Drum* generation of writers, and also a 'remarkable judge of character', according to former *Drum* journalist Doc Bikitsha. It was Nkosi's belief that Themba had the 'liveliest mind and the best command of the English language' of his generation. Bikitsha agreed: 'Can's beauty and talent lay in his prowess of thought, writing and debate.'[5]

It is no wonder his writings have outlived him and many of his contemporaries, garnering wide readership and filling theatres more than five decades after his passing. His works continue to inspire different generations of readers and writers alike.

Themba's intellectual disposition has been widely recognised and celebrated by his contemporaries and successive generations in journalistic, literary and academic spaces. But he was no ivory-tower academic; trained as a teacher and plying his trade as a journalist, he staged his debates and discussions in the shebeens of Johannesburg and in his abode, the aptly named 'House of Truth'. Mcebisi Ndletyana's adaption of Antonio Gramsci is useful in expanding on what is meant by describing Themba as a public intellectual: 'Intellectuals are individuals who, by virtue of their position in society and intellectual training, are preoccupied with abstract ideas, not only for self-gratification, but also to fulfil a public role.'[6] As an 'intellectual tsotsi', Themba's intellectual disposition defied orthodoxies and often allied him to those resented, rendered invisible and excluded in society (see Chapter 12).

In juxtaposing Themba's intellectual acumen with the cult of a tsotsi, Nkosi alluded to his former colleague's social and historical location. A tsotsi can be described as a slick township thug or criminal who terrorises communities through violent attacks, assault and robbery; a robust subculture, they are often distinguishable through their attire and patois. Father Trevor Huddleston, in his memoir of his years in Sophiatown, *Naught for Your Comfort*, notes that 'the tsotsi is the supreme symbol of a society which does not care. His knife and his revolver are significant not only for today but for tomorrow.'[7]

Huddleston's claim that tsotsis were part of the societies they tormented was shared by Themba's contemporary and fellow journalist Henry Nxumalo, who argued that tsotsis were not an exotic tribe situated outside society, but a product of the socio-economic conditions of black people in South African townships of the time:

> Of course, tsotsis are made as well as born: they are made every day on the Reef, it is true that when a young boy takes a wrong turning it is partly his own fault; but the amount of crime in a city varies with the well-being or poverty of the mass of its citizens. With the grinding poverty and the sea of squalor that surrounds the 'Golden City', it is not difficult to understand the rest. There is a struggle for existence, and the individual intends to survive.[8]

While Nxumalo, Arthur Maimane, Bloke Modisane and other scribes from the 1950s' generation wrote about the tsotsi phenomenon, according to Muxe Nkondo in an exclusive interview in 2015, Themba stands out for 'humanising', perhaps even romanticising, the tsotsi in his writings.[9] Many of his stories, both fiction and non-fiction, feature the tsotsi character, whether referred to as a thug, an urchin or a gangster. As a writer who chronicled and interrogated the stories of the black urban world, Themba was able to locate the tsotsi and the intellectual in the same social and cultural space.

Themba might not have been a knife-wielding or gun-toting criminal, but he immersed himself in the lives of tsotsis: he spoke their language, dressed like a tsotsi and drank with them in shebeens. They have an almost permanent presence in his writing, and the relationship flowed both ways: poetry became one of their meeting points, as the Sophiatown tsotsis had a penchant for Shakespeare's sonnets (which they would force the local intellectuals to recite). Themba, in particular, used to write poetry for some of the gangsters, which they intended to use to impress girls. In the film *Come Back, Africa*, in which he had no script to follow but had to improvise a debate with friends, Themba appears sympathetic to Marumu, the tsotsi character, and explains how the trauma of losing his father at an early age, and the poverty that led him to desiring small things like sweets, might be the cause of his aggression: 'He wanted bigger things, he wanted to grab things that were bigger and the only way you could get those things was through force, and so he thought in terms of force …'[10]

Themba and his peers often suffered the same fate as the tsotsis – arrest and imprisonment, even if for different reasons. It was because of their proximity to the tsotsi, their intertwined lives, that Themba claimed that the tsotsis 'saw us as cousins'.[11] It was because of this connection that Nkosi saw Themba as the embodiment of the 'intellectual' and 'tsotsi' paradox.

Paul Gready expands on the ways that Themba embraced the tsotsis to the extent of romanticising their ways, even seeing his own condition mirrored in theirs: 'Themba tried to ally himself with a private conception of the tsotsi, and thereby to the people. He was the supreme "intellectual tsotsi", who eventually romantically compared the violence of the gangs to that of the possessed, self-destructive artist, that is, himself. Onto the romantic myth of the gangster Themba super-imposed his own myth of the artist.'[12]

Gready's words remind us that Themba was in many ways a troubled genius. In addition to the challenges of being a black professional operating within the confines of the apartheid state, Themba was frustrated by the system that did not recognise his hard-earned qualifications, had no appreciation for his experience, and certainly paid no regard to his intellectual contribution, talent and accomplishments. His reliance on alcohol to cope with his personal troubles is well documented.

In the end, he was overwhelmed by a combination of forces that left him in despair. Driven out of his home country, he lived a destructive life in exile, leading to his untimely demise in 1967, thus depriving the literary world of the opportunity to benefit further from his potential. Themba's protégé and veteran journalist Harry Mashabela put it succinctly in his tribute to the fallen scribe when he said: 'Can Themba was what he was and not what he could have been because his country is what it is.'[13] Hence Nkosi's lament in his tribute to Themba: 'We mourn what might have been.'[14]

At the time of his passing, Themba's works were banned in South Africa under the Suppression of Communism Amendment Act of 1965. In yet another paradox, his passing sparked interest and breathed new life into his oeuvre, thus entrenching his name in the annals of journalism and the literary landscape in South Africa. While his works are widely celebrated today, reference to his biographical background is scant. Where reference is made to biographical details, there are barely any substantive facts that give an epistemological account.

Another trend that has perhaps skewed our ability to gauge Themba's life and works clearly is the established pattern in scholarship of discussing Themba as part of a discursive analysis of a generation. Perhaps the most intensive of the texts in grappling with Themba as a person is Nkosi's tribute, in which he pays homage to two of his contemporaries – Can Themba and Nat Nakasa.[15] Many scholars, however, focus on Themba's works without making any direct links to his life experiences, and reference to his personal traits are made only glibly.

This is true not only of scholarly discussion of Themba, in particular, but of the entire generation of '*Drum* Boys', who are often treated as a homogeneous group. This is reflected in Lucky Mathebe's claim that 'during most of the time when the history of the *Drum* school is written and discussed, the writers are singularly treated as an inferior type of elite'.[16] In many ways, Themba has become the primary victim of the wholesale packaging of this generation of writers. He is projected as a representative of a generation: the reflection of the much-romanticised African urban world, the epitome of black writing in the 1950s and 1960s in all its glory and defects.

Themba joined *Drum* magazine at the point of its transformation in 1953, and became a formidable force in its renewal at a time when it was reinventing itself as a publication for urban Africans – a far cry from the initial *African Drum*, which presented a 'return to the tribe' mantra. There is no doubt that *Drum* magazine played a pivotal role in chronicling the emergent black urban world of the 1950s and providing a publishing platform for authentic black voices, thus speaking directly to black audiences about their own life experiences and perspectives. However, the treatment of these writers as a collective comes at the expense of their individual qualities, and carries the risk of distorting their distinct characters, capabilities and experiences.

This is an important point of departure for this book: I try to go beyond the usual focus on the pinnacle of Themba's journalistic and writing careers and pay particular attention to his educational and intellectual journey prior to joining *Drum* magazine, as well as the post-*Drum* years of deterioration and eventual demise.

In its most prosaic sense, then, this book endeavours to answer the basic question, 'Who was Can Themba?' Answering this central question means investigating Themba's biodata and linking this both to what he wrote, and what has been written about him and his work. In grappling with this question, particular attention has to be paid to the making and the breaking of Themba; how he immortalised himself in his writing, while at the same time needing to be recreated through various projects of recovering his work over the years. This approach compels us to go beyond the stereotype of the venerated writer and journalist, to try to trace how he became the iconoclastic figure that we know today, and the factors that contributed to this.

The decision to select Can Themba as the subject of this biographical text is obviously premised on recognition and appreciation of his work, and is therefore subjective. I have had to consciously suppress the temptation to write a hagiography instead of objectively engaging with biographical elements. My juxtaposition of the construction and destruction of Themba acknowledges that an honest account of his life history entails both positive and negative elements. Yet, I have tried to both explore and evade the binaries of the apparent contradictions and paradoxes of his life. In writing this biographical text, I have tried to cast the net wide to include aspects that either have not received adequate attention or have been overlooked in the past.

In any attempt to trace Themba's literary and journalistic trail, it soon becomes evident that his trajectory is complex and multifaceted, branching through the history of his education, romantic and domestic life, politics and professional experiences.

A biography is often understood as a text that mirrors the life and times of specific individuals and their societies. Yet, a mirror is a passive object that only reflects what is put in front of it. My interest goes beyond documenting or mirroring a series of dates and facts. My intention is to wrestle with the experiences and the emotions behind the facts, to come as close as possible to representing Themba in human form, while at the same time juxtaposing his life with his works. This compels us to trace the contours of Themba's trail, taking stock of each and every mound and mountain on which he left his footprint. This book, therefore, goes beyond the biographical. It is an attempt to present an integrated construct that draws parallels between the life and times of Themba and his entire body of work.

One constant challenge in writing the life history of someone long after their death is that there are often hidden stories, contradictory facts, subjective memories and contending narratives about such individuals. In addition to this, there are the dangers of anachronism, in which the biographer situates the story in a discordant historical context. To avoid this in researching the life of this enigmatic personality, I had to 'generate' primary material as well as consult texts, scholarly resources, archival material and oral narratives. A substantial amount of the information included in this book comes from more than twenty exclusive interviews I conducted with people who knew and interacted with Themba personally, or were touched by his work. These oral sources have provided elements and information not previously featured in any other research on Themba. The fact that so many of those who kindly shared their memories and reflections with me have passed away since I began the interviews in 2013 is an indication of how fragile our past is, and how important it is to uncover its truths before they are lost to us.

The telling of the truth in all its glory and defects was central to Themba's being. As a teacher, journalist, short story writer and philosopher, he was a man in search of truth. Naming his modest dwelling the House of Truth was a declaration of the ideals he cherished. The House of Truth may once have been a physical place (long since crushed by apartheid bulldozers), but it lives on today as a metaphor for Themba's dynamic but incomplete life project. It represents the vibrancy of the debate and intellectual engagement in which he so fervently believed. It represents the reading and writing culture that was his forte. It also symbolises the dreams he cherished and pursued, but could never realise in his lifetime. Most importantly, it represents who Themba was and what he stood for. The re-emergence of the House of Truth in various forms, including in the shape of a play, is a clear demonstration of the resilience of his intellectual legacy. To understand Can Themba, to understand the forces that made him and broke him, we need to get inside the House of Truth where his life unfolded. Let us open the door and step right in.

PART I

Death and Birth of a Scribe

1

A Knock on the Door

We were those sensitive might-have-beens who had knocked on the door of white civilisation (at the highest levels that South Africa could offer) and had heard a gruff 'No' or a 'Yes' so shaky and insincere that we withdrew our snail horns at once.

Can Themba — *Requiem for Sophiatown* (2006), 57

He knocked on the door. There was no response. He knocked again, and listened. All was quiet. He tried to turn the doorknob and push the door open. It was locked from the inside. He knocked once more, harder this time. Nothing. He pressed his ear against the wooden door. Silence.

With one eye closed, he peeped through the keyhole. He could make out a lanky man lying in bed with his feet pointing heavenwards. It was definitely the man he was looking for. Why on earth was he not opening? He banged on the door with his fist, shouting his name: 'Bra Can! Bra Can Themba!' No response. He hammered on the door. Silence.

It was Friday, 8 September 1967. The 25-year-old Pitika Ntuli had travelled all the way from Lubombo, a journey of about 25 kilometres, to Manzini in Swaziland (now the Kingdom of eSwatini), where his mentor rented a flat. At the time Can Themba – full name Daniel Canodoce Themba, also known as Dorsay – was a teacher at St Joseph's Catholic Mission School in Umzimpofu, about five kilometres outside Manzini. He often hosted young men in search of knowledge and intellectual stimulation.

Now Ntuli's friend, Bicca Maseko, suggested that they go watch a film at the bioskop (cinema) and come back later. It was a Friday afternoon, and the schools had closed for the September holidays. Teacher Can Themba had probably drunk a little too much, a little too early, and had passed out, Maseko reasoned. With little choice, Ntuli concurred, and left reluctantly. He kept looking over his shoulder as they walked away, hoping that the door would fly open.

Ntuli, a young South African student exiled in Swaziland, was intending to visit the man who had been his role model and mentor since higher primary school days. Growing up in Witbank (now eMalahleni) in the former Eastern Transvaal (now Mpumalanga Province), Ntuli often visited Sophiatown, a culturally and politically vibrant township in Johannesburg, during holidays and over some weekends. Here he came to know of one Can Themba, a former teacher who had become famous as a journalist plying his trade with *Drum* magazine. Despite his fame, Themba remained humble and opened his door to everyone. He had turned his abode in Sophiatown, which he named the House of Truth, into a place for candid debate and intellectual engagement.

Themba was regarded by many as a 'people's person', and by opening his house to the community of Sophiatown, he demonstrated his lifelong commitment to teaching and mentoring. The House of Truth was one of the vehicles he employed to execute his mission of intellectual engagement and education. His teaching was never confined within the walls of the classroom.

Ntuli was at first simply a curious boy who had stumbled into a hub of intellectual debate at Themba's House of Truth, and was fascinated by how well black men like Bloke Modisane, Nat Nakasa and Themba spoke English. This exposure would prove to be a life-changing experience for him, and would play an important role in the development of his consciousness.

According to Ntuli, who had imbibed wisdom directly from the source at the House of Truth, Themba would take a nonchalantly uttered word and decipher profound meanings from it: 'Can Themba was absolutely one of a kind, the warmness of his spirit, the sharpness, the witticism. You'd utter a statement and immediately you've uttered a statement, he's going to pick one word out of that statement and turn it actually upside-down and make you realise what you've actually said, how profound the statement you've made is.'[1]

A culture of debate and intellectual engagement had been part of Themba's social milieu since his days as a student at the University of Fort Hare, where he engaged in discussions with fellow students – including the likes of Robert Sobukwe, Duma Nokwe, Dennis Brutus and many others who would later become prominent political and cultural leaders of society. Former cabinet minister, leader of the Inkatha Freedom Party (IFP) and prime minister of the Zulu Kingdom, Prince Mangosuthu Buthelezi, has fond memories of Themba hosting gatherings in his room at university.[2] The establishment of the House of Truth, and the activities it hosted, continued this tradition. The subjects of interest included a wide range of topics and issues, from literature to history, philosophy to politics, education to journalism, and these conversations fed into Themba's stories.

In all his engagements, whether formal or informal, Themba's mission was to impart knowledge. His determination to nurture young minds, inside and outside the classroom, speaks of a visionary committed to the future of the intellectual tradition in Africa. His various teaching stints, the conversations he anchored in the newsroom, the intellectual engagements he embarked upon in the House of Truth, the private lessons he offered to individuals, and his public speaking engagements bear testament to a man who was determined to share his knowledge with others. The House of Truth, a space where he could wield control, was a platform he established precisely for this purpose. It was a place not just of intellectual growth, but where strong bonds of friendship and mentorship were forged.

One man who benefited from Themba's teachings both inside and outside the classroom was Stanley Motjuwadi, a legendary journalist in his own right. Motjuwadi was Themba's matric student at Madibane High School in 1950. When Themba became the associate editor of *Drum* magazine, then news editor of the *Golden City Post* newspaper and editor of *Africa!* magazine, he recruited his former students. Motjuwadi and his friend Casey Motsisi came to work with him, both establishing themselves as formidable voices in the world of journalism. According to Motjuwadi's tribute to Themba, published in *The World of Can Themba*, the House of Truth was 'Can's way of cocking a snook at snobbery, officialdom and anything that smacked of the formal. Everybody but a snob was welcome at The House of Truth.'[3]

Indeed, all and sundry were welcome at the House of Truth. It was where everything concerning human experience in Sophiatown was told with candour, often inspired by liquor. There were no secrets, or, at least, there were not meant to be any. 'Can loved company and he was superb company himself, a sparkling conversationalist with razor-sharp repartee,' Motjuwadi elaborated. 'Aspiring writers, unemployed journalists, frustrated artists, women in search of a good time – all thronged to the House of Truth. The only passport to enter it was to slough off hypocrisy when stepping on the threshold.'[4]

Motjuwadi's friend, former schoolmate and colleague, Casey Motsisi, was to become Themba's right-hand man for a number of years. Motsisi commented on the contradictions presented by Themba's influence on some of the younger people who flocked to the House of Truth. Much as he offered a platform for intellectual growth and honest debate, with the regular presence of alcohol in the conversations, it was inevitable that some would lean more towards the bottle than they did to intellectual rigour. Motsisi was nevertheless baffled by the view held by some of Themba's detractors – that he was a 'corruptor of youth', primarily through exposing them to alcohol. He believed that Themba was the 'very epitome of a man of genius', whose major preoccupation was intellectual development, fundamental for ambitious young people.[5]

While clearly the House of Truth meant different things to different people, with its legacy still a sometimes contentious issue, there is no doubt that both debate and alcohol flowed freely. In our interview held in 2015, Muxe Nkondo succinctly captures the paradoxes of the House of Truth: 'It was the only forum where the intelligentsia would meet with ordinary people to discuss issues. It went beyond just drinking beer and what have you, to providing a venue, a kind of parliament of the streets; it is where serious issues were discussed.'[6]

Sylvester Stein, *Drum* magazine editor and one of the white men who had the honour of setting foot in Themba's abode, reflected on the debates at the House of Truth: 'It was here in Sophiatown that Can Themba had matured in intellectual strength, and it was there at his home base, The House of Truth, where blacks and honorary blacks gathered together to debate a thousand topics ranging from Sartre's philosophy to the vintages of hooch.'[7] It is clear that for Themba, alcohol was a key ingredient in opening a path to good conversation.

At the official opening ceremony for the House of Truth, about thirty guests filled the small space, including community members, township drunkards, journalists and a lone white man. The event featured a live performance by one of the most famous women in the whole of Africa – Dolly Rathebe. Dolly was everybody's dream girl: she had made a name for herself as a cover girl, musician and a film star. She broke into fame in 1949, when she starred in a British-produced movie, *Jim Comes to Joburg*, one of the first films set in South Africa that portrayed urban blacks in a positive light. She was so popular that her name found its way into the slang of the time, wherein the tsotsis would say 'I'm Dolly', when they meant they were fine, and 'I'm double Dolly', when they felt really good. Dolly was there to honour Themba, who was already celebrated as a writer and popular reporter at *Drum*, the most widely distributed magazine in sub-Saharan Africa. The only white man present was Anthony Sampson, whose pen vividly chronicled this particular event in his 1956 book, *Drum: A Venture into the New Africa.*

Themba took the occasion so seriously that before addressing the guests, he put on his academic gown from Fort Hare University, where he had graduated with a BA degree. This was, of course, after he performed his famous clockwork dance. In describing the dance, Sampson writes, 'His whole body twisted into a sharp curve; one hand curled up behind his back, the other, tense with expression, gripped into his side. His feet jerked as if on hot coals; his body was consumed with the rhythm, lost to the world around him like an epileptic. His tongue slid between his teeth, and his face was contorted in a grimace.'[8]

As the master of ceremonies at his own function, Themba made a formal speech in which he explained that they were gathered there that evening to witness the christening of his 'noble mansion', which he had the honour to name 'The House of Truth!'.[9] It goes without saying that nothing but the truth could be uttered in the house.

His abode was not the only one that had a name in Sophiatown, but it was the only one reported to have had a formal opening ceremony. Each house name had a special significance in reflecting the vision of the proprietor. Themba's friend and colleague, Modisane, called his house Sunset Boulevard.[10] Others included the House of Commons and the House of Saints.[11] The House of Truth was obviously designed to stay true to its name – to be a free space where debate was shaped by objective truths.

One of the truths is that the House of Truth at 111 Ray Street was a one-and-a-half-roomed bachelor flat. It was in fact a single room, with a dividing curtain that separated the bed from the living area. The elaborate opening ceremony was typical of Themba's abundant wit and slapstick humour, features of both his personality and his writings. The House of Truth was to become a metaphor that epitomised Themba's life philosophy and legacy.

Pitika Ntuli, the young man knocking in vain at the door of Themba's Swaziland flat, imbibed more than just the culture of debate, a flair for language and passion for the written word from the House of Truth; he also adopted and replicated the idea of a forum for debate and intellectual engagement at later stages of his life. When he went into exile in Swaziland in the mid-1960s, he established his own version of the House of Truth in Lubombo.

In the 1960s, there was a large South African community in Swaziland. Following the Sharpeville massacre in March 1960, the banning of political parties and the Rivonia Treason Trial (which lasted from 1963 to 1964), many South African activists, including students, teachers, writers and other professionals, streamed out of the country, either to escape from the brutalities and crudities of apartheid, or to fight against apartheid from outside the country. Swaziland, as a British protectorate sharing borders with South Africa, was one of the frontline states to which South African activists travelled or escaped before moving on to other countries. It was not uncommon, therefore, to bump into South Africans on the streets of Mbabane, Manzini or any of the towns in Swaziland.

It was, however, a huge surprise when someone on the streets of Manzini called Ntuli to turn around. When he did so, he realised that the man hailing him was none other than Can Themba. After exchanging the normal pleasantries, Ntuli broke the news that he had established his own House of Truth in Lubombo.

Weeks later, while Ntuli was having a heated debate with his friends, with Solly Magwagwa holding the floor, the great Can Themba showed up. The discussion continued until Themba had to leave. The group arranged to meet on weekends, when the young men could visit their mentor in Manzini. The very next week, they had a discussion on the writer and philosopher Edward Said at Themba's place in Manzini. 'He liked talking about Edward Said; [he said] that Edward Said [was] somebody who studied English literature, but he understood that English literature [was] an embodiment of

English philosophy, of its psychology, of its economic structures, of its industrial structures,' says Ntuli.[12]

The man Ntuli had admired as a child, who had mentored him, and whom he had visited at his own House of Truth where he had taken part in intense debates while demolishing bottles of brandy, had not responded to his knocking on the door. When Ntuli sat in the bioskop watching a film, it felt like the longest wait of his life. Afterwards, he could not even remember the storyline. As soon as the film ended, he went back to Themba's flat, but his efforts were once again in vain. There was no response to his loud knocking, then banging with his fists, and finally his attempts to kick the door down. His friend Maseko was also concerned, and looked through the keyhole. The feet were still visible, but their owner was not responding. He was lying in exactly the same position he had been in a few hours earlier. Motionless.

Going back to Lubombo, Ntuli could not stop worrying. It would have been understandable if Themba had actually been absent, as sometimes he visited his family in the nearby city of Mbabane. While Themba taught in Umzimpofu, his wife, Anne, lived in Mbabane with their two daughters, Morongwa, who was six, and Yvonne, who was then eighteen months old. Anne was running a nursery school sponsored by the United Nations Children's Fund (UNICEF), the first such school in a township in Swaziland.

Themba had promised his wife that he would use the September holidays to finish a book he had been writing. One of the main reasons they had gone to Swaziland was so that he could be in an environment where he was free to write. However, his wife kept enquiring as time passed, and the book was not forthcoming. 'Sweetie, you think writing a book is sitting down and writing an essay?' he would say. Anne would have none of it, and even threatened to go back to South Africa if their purpose for being in Swaziland was not accomplished.

Themba understood the importance of finishing his writing project: 'All right, this holiday I promise you, I will write the book when the schools close. When the schools close I'm going to write the book so that when they open, I just give you your book and say, there's your book!' This, according to Anne, was the promise her husband made her.[13]

But Themba was spending the weekend of 8 September in Manzini, not with his family in Mbabane. Ntuli spent a sleepless night in Lubombo, tossing and turning, anxious about the non-responsiveness of his mentor. At the crack of dawn, he got up and retraced the 25-kilometre journey. He hitchhiked back to Manzini with a clear objective of kicking the door down if there was still no response from within. If he thought the hours he had spent in the bioskop the day before had dragged, they were nothing compared to his journey back to Manzini. Time seemed to have frozen.

Finally, he arrived in Manzini. Huffing and puffing, he ran towards Themba's flat. As fate would have it, there was no need for him to kick the door down. When he arrived, people were milling about the vicinity. Bystanders were anxiously looking in the direction of Themba's apartment. Mouths agape. Speaking in hushed voices. Faces revealing a mixture of anxiety, shock and sadness. The police demarcation tape, a lifeless body being wheeled out on a stretcher – these confirmed Ntuli's worst fears. Can Themba had passed away. He was only 43 years old.

Devastated, Ntuli stood there for a while, not knowing what to do next. Eventually, he went to the nearest watering hole. The Reeds had been one of the two popular venues for their meetings and debates – the other being the Punch Bowl. The proprietor of The Reeds, Aunt Jane, was sympathetic. She came to offer her condolences to the distraught Ntuli, recognising that Themba was his 'father and mentor'.[14]

Ntuli was inconsolable, and proceeded to drown his sorrows in memory of the man who had lived (and now died) by the adage, 'Live fast, die young and have a good-looking corpse'. This line, embraced by Sophiatown tsotsis and intellectuals alike, had been popularised by none other than Themba himself. He had appropriated it from Willard Motley's 1947 novel, *Knock on Any Door.*[15] It became even more popular in Sophiatown after the 1949 film adaptation, which starred John Derek and Humphrey Bogart, both very popular actors at the time.

Ntuli's unanswered knock on the door felt like being denied entry into the House of Truth, an antithesis to what Themba stood for. This, in both its literal and metaphoric senses, leaves a number of questions about Themba's passing. One question that nags when someone dies under mysterious circumstances is, 'What happened?'

Themba was alone when he died, and it took at least a day before his lifeless body was discovered in his flat. The biographical note in the compilation of his stories, *Requiem for Sophiatown*, as well as the write-up in the tribute publication, *The Fifties People of South Africa*, both state that Themba died while reading a newspaper.[16] One would imagine that as he gasped his final breath, the newspaper fell on his face, like the drawing of a curtain after a splendid stage performance. It was a spectacular exit for a writer.

Whatever happened, whatever the circumstances, the objective reality is that Themba died an outsider: away from his ancestral land, away from the House of Truth, and away from his family. Not only was he unable to return to his home country, but, as a banned citizen, he could be neither published nor quoted by any media in South Africa. It is fair to postulate that whatever the medical reasons for his passing, he did not die a happy man. His former editor, Stein, captured it succinctly: 'Whatever the actual mode of his going, he surely died of a broken heart.'[17]

To understand Can Themba's dying, we need to understand his living. To get to know what made him, and what broke him, we need to open the door and get inside the House of Truth where his life unfolded. Ntuli's incessant knocking on the door was to forecast this quest for the truth about the life and times of Can Themba.

2

The Poet Laureate of Fort Hare

Can Themba was the one who was preoccupied with … the poetry of immediacy, the poetry of proximity.

Muxe Nkondo — Interview (2015)

'The winning prize of £3 3s. 0d. goes to the writer of the following poem,' read a December 1949 article in *Zonk* magazine.[1] The poem was titled 'Recollection', written by someone simply called Doce. At the bottom of the page, the author byline read, 'This writer used to be known as the Poet Laureate of Fort Hare. He now lives in Sophiatown.'

The author was none other than the man who would emerge four years later as the winner of the £50 first prize for the *Drum* short story award. Daniel Canodoce Themba, popularly known as Can Themba, was born in Marabastad on 21 June 1924. At that time, Marabastad was an overcrowded, vibrant, colourful and multicultural place, consisting mainly of black, coloured and Indian communities. The severe overcrowding that characterised Marabastad was largely the result of its history as a trading area; the government of the time tried to control the congestion by establishing more housing units in the surrounding areas. Themba's family ultimately relocated to Attridgeville, a black township west of Pretoria, founded in 1939 as an attempt to solve the overcrowding problems in Marabastad. Here they lived at 5 Ntlatleng Street. He moved to Sophiatown once he started working as a teacher in Johannesburg.

Themba wrote under different pen names, including Doce, D. C. Themba, D. Canodoce Themba, D. Can Themba, Can Themba, Parks Mangena and Morongwa Sereto, amongst others. The first available record of his publications dates back to 1945, when he published a poem entitled 'Thirst in the Hearts of Men', in a journal of the South African Native College (SANC), the former name for the University of Fort Hare.[2] Coincidentally, this poem appeared alongside Dennis Brutus's first published poem, titled 'Rendezvous', under the pen name Le Dab. In 1947, Themba produced a poem titled 'Dedication', and a short story titled 'Revelation', both published in different editions of *The Fort Harian*, a student journal.[3]

While there is no doubt that winning the *Drum* short story award was a major breakthrough in Themba's writing career, his was a talent that had been simmering for a number of years. The SANC, in particular, played a pivotal role in cultivating Themba's literary aptitude. His love for reading and writing, and English literature in particular, was palpable while he was still at boarding school at Khaiso Secondary School in Seshego, outside Pietersburg, in the Northern Transvaal (now Limpopo Province). He enrolled for Standard Six at Khaiso in 1939, and completed his matric in 1944. Khaiso was a prominent school that attracted some of the leading minds in the country, including the famous painter Gerard Sekoto, who taught at the school in the 1930s. Themba's intellect, combined with his scholarly acumen and commitment, earned him good marks as a pupil in high school.

This was a turbulent period not only in the Union of South Africa, but also in global politics. Themba's schooling coincided with the duration of the Second World War, in which South Africa participated on the side of Britain and the Allied powers. Finishing his matric as the war approached its end, he became the first student to be awarded the Mendi Memorial Scholarship to study at the prestigious SANC at Fort Hare in Alice, in the Cape Colony. This scholarship was established during General Jan Smuts's second tenure as the prime minister of the Union of South Africa, in commemoration of the tragic incident in which 607 black volunteers supporting Britain in the First World War drowned after the SS *Mendi* troopship collided with the SS *Darro* in the English Channel on 21 February 1917. The 'Mendi episode' became a symbol of the bravery of black soldiers and co-operation between the 'natives' and the colonial powers.

Smuts, his history as a military man and leader of an oppressive state notwithstanding, took a personal interest in education. Early in his political and military career, he had worked closely with General Louis Botha, who opened the SANC in February 1916 in his capacity as the prime minister of the Union at the time. The historical sketch published in the 1946 annual calendar of Fort Hare reads: 'The South African Native College was declared open by the Rt. Hon. General Botha, in the presence of a large and representative gathering of Europeans and Natives on the 8th of February 1916. Thus, after many years, the ideal of a College for the higher education of the natives of South Africa reached the stage of working realisation.'[4]

The SANC (from 1951 officially called the University of Fort Hare), soon to become a crucible for the student resistance movement in South Africa, was founded only four years after the formation of the South African National Native Congress, the predecessor to the African National Congress (ANC).

The Mendi scholarship, administered by the Department of Native Affairs, helped Themba enrol as a first-year student at the SANC. He had sent his application to the institution on 24 October 1944, stating his ambition to become a teacher. In motivating for admission to the university, he wrote: 'I want to prepare for a B.A. degree and intend to become a teacher. I am twenty years of age and expect to complete my matriculation at the end of this year. For further particulars the Principal of the above school [Khaiso] is willing to speak on my behalf.'[5] Having sent this application a few months before getting his matric results, Themba became anxious when he received no response.

On 9 February 1945, Themba wrote another letter to the college asking about the results of his application. He also confirmed that he had passed his matric exams, as he had by then received his results. The Registrar wrote back to Themba on 15 February, confirming his admission: 'In reply to your letter of February 9th I have to inform you that a notice of admission, a railway concession certificate, and a list of your personal requirements were posted to you on February 7th, addressed to Eastwood Township Pretoria, which was the home address given on your application.'[6]

Armed with a confirmed scholarship, Themba boarded a train at Pretoria station. The metal snake rattled him through the mountains and gorges of the Union of South Africa and all the way to Alice, on the banks of the Tyhume River, nestled between the Amathole Mountains in the Cape Colony, land on which he had never before set foot. He was there to start a new life, in a region where the surrounding communities spoke Xhosa, a language he was not familiar with.

He enrolled as a first-year student at the SANC, an institution that had been established on strong Christian grounds (and partly funded by the Free Church of Scotland). This formed an integral part of almost every aspect of its existence. Accommodation was allocated according to the denomination of the students. This was partly because of the Christian origins of the university, but was also aimed at garnering still more converts, while at the same time entrenching a particular ethos.

In his application for admission, Themba had declared that he was Anglican. He was therefore allocated to Beda Hall, also known as the Anglican Hostel. According to the university prospectus of 1945, 'In the hostel erected by the Church of the Province [the Anglican Church] there is accommodation for sixty-six students.' Among the students in Beda Hall in 1945 were Themba and Brutus, the latter having arrived at Fort Hare a year before Themba. Both would in years to come establish themselves as prominent writers.

Commenting on the Christian foundations of the institution, Brutus's biographer, Tyrone August, says:

> For one, the idea of a 'Native University' was first proposed by the British missionary, Rev. James Stewart, when he was principal of the Lovedale Missionary Institution. Secondly, the university was built on the mission lands of the United Free Church of Scotland, right inside a fort built by the Cape Colony in 1946 as a bulwark against the indigenous people. And thirdly, and most importantly, it was conceptualised and constructed almost entirely on the foundation of a British world view.[7]

Each day started with the students assembling for prayer, and religion permeated almost every aspect of university life. According to August, 'Students were compelled to attend Sunday night church services as well.'[8] It is difficult to tell whether the students were indeed members of or earnestly committed to the various denominations to which they claimed to belong, or whether this was a matter of compliance, along with the resulting benefits. It made logical sense to declare their Christian faith while studying and staying at the institution.

Themba's benefactor was one Reverend H. G. Mpitso (not to be confused with Reverend Thuntsi, who championed him in his childhood), who served as the secretary of the Mendi Memorial Scholarship Fund. Reverend Mpitso, who lived in Pimville, Soweto, reported to the Native Commissioner in Johannesburg, and was accountable to the Secretary of Native Affairs. Reverend Mpitso had to write testimonials on behalf of Themba on an annual basis to motivate for the transfer of funds to cover his expenses at university. In return, at the end of each academic year, Themba was required to submit a performance and progress report.

The principal of the SANC was Alexander Kerr, a Scottish émigré who was only thirty when he took up the position upon the founding of the college in 1916. Themba enrolled for a Bachelor of Arts degree in 1945, majoring in English, which was taught by Kerr himself. The syllabus for arts students majoring in English included the history of English literature, the poems of Milton, Pope, Goldsmith, Coleridge, Keats and Tennyson, as well as works by Dickens and Wordsworth, amongst others. Shakespeare dominated the syllabus, with works such as *Henry IV*, *The Merchant of Venice*, *Hamlet*, *Richard III*, *The Tempest*, *Antony and Cleopatra*, *King Lear* and *A Midsummer Night's Dream* prescribed during the three years of the Bachelor of Arts degree. Exercises for students included essay writing and literary criticism.[9]

This syllabus established a solid foundation for Themba's literary appreciation and capabilities, and it is not surprising that his writing star began to rise while he was at university. The influence of this syllabus was later discernible in his opus as a writer, as will be seen when examining Themba's literary influences in later chapters.

While Themba and his fellow literary enthusiast Brutus chose writing as their vocation, many of his fellow students were destined to play equally impactful roles in the political arena. Brutus acknowledged the 'social, political and intellectual' exposure he gained at Fort Hare as having shaped his world view. In Beda Hall, it was policy since its inception in 1920 to 'mix the students of the various races – Bantu from various parts, Indian, and coloured'. He goes on to explain that 'when a permanent hostel was opened in 1935, Beda Hall introduced the rule that, in those dormitories which accommodate five students, no more than two in any dormitory should be non-Bantu'.[10] This was meant to encourage students to interact with cultures other than their own. (Brutus was classified as coloured, while Themba was considered Bantu.)

One of Themba's housemates at Beda Hall, Ntsu Mokhehle from Basutoland, took the political route and went on to hold the position of prime minister of Lesotho between 1993 and 1998. Other notable contemporaries during Themba's student days included Mangosuthu Buthelezi, an ANC Youth League activist who later became leader of the KwaZulu homeland, founder of the Inkatha Freedom Party (IFP) and cabinet minister in a democratic South Africa; Robert Mangaliso Sobukwe, former ANC Youth League activist and founding president of the Pan Africanist Congress (PAC); Duma Nokwe, former secretary general of the ANC; Joe Matthews, ANC Youth League activist, who later joined the rival IFP; and Robert Gabriel Mugabe, who fought for independence for Rhodesia and eventually became president of Zimbabwe.

In the 1940s, Fort Hare was fast becoming a hub for political ferment in South Africa. As the institution was establishing itself as a breeding ground for young intellectuals, who were naturally at the coalface of unfolding political unrest, the ANC targeted it as an incubator for future leaders, as the youth are traditionally frontrunners of unfolding political dramas in society. Sobukwe was a student from Graaff-Reinet whose star was fast rising, and who was destined to make a mark in the political arena.

Parallels can be drawn between Themba's and Sobukwe's career choices, and the paths they would tread after university. While Themba made his mark in student journals such as *SANC* and *The Fort Harian*, Sobukwe was a regular contributor to *Beware*, a pamphlet that offered a platform for daily commentary on political issues. 'Hand-written, the topic of choice of these daily manifestos was non-collaboration, with fierce attacks on such advisory bodies as the Natives' Representative Council (NRC),' writes Daniel Massey in *Under Protest: The Rise of Student Resistance at the University of Fort Hare*.[11]

In 1948, the year of Themba's graduation, the National Party came to power, and apartheid, with racial segregation and discrimination as a formal means of control, was established as official government policy. Themba was about to move to Sophiatown, a crucible of South African opposition politics at the time, where the likes of Walter Sisulu, Oliver Tambo and Nelson Mandela lived. Mandela and Tambo had studied at Fort Hare before Themba. In his account of this period, Lewis Nkosi gives a brief overview of the political condition: 'My generation came to maturity just before or soon after the Second World War, at about the same time that Dr Malan was taking over the country on a mandate to apply more rigidly apartheid than the Smuts Government before him had seemed prepared to do.'[12]

These drastic changes in the national political landscape profoundly affected the young Themba. During this volatile period, the student activists at Fort Hare were fortunate to have the support of some progressive lecturers (even though they were a minority), some of whom were active members of the ANC, including Godfrey Pitje, himself a graduate of Fort Hare.

The man at the forefront of youth activism in the ANC was A. P. Mda, who was determined to ensure that the university boasted one of the most politically vibrant campuses in the country. Mda wrote a letter to Pitje suggesting that Fort Hare was fertile ground for future leaders of the national liberation struggle, and the best place to start an ANC Youth League branch. This was a vital step in the politicisation of the student movement, and it also planted seeds for grooming future political leaders. Massey describes the reasoning for the formation of the Fort Hare branch of the ANC Youth League as follows: 'In 1948, the YL [Youth League] began to grow under the direction of A. P. Mda. Because Fort Hare was home to the leading members of South Africa's black intelligentsia, and because teachers trained at Fort Hare went on to educate people around the country, the university was strategically important for Mda, who grew determined to establish a branch on campus.'[13]

Buthelezi attributed a fundamental part of his own political consciousness to this epoch during his time as a student at this university. At the time, Buthelezi, like his fellow IFP party man Joe Matthews, as well as Sobukwe, was a member of the ANC Youth League. Buthelezi feels that in the highly politicised environment on campus, it was inevitable that one would be political: 'It was inevitable, of course, that political issues would be talked about at that time as well, because at Fort Hare I was a member of the ANC Youth League, and therefore my interest in politics … was ignited. One of our lecturers, Advocate Godfrey Pitje, was our chairman [of the ANC Youth League at Fort Hare]; [after] he left, Mr Mangaliso Robert Sobukwe [became] our chairman too.'[14]

Given the nature of political dynamism that was prevalent at Fort Hare, the products of the university were driven by equally diverse schools of thought. There were communists like Govan Mbeki, nationalists like Tambo and Mandela, Pan Africanists like Sobukwe, and traditionalists like Kaiser Matanzima and Buthelezi, all of whom cut their teeth on student politics. Furthermore, there were clandestine associations of secret agents within the student community. In his *Drum* article 'Special Branch Tries to Keep the Lid on Political Change', which he co-authored with Todd Matshikiza, Themba wrote: 'Fort Hare has for a long time been under guard. There has always been a student whose presence and practice have been suspect. In times of student crises these spies get sorely embarrassed. Their behaviour is the first to be scrutinised by the students; they are the first to be blamed for any action taken by the college authorities against the students.'[15]

In short, Fort Hare was a microcosm of a dynamic and complex political world. Themba navigated his way through this tumultuous period, which marked both increasing viciousness and rigidity in apartheid legislation, as well as growing and steadfast opposition to the new regime. The likes of Mandela, who had already left Fort Hare by that time, often visited the campus in their quest to establish a branch of the ANC Youth League there, or at least in the town of Alice. Themba participated in some of these political debates, and even hosted some in his own room at Beda Hall.

Buthelezi remembers him as a popular student: 'We tended to crowd around him, he almost had a following because … we used to enjoy … his witticisms and his wonderful sense of humour. He was a very brilliant person.'[16] One of Buthelezi's most vivid memories of his student life was when Themba hosted a mock graduation, in which he acted as the chancellor of the university. 'The day before the graduation, there used to be a mock grad at Beda Hall, and I recall vividly that Can Themba was [the] chancellor of that mock graduation … He dressed up in some very shabby garments and actually capped those who graduated [at the mock ceremony].'[17]

In the midst of political ferment in the rest of South Africa and the growth of the student resistance movement on campus, Themba was determined to flex his literary muscles. It was during this time that he published his first stories and poems in several magazines. As a budding writer, Themba published poetry, mostly in student journals such as *SANC* and *The Fort Harian*, as well as in *Zonk* magazine, from 1945 to 1951. The work that he published during these early years is not available in the public domain, so it remains little known.

His publications during this period demonstrate a great talent yet to be discovered by mainstream magazines and newspapers. It is worth noting that Themba largely wrote poetry during this time, even though he would publish a short story or essay here and there. His choice of literary genre in the early years of his career was no doubt associated with his major literary influence – William Shakespeare. Even his short stories contained Shakespearean poetic diction in their dialogue.

His earliest available poem, 'Thirst in the Hearts of Men', published as far back as 1945 during his first year at university in the *SANC* summer edition, clearly shows this. While the poem does not contain specific phrases directly derived from any of Shakespeare's poems, the rhyme and rhythm of the poem reflect a strong Shakespearean influence, as can be seen from the following excerpt:

What see we all over the land
Burning thirst, throats are dry;
'Tis thirst, thirst in the hearts of men.[18]

The metrical feet and rhyme are typical of the linguistic nuances and the quintessential Shakespearean rhythms conspicuous in Themba's early writings, particularly those he produced while he was still a student, and published when first entering the literary scene.

To illustrate this further, take two stanzas from Themba's poem 'Ciskeian Maid', published in *The Fort Harian* in 1951:

Wordlessly we appointed our secret tryst
To meet at Ramona at dead of night
There to calm the soul that piteously cry'st
So against his wicked world's law of blight

And, true, at dead of night there I met thee
Waiting, wondering, 'Would he fail at the last?'
And looking around, making sure to be free
I clasped thee in my arms and held thee fast.[19]

The evocation of Shakespeare can be readily deciphered in the somewhat archaic English lexicon Themba employs in the lines above. The consistent use of pronouns such as 'thee', 'thy' and 'thou' in this poem further reflect the transposition of language from England's Elizabethan era. The entire poem is awash with formalised and perhaps esoteric vocabulary not commonly found in the works of writers who were Themba's contemporaries. This once again had its roots in his Fort Hare education, which Brutus described as steeped in the English literary canon, which in turn influenced his own writing: 'These were very much in hybrid Victorian or Elizabethan mode, because that's what I was being exposed to, rather than South African ones.'[20]

The dominant themes in Themba's early writings hinge on the politics of difference where feuding families or clans are brought together, another indication of Shakespearean influence, which I discuss in more detail in Chapter 14. This aspect is clearly shown in 'The Ciskeian Maid'. Although this is a poem, it bears strong similarities to Shakespeare's tragic play *Romeo and Juliet*. The differences between the two prominent families in *Romeo and Juliet*, the Capulets and the Montagues, could be paralleled with Themba's own personal history as a young man seeking love in the hinterlands of what was to him an alien rural environment. As a man of Zulu ancestry who grew up in Marabastad, Pretoria, and spoke Afrikaans as his first language, Themba managed to fall in love with a Xhosa woman whose language he could not even speak. In this instance, Themba selected a single aspect from Shakespeare's narrative – that of the 'star-crossed lovers' whose families were traditionally enemies – and developed a poem around it.

Themba's reflections of his student days are captured in his earliest poetry and short stories, and these epitomise his English studies, which were dominated by Shakespeare. Having published poetry from his very first year as a student, and continuously during his two stints at Fort Hare, it is little wonder that he was known as the 'Poet Laureate of Fort Hare'.

3

The Teacher of Life and Letters

You know, sometimes he would probe you with questions and then when you're frustrated and fed up and … searching for words and you are actually talking, you see a glint on his face, like a sadist, you know, like a glint actually on his face – then he says: 'You've got it.'

Pitika Ntuli — Interview (2013)

After finishing his studies at Fort Hare, Can Themba went to teach at the Western Native High School (also known as Madibane High School) in the Western Native Township. However, throughout his career he practised teaching and journalism interchangeably. These intertwined professions defined his career.

Themba started teaching at Madibane High School in 1949. His arrival at Madibane was anticipated as a momentous occasion. Among the students at the school who remembered this was one Stanley Motjuwadi, later to be known as 'Black Stan' during his days as a journalist for *Drum* magazine and *Golden City Post*. Motjuwadi penned an ode to Themba as part of the 1968 tribute edition of *The Classic*. In paying homage to Themba, Motjuwadi recalled his anticipation: 'Like all the other pupils at Madibane High School in Western Township, I eagerly awaited the arrival of the new English Master from Fort Hare. More especially as we had been told that he was brilliant and had passed English with distinctions at the University.'[1]

Upon arrival, Themba did not match up to the hype, certainly not in terms of his appearance; he did not even try to impress. In a reworked version of the same article, published in *The World of Can Themba*, Motjuwadi contrasts their level of anticipation with the actual outcome. Because Themba had passed English, the language of the colonial master and the British Empire, with a distinction from the prestigious Fort Hare, the scholars' level of respect for the new teacher was already sky-high. But this changed when they were confronted by his unimpressive appearance:

> You can imagine our disappointment when the principal Mr Harry Madibane proudly stood on the stage and introduced the new Wonderboy. He was scrawny with an incongruously puffy, rubbery face. At my most generous, I would not say he looked a 'bit' distinguished. Sartorially he was a disaster. No tie, a cheap baggy grey workman's gabardine trousers, a khaki shirt, shoes that had an overdue date with the repairers and the kind of jacket a fussy student would not be seen dead in. Quite a let-down after the imposing figure we had over the days built up in our minds.[2]

Themba's disappointing appearance seems to have been an antithesis of what happened once he started addressing the school assembly. The impression he created is similar to the effect S. E. K. Mqhayi had on the young Nelson Mandela, when the famous poet visited their school in Healdtown. In his autobiography, Mandela shared his experience of seeing Mqhayi in person for the first time. He had considered Mqhayi his hero because of his impressive poetry, but when he finally got to see him, the 'heroic' figure seemed too ordinary – short and unassuming. But as he began to speak, Mqhayi grew in stature, and the respect that Mandela had for him was restored.[3] Likewise, Motjuwadi reported seeing Themba's stature grow as he spoke:

> Fortunately our disappointment was short-lived. From the moment he opened his mouth to address us, we were, to use a cliché, eating out of his bony palm. Blinking all the time like something unused to harsh lights, he spoke in a cool, sophisticated voice. He used words we were accustomed to, but he used them the way only he could. Eloquent and articulate, he really made the occasion his show without being pompous. On the contrary, he made us feel like his equals.[4]

Themba's oratory skills had an impact on many other students in the school. Yet, it was not only his inaugural speech, nor his appearance on the day that created a lasting impression on the minds of his students, but his teachings. Former students of his continue to affirm the positive impact he had on them, and the guidance that he gave to them as a mentor – even outside the classroom. A number of prominent South Africans were beneficiaries of his teaching skills, including Desmond Mpilo Tutu, Anglican archbishop emeritus and a Nobel Peace Prize winner, and the witty journalist Casey Motsisi, who followed in Themba's footsteps both in his profession and in his lifestyle.

The relationship between Themba and Motsisi, as mentor and protégé respectively, is one of the most legendary and well-documented partnerships in the history of journalism in South Africa. Motsisi, an iconic journalist in his own right, also shared his memories in *The Classic*, claiming that Themba not only taught him literature; he taught him about life. 'I first came in touch with Can during my search for knowledge at the then Western High School on the outskirts of Western Native Township where he taught literature, poetry appreciation and history in Matric,' Motsisi said.[5]

Former teacher and student formed a mutual admiration society. In his article 'Zeke Past Bachelor of Arts! Casey Past Bachelor of Hearts!', which jointly pays tribute to Es'kia Mphahlele and Motsisi, Themba describes the latter as that 'irrepressible, fun-loving, humour-packed, pocket-sized young man, Moses Casey Motsisi'.[6] He goes on: 'During his high school days I used to teach him English – I heartily apologise for it. But he got by.'[7]

After matric, Motsisi studied to be a teacher at the Normal College in Pretoria, where he co-edited a student magazine called *The Normalite* with Motjuwadi. Motsisi got into trouble after a student, later identified as Doc Bikitsha, but writing under the pseudonym Abdool, wrote a 'naughty article' that did not meet the approval of the principal. When the principal and other authorities wanted to know the real identity of Abdool, Motsisi would not reveal his sources. Motsisi was promptly expelled, after which he wrote the principal a five-page 'thank-you' letter, which began thus: 'The worst thing that ever happened to me was being admitted to the Normal. It is anything but normal. The best thing that ever happened to me was to be dismissed by you.'[8]

This, at least, is one version of how Motsisi left the Normal College. The other, which does not necessarily contradict this one, is that following the establishment of *Africa!* magazine under Themba's editorship, Motsisi sent a story for publication. Themba's response was to offer him a job: 'Instead of sending payment, Themba sent a telegram suggesting that Motsisi start work on the magazine pronto.'[9] The invitation to come and work for the magazine may well have coincided with Motsisi's troubles at the college. Either way, he accepted Themba's offer with alacrity.

Motsisi and Themba were to work very closely together as editor and associate editor of *Africa!*. Their partnership was one of great chemistry; they were sometimes dubbed 'David and Jonathan, sometimes Laurel and Hardy' – but whatever they were called, the pair were inseparable.[10]

The 'life coach' that Themba became to Motsisi and other young people reflected his own personal weaknesses, and those who learned from him did not always distinguish between what behaviours ought to be emulated and what might have been wiser to avoid. As a result, young men like Motsisi tried to imitate everything Themba did. This blind loyalty might have bordered on exuberant deification of Themba, but Motsisi does not seem to have any regrets: 'I followed him like a second shadow through the cracks, crannies of a fated Sophiatown as he hobnobbed from shebeen to shebeen … I so idolised him that I even tried to walk like him, speak like him and to be a woman chaser. But I realised at a certain point that I was made of less stern stuff.'[11]

While Motjuwadi and Motsisi speak fondly of the man and how much they admired him as a teacher, Sol Rachilo speaks more explicitly about how Themba fared as a teacher in the classroom. Rachilo credits Themba as his English master for his own proficiency in speaking and writing English. He admired and appreciated Themba no less than the pair of protégés already mentioned: 'We enjoyed being in Dorsay Can Themba's class because he was our English master. Very wonderful intuition and imparting [of] knowledge, applying the Socratic method all the time.'[12]

It would appear that imparting knowledge is what Themba enjoyed the most in his twin vocations: education and journalism. Even when he was not employed as a teacher, he would pay special visits to different schools. Distinguished intellectual and academic Muxe Nkondo, who in the late 1950s was a student at Orlando High School in Soweto, had the privilege of receiving this knowledge directly from the source.

Themba was invited to the school by a certain Mr L. Makubalo, who was with him at Fort Hare and who, like Themba, had majored in English. At that time, the English examination had three parts, including one on poetry. As part of the poetry component, pupils were required to write an essay on one of Keats's poems, 'The Eve of St Agnes', a poem set in the early hours of a cold wintry morning in England. The Johannesburg winter, while chilly, is definitely nothing compared to the climate of the British Isles, where snow falls in the winter. This was a very difficult poem to teach to young South Africans who had no idea of what a European winter felt like, so the great English master was called in to share his insights with the students. The fact that the lesson took place on a hot day in October must have made it even more challenging to explain the poem.

Nevertheless, Themba read the poem to the class, explained its meaning and described its sensations so vividly that the students started feeling cold. Nkondo tells how his classmate, Nana, started having illusions: 'The way he commented on the cold, on the chill, my classmate Nana, we all felt an immediate chill, so much that she stood up and in a kind of hypnosis, started closing imaginary windows. There were no windows, but it became so cold in that room because of the evocative power of Can Themba's understanding and his hold on words.'[13]

Nkondo argues that the evocative power with which Themba interpreted Keats's poem can be found throughout Themba's works. He had this ability to connect with his audience, to engage them fully to the extent of creating the illusion that the reader was part of the story. He was determined to penetrate the subconscious of both his readers and his students.

In the classroom, Themba was equally dedicated to ensuring that the full potential of his students was realised. Rachilo elaborates: 'Immediately he was aware of my potential as far as English was concerned, he was helping me even after hours. He'd say, listen, your essay was good, this is how in future you must build up what you write. When he was around, he was already guiding me on how to go on about the English language, especially writing.'[14]

While many students were happy with his lessons and the way he related to them, Themba was not entirely happy working as a teacher. He was regarded as an 'uncertified' teacher and did not get a full teacher's salary, owing to his lack of a teacher's diploma. In 1950, he returned to the Cape, and registered for the University Education Diploma (UED) offered by Rhodes University in Grahamstown (now Makhanda). As Rhodes was an institution exclusively for white students, this meant Themba had to be resident at Fort Hare for the duration of his studies.

The Uncertified Teacher

Can Themba's return to university to study towards a teaching diploma clearly demonstrates his fervent desire to be recognised as a teacher. He taught intermittently during this period, as practice teaching was a requirement for the diploma he was pursuing. However, after sacrificing his job and studying for two years, he never received the certificate that confirmed him as a qualified teacher.

First came delays in receiving his results, partly due to his failure to pay his outstanding university fees. Then endless complications led to deferrals in the issuing of his diploma. The flurry of correspondence that followed exposed glaring inconsistencies between the various universities and government departments. For the next two years, from 1952 to 1953, Themba went to extraordinary lengths to meet the necessary bureaucratic requirements. He was in constant correspondence with the University of Fort Hare, Rhodes University and the Transvaal Education Department regarding his qualification, exchanging no less than thirty letters with the education authorities during this period.

A close look at these letters reveals the seriousness with which Themba took the teaching profession, and his determination to get professional recognition as a teacher. On 19 March 1952, Themba wrote to Fort Hare and paid his outstanding fees so that he could receive his results. The letter reads:

> Find enclosed the sum of five pounds, ten shillings and no pence, which I believe settles my account. Kindly arrange to have my examination results sent to the above address. I regret the delay which is due to the fact that I have only just received my first salary.[15]

Themba was eager to possess the formal accreditation he had worked for so that he could be paid accordingly. At the time, he was working as a teacher at Madibane High School under the auspices of the Transvaal Education Department. The regulations of the department demanded that he hold a teaching qualification in the form of a UED in order to be recognised and given the appropriate salary.

Rhodes University finally issued his UED to Fort Hare, which acknowledged its receipt in a letter sent to Themba on 27 March 1952. A couple of months passed, and Themba had still not received the diploma. He kept sending letters to the respective institutions, pleading for the issuing of his certificate. In a letter dated 25 June 1952, he sent another reminder to Professor Dent, the principal of Fort Hare:

> Up to this moment I have not received the U.E.D. certificate to which the Registrar assured me I was entitled. It would be a great kindness if you could arrange that it is made and sent to the above address.
>
> The Transvaal Education Department under which I serve as a teacher employs me as an uncertified teacher 'pending the production of certificates', and pays me accordingly. You will appreciate therefore that the delay is causing me hardship.
>
> I have also asked the Registrar for a statement to the effect that I was in residence at Fort Hare as a student for the following periods: 1945–1947 and 1950–1951, both inclusive. I wish to apply for tax exemptions for those periods and therefore need the statement.
>
> Yours faithfully,
> D. C. Themba[16]

Rhodes University at last issued Themba with only a provisional Education Diploma, owing to the fact that he had failed History of Education III, a requirement for qualification for the diploma. The rules for the issuing of the provisional UED seemed to be ambiguous; Themba challenged their validity, as it was clear that there were contradicting interpretations of legislation between Rhodes University and the Transvaal Education Department. After a protracted exchange between Themba and the respective institutions, he was advised to register for an additional subject with the University of South Africa (UNISA) in order to qualify for a full UED. He sent a letter to Fort Hare enquiring whether the procedure was valid and acceptable, which the university confirmed.

He subsequently registered with UNISA, studying and passing Philosophy I. Following the successful completion of the course with UNISA, he informed Rhodes University, and on 3 February 1953, wrote again to Fort Hare pleading for the release of his UED:

> In accordance with your assurance made to me in a letter dated 28.3.52, that the procedure I suggested of taking Philosophy I as an N.D.P. subject with the University of South Africa, is quite correct, I have done so and have passed as the enclosed Statement of Results testifies. Kindly pass this on to Rhodes University with the enclosed exemption fee of one pound, payable to Rhodes.
>
> I shall be pleased to receive my U.E.D. certificate as soon as possible for registration with the Transvaal Education Department whom I serve.[17]

It is likely that by the time the letter above reached the university, a positive response was already on its way to Themba. The confirmation of the issuing of the certificate was sent to Themba on 5 February 1953, a month before he was announced as the winner of the *Drum* short story competition (an achievement of which he was already aware). The letter sent by Rhodes University to Fort Hare read:

> This student completed in 1951 all the requirements for the U.E.D. except for the academic subject in the place of History of Education from which he was exempted. He has now passed Philosophy I as an external student of the University of South Africa. I am enclosing his certificate and £1 note for exemption fee. I should be glad to know that he has now fulfilled all requirements for the U.E.D. and that the diploma will be issued to him in due course.
>
> Yours faithfully
>
> Registrar[18]

However, 'due course' seemed indefinite. Themba never received the certificate as promised in this correspondence. After numerous unsuccessful attempts to extract it, he next sought to establish whether his provisional diploma had any professional value. In a letter dated 29 June 1953, by which time he was already working for *Drum*, he wrote to Fort Hare enquiring about the conditions of the provisional diploma, as the information was required in connection with the adjustment of his salary. He seemed to be particularly frustrated during this period, and the final nail in the coffin was this letter from the Registrar of Fort Hare, dated 18 August 1953:

> Each Education Department has a right to accept or reject whatever Diplomas it chooses. In fact, the Cape Education Department has sometimes accepted a provisional diploma. But that does not oblige the Transvaal Education Department to do likewise. If the Transvaal Education Department regards a provisional [diploma] as not entitling the holder to an increase in salary the University which issued the Diploma can do nothing to change the situation.[19]

This particular letter dashed all Themba's hopes of finally getting a full teaching salary. It is clear from the amount of energy he expended in pursuing his certificate that the issue of his recognition as a teacher weighed heavily on him.

Worse still, the introduction of deliberately inferior Bantu Education policies in 1953 must have been immensely discouraging. They would have been a reminder that his difficulties with the education authorities were part of the systematic abuse of the rights of the broader African community under the apartheid regime.

In 1953, the Minister of Native Affairs, Dr Hendrik Verwoerd, had introduced Bantu Education as a system that offered deliberately inferior education for black people in line with the ideals of the National Party government's apartheid policy. In justifying his reasoning, Verwoerd said in June 1954:

> The Bantu must be guided to serve his own community in all respects. There is no place for him in the European community above the level of certain forms of labour. Within his own community, however, all doors are open … The effect on the Bantu community we find in the much discussed frustration of educated Natives who can find no employment which is acceptable to them. It is abundantly clear that unplanned education creates many problems, disrupts the communal life of the Bantu and endangers the communal life of the European. For that reason it must be replaced by planned Bantu Education.[20]

This is the environment within which Themba would have had to operate should he have returned to teaching in a state school. The offer to join *Drum* magazine came in the midst of all these frustrations. At the time, the magazine was showing glimpses of growth as it underwent major transformation. The beat of the drum was too seductive for an uncertified teacher to resist.

The Teacher in the Newsroom

Can Themba's influence was not confined to the classroom: it stretched across the realm of society. A writer *is* a teacher – as Chinua Achebe pointed out in his essay 'A Novelist as a Teacher' – one who shares a point of view through their writing.[21] Themba's writings were widely circulated. *Drum* magazine, as the platform on which he plied his trade in words, was distributed across the continent, and thus reached audiences in places that Themba himself had never been to. He was later published on other platforms, locally and internationally, and this expanded his realm of influence.

But while he did not go back to the classroom to teach full-time during the period he was working at *Drum*, Themba remained hands-on in extending his reach as a writer, teacher and mentor. Many young scribes got their break in journalism or honed their journalistic skills under the tutelage of Themba.

Joe Thloloe was one of them. In his case, Themba's intervention gave wings to a career that has lasted over fifty years, and which has included serving as a field journalist, a columnist, an editor, the country's press ombudsman and the director of the Press Council. It was in recognition of Themba's role in mentoring him that Thloloe says of the period Themba was the acting editor of *Golden City Post* that he had 'a teacher in the newsroom'.

At the Can Themba Memorial Lecture in 2013, Thloloe shared this anecdote:

> The first person who gave me a chance was Can Themba. He was acting News Editor at the time and I took a story to him and he looked at it and said please change this, please change that, like the teacher he was. I took the stuff that I wanted and I rewrote it the way that he had suggested and lo and behold it was published and for the first time I had been published in the *Golden City Post*.[22]

'The teacher in the newsroom' stands as an apt label for a man who continued with his vocation of teaching even in an altogether different landscape. Journalist and author Lucas Ledwaba likens Themba to a farmer who sprinkled seeds on fertile soil; the writing world of South Africa reaps the rewards to this day.[23] This assertion is echoed by Thloloe, whose lasting memory of Themba was 'somebody who could teach, and somebody who could nurture young talent'. According to Thloloe, Themba 'replicated himself', thereby ensuring that he left a positive legacy.[24]

Juby Mayet shared similar sentiments, saying: 'He gave a lot of other people, apart from me, the inspiration to always try to be better or to reach greater heights. And, as I say, always to tell the truth in whatever situation.'[25]

Similar testimonies have emerged from Swaziland, where Themba spent the last years of his life. Lindiwe Mabuza, a South African exile teaching at Manzini Central School in Swaziland in the early 1960s, also testified to Themba's influence. She explained that 'Swaziland at that time in the early sixties was a safe haven for many politically minded teachers, professionals; everybody who was sick of apartheid went to Swaziland, Lesotho and Botswana'. Her uncle, George Nxumalo, brother to former *Drum* journalist Henry Nxumalo, informed her that Themba would be visiting, and that he wanted to see her in particular as she was a student of literature. When they met, Themba interrogated her about her career choices. She was found wanting, but he insisted that she write a book, because he saw potential in her. To her protestations and claims of ignorance about what to write, or even where to start, Themba responded: 'When you start writing the first thing you must say is "I do not only menstruate, I think because I've got a brain".'[26] Although it took years for Mabuza to finally put pen to paper, these words stayed with her, and she eventually heeded Themba's injunction.

In some ways, Themba came full circle in returning to teaching while exiled in Swaziland. Simon Maziya was a Form I (Grade 8) pupil at St Joseph's Catholic Mission School in 1967, and was taught by Themba. He has memories of Themba teaching him Biology; the teacher happened to be fond of Maziya because he was one of the best students in his class. It was after the holidays in September that he heard the devastating news of the passing of his teacher. He also found that Themba had left a message saying that Maziya and another student should be promoted to the next class before the end of the year, as they had demonstrated knowledge beyond their current level. Themba's wish was granted, and Maziya progressed to Form II before the end of the year. He later qualified as a teacher and taught at his alma mater.

Themba was a teacher in the classroom, in the newsroom, and wherever he found himself. He was a teacher both by profession and by inclination. The likes of Casey Motsisi, Stanley Motjuwadi, Joe Thloloe, Juby Mayet, and many others who were touched by Themba in a variety of ways, all stand as testament to Themba's passion for teaching. Talking about their reunion in the newsroom, Motsisi put it eloquently when he said, 'Can at this stage was not teaching me how to appreciate the sonnets of Shakespeare ... but was teaching me LIFE'.[27]

4

From Marabastad to Sophiatown and Beyond

For Can Themba, the African township represented the strength and the will to survive by ordinary masses of the African people. In its own way the township represented a dogged defiance against official persecution, for in the township the moments of splendour were very splendid indeed, surpassing anything white Johannesburg could offer.

Lewis Nkosi — *Writing Home* (2016), 206–207

After completing his studies at Fort Hare, Can Themba moved back to the Transvaal in 1949, where he settled in Sophiatown, a freehold township outside Johannesburg. He was soon to become one of its most iconic figures.

Today he stands out as one of the most prominent chroniclers of Sophiatown of the 1950s. This is evident both in his fiction and in his journalistic pieces, in which Sophiatown is the dominant setting. He writes with great conviction about its personalities, its shebeens, the poetry and politics of the place, some of the key historic moments, and, finally, its destruction. Sophiatown is where he came of age as a writer and journalist, earning himself yet another moniker: the 'Sage of Sophiatown'.

Themba wrote about the cracks and crannies of Sophiatown with cinematic vividness, great passion and unparalleled erudition, demonstrating intimate connection with the area. In *The Beat of the Drum*, his reflections of the period, Jim Bailey writes that Themba's 'understanding of the black townships of Johannesburg was intuitive, complete and magical'.[1] In his own 'Requiem for Sophiatown', Themba describes life in the area as 'swarming, cacophonous, strutting, brawling, vibrating ...'[2] Stories like his much-celebrated

'The Suit', 'The Will to Die' and 'Bottom of the Bottle' all explore the anxieties and the ecstasies, the crudities and crevices of everyday life in Sophiatown.

The social architecture of Sophiatown went against the newly enacted Group Areas Act, which classified South Africans according to race and dictated where they were permitted to live, thus preventing harmony and equality. One of the many reasons it was targeted by the apartheid government was because of its multiracial character, as it was a freehold township, one of very few areas in South Africa where Africans could and did own stands or property alongside their white counterparts. Its very existence made a mockery of the divisive policies of the apartheid government. Nelson Mandela, who had been one of the more prominent personalities in Sophiatown, elaborated on this: 'At the top of the list for removal was Sophiatown, a vibrant community of more than fifty thousand people, which was one of the oldest black settlements in Johannesburg. Despite its poverty, Sophiatown brimmed with a rich life and was an incubator of so much that was new and valuable in African life and culture. Even before the government's efforts to remove it, Sophiatown held a symbolic importance for Africans disproportionate to its small population.'[3]

Sophiatown holds an exceptional position in the history of urban townships in South Africa as a breeding ground for both cultural and political activists such as Oliver Tambo, Miriam Makeba, Dolly Rathebe and many more. It was here that Themba reunited and interacted with the likes of Duma Nokwe and Robert Sobukwe, who had been his peers at Fort Hare.

Writers such as Bloke Modisane, Don Mattera and Themba himself documented the demolition of Sophiatown extensively in their writings. They all offered authoritative voices from the perspective of both residents and eye-witnesses. Themba and Modisane, in particular, write from the points of view of victims and observers. As residents, they had to watch their homes being razed to the ground; as observers and journalists, they had to chronicle the story of the destruction of Sophiatown and the forced removal of its inhabitants. Their accounts, although differing in experience and perspective, present a vivid picture of the situation, demonstrating astute awareness of the political condition of the time.

Johannesburg remains a city of migrants, and this was even more so during the 1950s, the period during which Themba lived in and wrote about Sophiatown. The Nxumalos, Rathebes, Mandelas, Sobukwes, along with many others who became prominent personalities in Sophiatown, and about whom Themba wrote, had, just like Themba, come from elsewhere. 'Sage of Sophiatown' or not, Themba actually came from Marabastad in Pretoria, a location that barely features in his writings.

The near absence of Marabastad from Themba's writings led to certain perceptions about his attitude to his origins. His former colleague at *Drum* and the *Golden City Post*, Obed Musi, shared some views about Themba's apparent dissociation from Pretoria that were not very flattering. In an interview with Mike Nicol, Musi said: 'There was a rivalry between the guys from Johannesburg and those from Pretoria: the Johannesburg people considered themselves superior and vice versa. Can did not want to identify with Pretoria, he wanted to be one of the slick guys from Johannesburg, and this also made him live in two worlds. He wanted to be all things to all men.'[4]

Themba gained prominence while he was living in Sophiatown. The articles he authored, articles about him, and most of the coverage he received in the 1950s associate him with Sophiatown; his rise and Sophiatown's cultural and political ascendancy soared together. This was the period during which the likes of Dorothy Masuka, Miriam Makeba and Dolly Rathebe were making a name for themselves in the music industry; Nelson Mandela, Robert Sobukwe and Robert Resha were leading political campaigns. It was at this time of ferment that Themba joined *Drum* magazine alongside the likes of Henry Nxumalo, Todd Matshikiza and a host of '*Drum* Boys' who revolutionised journalism. Sophiatown was front and centre in all these activities.

Marabastad, on the other hand, received no such attention. The majority of the families that resided in the area were not forcefully removed en masse and their houses demolished, as was the case in Sophiatown. Instead, new settlements like Attridgeville emerged, and while many residents relocated to the surrounding townships, some remained. As much as Marabastad could not compare with Sophiatown in terms of the latter's prominence, its residents were equally victims of the oppressive apartheid laws; many of them cherish their memories of having lived there.

Themba's short story 'Ten-to-Ten', first published posthumously in his collection *The Will to Die*, is his only published story in which Marabastad is the setting. In his opening paragraph, he writes: 'The curfew proper for all Africans in Marabastad, Pretoria, was 10 p.m. By that hour every African, man, woman and child, had to be indoors, preferably in bed; if the police caught you abroad without a "special permit" you were hauled off to the battleship-grey little police station in First Avenue, near the Aapies River, and clapped in jail.'[5]

Themba's reflections of Marabastad are memories from childhood, which he documents with vivid imagery. In this excerpt, Themba refers to First Avenue, a street away from Second Avenue, the golden thread in Ezekiel Mphahlele's autobiographical text *Down Second Avenue*.[6] We can speculate as to why Themba did not explore Marabastad in his writings the way Mphahlele did. Perhaps he was far less attached to Marabastad than Mphahlele was; or he did not want to be associated with the area, as alleged by Musi; or he had relatively few striking memories of his life there.

Can was the third of five siblings: George, Baby, Can, Maide and Peter. His mother, Angelina Mgole, worked as a seamstress at the Pretoria General Hospital. Themba's father passed away at a young age, and his maternal aunt, from the Phahlwa family, also lost her husband at about the same time. The two widows joined their families, and the children from the Themba and Phahlwa families grew up as a single unit. Can was closest to his cousin, Percy Phahlwa; the pair were brought up almost as twins.

The young Can showed flashes of brilliance from a very young age; according to Sylvester Stein, Themba's uncle told him that 'you could already have a forecast of a great future for Can at two years old'.[7] The moment that turned things around for the youngster was when Reverend Thuntsi, who recognised the boy's intellect, took him under his wing. He supplied the youngster with reading material and encouraged him 'never to part with a book'.[8] This invocation was to have a long-lasting impact on Themba. It was his resulting obsession with books, coupled with scholarly aptitude, that saw him dispatched to board at Khaiso Secondary School.

During Themba's final year at Fort Hare, another historic landmark occurred: the 1948 whites-only elections, which ousted Jan Smuts of the United Party as the prime minister of the Union of South Africa, and replaced him with D. F. Malan of the National Party. This meant the formal introduction of apartheid as an official system of government; the mastermind in engineering it was Dr Hendrik Verwoerd, the political strategist of the National Party in the run-up to the May 1948 elections, also notoriously known as the 'architect of apartheid'.

In 1949, after graduating with his BA, Themba enrolled for an Honours degree at Fort Hare, while at the same time teaching at the Bantu High School (later known as Madibane High) in the Western Native Township.[9] The school was founded in 1939 under the leadership of the founding principal, Harry Madibane, for whom it was later renamed. Since its establishment, Madibane High School had grown in prestige both in terms of its academic performance and in sports achievements. Themba was not the only prolific writer who taught there. One of his colleagues was the prominent Setswana novelist, Daniel Phillip Semakaleng (D. P. S.) Monyaise, who taught Setswana and Afrikaans literature.

Themba rented a room at number 81 Victoria Street in Sophiatown, not far from the Western Native Township, and lived there from 1949 to 1953. After enrolling for the University Education Diploma (UED) at Fort Hare, which meant he could teach only intermittently as he commuted between the Transvaal and the Cape Colony, he used the same address in Sophiatown even while he was in university residence for part of 1950 to 1951, including for most of his correspondence with the University of Fort Hare and other institutions during this period.

This was also the address where *Drum* magazine journalist Henry Nxumalo, accompanied by photographer Jürgen Schadeberg, met Themba in December 1952. Themba had submitted his story 'Mob Passion' for the inaugural *Drum* short story competition, an idea hatched by the proprietor, Jim Bailey, and the British editor, Anthony Sampson, who had met as students at Oxford University, and were passionate about literature and the English classics in particular.

The idea to run a short story competition was part of a broader strategy to transform *Drum* magazine and attract wider audiences among the black population. The two men from *Drum* were visiting Themba to break the news that he was the first winner of *Drum*'s 'Great International Short Story Contest', which had attracted thousands of entries. He had beaten hordes of talented writers from across the continent, including some who would soon form part of the African canon, such as Nigerian writer Cyprian Ekwensi and South Africa's Bloke Modisane. Nxumalo reported on this first visit: 'At the top of a noisy street in Sophiatown, sitting reading on the stoep of his home, we found *Drum*'s winning author Dorsay Can Themba. He took us into his tiny bed-sitting room which he shares with an old friend.'[10]

The article was accompanied by what would be Themba's first photo to appear in the magazine, taken by Schadeberg. 'I took a photo of Henry presenting the cheque to Can on the stoep and then asked him if I could take a picture in his room, which he rented from the family who lived in and owned the house. It was extremely tidy. There were bookshelves full of textbooks and literary magazines. On his desk books were piled one on top of the other, and there were papers and open textbooks. I asked him to sit behind his desk at the keyboard of his typewriter (a modern one, not the usual upright typewriter) and he happily obliged,' Schadeberg recalled.[11]

Following his sensational win, Themba left teaching and went to work for *Drum*, first as a reporter and later as the assistant editor. 'When we launched the short story competition the winning entry was a sardonic tale written by a school teacher, Can Themba, who then joined the staff; he was a magnetic character, philosophising with his own special irony, licking his lips as he constructed elaborate new theories about women or politics, and bringing a new cast of acolytes into the office,' according to Sampson.[12]

Themba worked for *Drum* from 1953 until he lost his job in February 1959. His unceremonious departure from the newsroom (see Chapter 8) raised the prospect of going back to teaching, but by now the repellent Bantu Education Act was in full force in South Africa. Nonetheless, Themba turned his sights to the private sector and found a teaching job at the Central Indian High School in Fordsburg. However, this return to teaching was short-lived as he made his way back to the newsroom after the Sharpeville massacre in March 1960, in which 69 protestors were brutally killed by apartheid security forces.

Themba was by now working as a reporter for *Golden City Post*, which was also owned by Bailey, and shared a building with his former employer, *Drum* magazine. This was a significant demotion for a man who for the largest part of his journalism career had been second-in-command at *Drum*. Journalist Harry Mashabela reminisced about witnessing Themba's return to the newsroom: 'I was sitting at my desk in the offices of *Post* at Samkay House, still planning the day's work. A lanky man, sweat glistening on his freckled face as if he had been running, strode in with a kind of limp. With hands raised and spread out and a broad, mischievous grin on his freckled face, he beamed a hi! to us boys, and headed for the editor's office. Almost unmindful of the excitement he had roused among the other fellows who sat or stood around in the office.'[13]

Mashabela was thrilled to see the man whose writings he had admired for years. He goes on to say, 'Later, he strutted round the newsroom, overwhelming without any inhibitions those of us he did not know. Can was back in journalism again, after a year or so of conspicuous absence. We were to become pretty close.'[14]

By now, however, Themba was sadly nearing the end of his journey as a journalist, a teacher, and indeed a South African resident. At the time, he was living with his in-laws at 479 Ngwenya Street, in Dube, Soweto. His beloved Sophiatown had been razed to the ground; the destruction that began in February 1955 had been completed by 1959, with all residents moved out of the area. What Lewis Nkosi had dubbed *Drum* magazine's 'Fabulous Decade' was coming to an end. The House of Truth had been reduced to a heap of rubble, along with the rest of Sophiatown.

In 1959, Themba published his essay 'Requiem for Sophiatown', in which he paid tribute to his beloved Sophiatown, or Kofifi as it was fondly called, with a mix of nostalgia and despair. 'I still wander among the ruins, trying to find one or two of the shebeens that Dr Verwoerd has overlooked. But I do not like the dead eyes with which some of these ghost houses stare back at me. One of these days I, too, will get me out of here. Finish and clear!'[15]

In 1962, Can Themba left for Swaziland.

PART II

'Live Fast and Die Young'

5

The *Drum* Seduction

There has been no one I have admired more, in a lifetime of mixing with the great and the little, than Canodoce Dorsay von Themba, and no one I've hoped more to be fulfilled. A man of great reading, a working philosopher, a witty and wise companion, a gifted editor and writer.

Sylvester Stein — *Who Killed Mr Drum?* (2003 [1999]), 95

Can Themba had a certain presence that made even the authorities afford him respect. He was a towering figure, not only physically, but also intellectually, with a magnanimous personality and a confident demeanour. Witty, articulate and erudite, he could hold up a discussion on any topic, and it was this aura that he brought to the *Drum* newsroom.

The *African Drum*, as *Drum* magazine was initially called, was founded in 1951 as a quarterly by former cricketer Robert 'Bob' Crisp, with Jim Bailey, the son of a mining magnate, coming on board as a financier. Although the black urban population was its target market, Henry Nxumalo was the only African journalist in the initial team of reporters at *Drum* magazine. He had been a messenger for the *Bantu World* newspaper, had worked for the *Post* and had read extensively while serving on the side of the Allies in Egypt and during trips to London (where he met with other displaced South African intellectuals) during the Second World War. He was nevertheless considered suitable only for the position of sports editor, probably because only he could go into the townships to watch soccer and boxing matches and report on them.

The evolution of *Drum* magazine during its first decade reflects a complex and fast-changing world. *Drum* was established to appeal to the cultural nostalgia of the black urban population, whose rapid increase in the Transvaal region could not be ignored.

After the discovery of gold in the 1880s on the Rand (or 'Reef', a geological formation that was to establish Johannesburg as a city), movement to and urbanisation in the area exploded. At the time, the Transvaal was a 'Boer Republic'; in other words, it had been colonised by the descendants of Dutch immigrants who had spread northwards. Its mineral wealth led to the British fighting two wars (formerly known as the Anglo-Boer Wars, now more correctly termed the South African Wars) to seize the Boer regions in order to serve the economic interests of the British Empire.

After these conflicts, and the formation of the Union of South Africa in 1910, there was an urgent need to rebuild the country and its economy. Gold mining was rapidly becoming a major economic driver in South Africa, and there was a need for a fixed labour force to work in the mines. Every occasion of major strife in the world is followed by an urgent need to rebuild, to reconstruct the affected country and revitalise its economy. These projects of renewal and rebuilding rely on a substantial workforce, often in the form of cheap labour.

In the case of South Africa, this led to major movement of black people from the rural areas of the Union and the southern African region to the rapidly growing industrial and urbanising areas. This growth was evident in the Transvaal area after the First World War (1914–1918), but it was after the Second World War (1939–1945) that the Baileys realised the potential market presented by the burgeoning black middle class of Johannesburg.

According to Nxumalo, '[Bob] Crisp did not grasp the full extent of the urbanising process. This had accelerated tremendously during the war years when shortages of white labour (as many men joined the army) led to a temporary relaxation of influx control.'[1] *Drum* magazine was established with this growing black urban population in mind. From the perspective of the proprietor, and given the perceived loyalty of Africans to their cultural values, the expectation was that they would embrace a magazine that championed their traditional ways. This was a fundamental mistake.

Feeding the urban Africans' content about their traditional heritage and appealing to nostalgia for rural life did not prove to be a wise strategy to lure readers. The first few issues of *Drum* magazine were monumental failures, with virtually no interest shown by the targeted urban African audience. According to David Rabkin, 'After the first four issues (March–June 1951) the circulation was only twenty thousand, and Bailey was losing £200 a month.'[2] These losses demanded an urgent review of strategy to save the magazine from an untimely death.

In November 1951, Crisp resigned as the editor and was replaced by Anthony Sampson. By this time, Jim Bailey had taken over as the proprietor, and had also decided to relocate the magazine from its original base in Cape Town to Johannesburg. According to Sampson, 'I became editor of *Drum* when it was six months old. I had been invited to South Africa three months earlier by an eccentric drinking friend called Jim Bailey, whom I had met at Oxford. He had cabled me to join a new black magazine: I regarded myself as unemployable. I knew nothing about Africa or journalism, so I went.'[3]

Even though Sampson had no prior editorial experience, he was wise enough to survey the opinions of the target market. It soon became apparent that the urban black community did not relate to the content that harked back nostalgically to tribal lifestyles; this, in fact, ran counter to their current circumstances in the urban spaces they had embraced, and in which they aspired to a better life.

Following these observations, and in an effort to bridge the gap between the magazine and its target market, an advisory board comprised of individuals from the targeted communities was established. Furthermore, Sampson allowed the black scribes to follow their own style of writing, which was presumably the style fancied by their target market. 'I was diffident about writing so I left the black journalists to write in a style that offended all the laws of Fleet Street, but which had a vigour and freshness that came from the heart of the townships.'[4]

As part of its ongoing transformation, in 1952 *Drum* initiated a short story competition. Over a thousand entries were received from across the African continent and the diaspora. The judging panel was chaired by the distinguished South African novelist Peter Abrahams, who said of the winning story: 'I should say that we have in this story notice of unusual literary promise and I can think of nothing more encouraging than that such promise should be rewarded with the *Drum* prize.'[5]

This story was 'Mob Passion' – penned by one D. Can Themba, a 28-year-old teacher living in Sophiatown. Winning this competition was a major breakthrough in Themba's career as a writer, and it also led to a transformation in his professional life. Shortly after winning the coveted prize, he was invited to work for *Drum* magazine full-time, a shift that catapulted him into stardom.

But this did not happen immediately. In the article announcing his win in the *Drum* issue of March 1953, Themba was introduced as a teacher who wrote in his leisure time: 'When his work as a teacher is over for the day, Themba seeks the peace of his room, where he can work.'[6] Little did he know that he would soon be reaching for fame as a journalist for the same magazine.

Themba saw winning the *Drum* competition as a vital step towards the fulfilment of his dream of becoming an author, saying: 'Winning the *Drum* contest, I feel inspired to go on writing and writing until one day, perhaps I'll be a really famous author.'[7] At that point, he envisaged keeping his job as a teacher, to which he had a special attachment, if not a lifetime commitment.

So the offer to join *Drum* magazine as a reporter, in the midst of his struggles with the education authorities, must have seemed like a golden opportunity. According to Jürgen Schadeberg, initially Themba seemed like a misfit. He wore a suit to work and seemed too serious for the newsroom. 'It took two or three days, [then] he adapted and he got used to it and he started taking off his tie and his jacket and he started to relax. He was fascinated by Anthony Sampson and Jim Bailey, who were both sort of former Oxford intellectuals and continuously discussed Shakespeare and Dickens.'[8]

Themba connected with both Bailey and Sampson, proprietor and editor respectively, largely because of their mutual interest in the classics of English literature. Themba, a fierce debater who was known for reciting Shakespeare at will, could engage on any intellectual subject with the two white men. They respected him both for his extensive knowledge of the English literary tradition, and his superior knowledge of township life, which was now the focus of the magazine. 'In fact, I discovered that Arthur [Maimane] and Can understood *Julius Caesar* much better than I did, as a study in revolution,' said Sampson.[9]

They were so pleased with Themba that by 1954, he was appointed editor of the newly established *Africa!* magazine. 'In order to give Can Themba an opportunity to use his talent better, Jim and Tony decided to start a new magazine, small in size (7 × 10 inch) and 60 pages in length, using the overflow material from *Drum*. Can would be the editor. Can was delighted. He brought in one of his former students, Casey Motsisi, as his assistant. They decided to call the magazine *Africa!*,' according to Schadeberg.[10] In addition to working as a reporter for *Drum* and serving as the editor of the newly founded *Africa!*, Themba also wrote for *Drum*'s sister newspaper, *Golden City Post*.

Themba served under three different editors at *Drum*. When he joined the magazine in 1953, it was under the editorship of Sampson. Sampson left his job and South Africa in 1955, and returned to his ancestral land. He was replaced by a South African journalist who had been based in Britain, Sylvester Stein. Sampson's departure actually worked in Themba's favour, because, upon his arrival, Stein appointed him as his associate editor, the number two position. Stein confessed that Themba, whom he described as a 'man of personal leadership and profound reasoning power', took responsibility for educating him, the new arrival, even though his was the senior position.[11]

Can Themba's colleagues and the new friends he made through his work were to have a dramatic impact on his professional and personal life. The pressures of journalism in the apartheid state created close bonds between Themba and his peers, and together they became a band of troubadours often referred to as the '*Drum* Boys'. His circles expanded to include friendships with white left-wing intellectuals and artists, who often gathered in his House of Truth and in shebeens. His work and location in Sophiatown placed him at the heart of the urban cultural ferment of the time. The *Drum* seduction was complete.

6

Occasions for Loving

The art of making love is lost in the townships, forgotten under the crush of hard living; the hardening of hearts and the coarsening of words and attitudes. A boy meets an attractive girl at a street-corner, twists her arm or wields a menacing blade, and if there is not another strongman in the neighbourhood who has already claimed her, she becomes his.

Can Themba — *Fighting Talk* (1961/962), 16

'Why would you marry me?' Can Themba asked his 32-year-old girlfriend, Anne Sereto. It was 1959, and Can was a 35-year-old bachelor. This was an odd way of proposing marriage, but then again Can von Themba was no ordinary man – he was 'the lanky, shambolic of dress, elegant in speech and writing, boozing, impish, scholarly journalist', as Aggrey Klaaste described him.[1]

Themba had been in the public eye since winning the *Drum* short story competition and subsequently joining the stable in 1953. Shortly after he joined *Drum*, the magazine was inundated with correspondence from readers seeking advice relating to matters of the heart from the young bachelor. In his editorial comment of the August 1953 issue, Anthony Sampson wrote that most of these letters were from students who knew Themba as their English master and admired him 'as both a teacher and a love expert but felt shy of asking him direct questions about these things'. According to Sampson, Themba's fan mail came 'as far afield as from Nigeria'.[2]

Themba jokingly wrote that readers seeking his romantic advice tended to take his surname 'Themba' (meaning 'trust') literally. 'After all I am an ignorant bachelor. The problems they send me help me swell my ideas for future "passionate stories" – and moola!' At the time, Themba had published two short stories with *Drum* – 'Passionate Stranger' and 'Mob Passion'.

Like most other young men about town, Themba had had occasions for loving. Some of these romantic associations were documented and publicly spoken about; others were not publicly known; others remain unsubstantiated rumours to this day.

It is important that we take an interest in Themba's personal life in an attempt to know him as a person beyond the popular public figure. Although a number of texts refer to some of his relationships, other fundamental aspects, such as his marriage, are hardly ever mentioned; nor is his family life explored in any depth.

Writing about the origins of their relationship, Anne said she was introduced to Can by a mutual friend, Lefinah Tsele, back in 1947. At the time Can was pursuing his BA degree at Fort Hare in Alice. The introduction emanated from an argument Can had had with Tsele about exercising restraint when faced with an attractive girl. His friend promised to introduce Can to a beautiful girl who would break his resistance. Can lost that round: he found Anne Sereto irresistible. It turned out the feelings were mutual, and the couple hit the ground running. After two years, Anne broke things off with Can, while he was working as a teacher at Madibane High School in the Western Native Township. Anne went on to work as a nurse.

The pair ran into each other ten years later, in 1959, and this time Can did not waste the opportunity. 'Nice to meet you again,' he had said. 'Who's the lucky guy?' Upon hearing that Anne had not yet gone down the aisle, he wondered aloud why such a beautiful girl had remained single all those years. 'If the guys don't want to lend a hand in marriage, there's nothing I can do about it,' Anne had explained.[3]

Can made his intentions very clear. 'Sweetie, as long as you can still raise an orgasm, let's get married right away. You have wasted ten of my precious years. I could have kids as big as myself by now! One question: Why would you marry me?' This question was some kind of a litmus test for Can, who was known as an expert on existentialism and had a penchant for irony. 'Because you are a loveable man. A complete being – a human being,' replied Anne.[4] This was all Themba needed to hear to put an end to his bachelorhood.

When Anne, in turn, asked him the reason for his prolonged bachelorhood, his explanation was that the many women he had courted were interested in marrying the titles instead of the man. '[Yours] is the answer I wanted from women; whenever I asked someone to marry me and when I asked her why she would marry me, she'd tell me that I'm Can Themba the BA; Can Themba the English teacher; Can Themba the journalist; you name it. Never Can Themba the human being.'[5]

The response he got from Anne convinced him that he had finally met someone who loved him for who he was as a person: 'For goodness sake, let's get married soonest!'

Can and Anne tied the knot on 10 November 1959. A year later, they were blessed with a daughter, Morongwa, with whom they later went to live in exile in Swaziland. They lived the largest part of their family life exiled in the British protectorate. In 1965, they had another daughter, Yvonne.

Can Themba might have been a public figure, but his family life remained private to the extent that even his colleague at *Drum*, Obed Musi, did not know the intimate details of his family. In *A Good-Looking Corpse*, Musi is quoted saying, 'Can was a very ebullient man, larger than life in a way. There was a bit of loneliness one could detect under the hard-drinking Can. *Because to this day I've never met anybody who says, I'm Can's brother or Can's cousin* [my emphasis].'[6]

In his very first appearance in *Drum* magazine in March 1953, Themba spoke freely about his life in general, including the romantic side. Following his announcement as the winner of the *Drum* short story prize, the 28-year-old bachelor revealed to Henry Nxumalo that he had a girlfriend. 'I like women, although I'm still a bachelor. But all my love affairs until now have been tragic ones. But at last I'm lucky, my girlfriend – she's a 22-year-old nurse – is one of the prettiest girls on the Reef. At least I think so.' Indeed, the pictures of Elizabeth Maizzie Maphisa confirm that she was a sight to behold.

Themba was himself not a bad-looking lad. He appears in the picture taken by Jürgen Schadeberg on the day of the interview wearing a crisp white shirt, a tie and fashionable glasses with round frames. He was a lanky fellow, fairly light-complexioned, with short and neatly combed hair. As a teacher and later a senior journalist, in most photos he appears in formal attire. Even before winning the prize, as a young, good-looking professional, he was an eligible bachelor. As for his beautiful girlfriend, her identity would not be publicly known until the product of that relationship introduced himself to Can's family more than three decades later.

In 1954, Maizzie Maphisa gave birth to a baby boy and named him Linda. He was to be her only biological child. She was working as a nurse at Baragwanath Hospital in Johannesburg at the time. Maizzie informed Linda that his father was one Can Themba, a legendary journalist who died while exiled in Swaziland. Linda does not have any recollection of ever meeting his father. Maizzie and Can were not married at the time she became pregnant.

In many African communities, it is customary for the family of the impregnator to pay for damages, or 'go up with the arm' and ask for a hand in marriage. For this to happen, a delegation from the family of the impregnated woman visits the impregnator's family, and informs them of or shows them the 'damage'. Alternatively, the family of the impregnator sends a dignified delegation comprised of elders to the girl's family. The family of the 'damaged' girl usually determines the worth of the damages, or the lobolo (bride price) in a case where marriage is proposed. The negotiations often begin on an adversarial note, especially on the part of the girl's relatives, as it is seen as disgraceful for the girl to be deflowered and impregnated out of wedlock. The 'worth' of the girl is usually measured according to whether she has had a child before, her level of education, and whether she has a job.

In the case of Maizzie, her family had invested a lot in her education by 1950s' standards. She had completed her Junior Certificate at Orlando High School, where Themba was often invited as a guest teacher. She then trained as a nurse at the Coronation Hospital in Johannesburg; King Edward VIII Hospital in Durban (where she completed her midwifery nursing); and Baragwanath Hospital, where she completed paediatric nursing. Just as she was beginning to earn a living working as a nurse, she became pregnant. These factors most likely amplified the rage and disappointment her family felt, hence the antagonistic atmosphere when the delegation representing Themba approached them. It is possible that the arrival of the delegation incensed the Maphisa family even further. The result was that the party representing Themba was chased away, for reasons that can only be left to speculation. They apparently called them 'uncouth boesman', probably because they did not observe the customary protocols, and did not speak any African languages. The use of the derogatory and racially offensive term 'boesman' to refer to the delegation is telling of the animosity that prevailed. It remains unknown whether Themba's party was there to take responsibility for the damages or to ask for Maizzie's hand in marriage.[7]

Meanwhile, far from the traditional drama, Themba was into his second year as a journalist at *Drum* and fast becoming a sensation in the media fraternity. A fun-loving, playful and yet sophisticated public intellectual, Themba soon became one of the most well-known and celebrated figures in Sophiatown. His influence spread across the continent, as *Drum* was also distributed in East and West Africa.

As a journalist working for *Drum* magazine, which thrived on creating posters of pin-up girls, film stars and beauty queens, Themba worked closely with a number of models, actors and musicians, in an era in which sexual stereotyping was a normal part of creating glamour and intrigue.

In one 1956 file image, Themba and Arthur Maimane are posing with dancer, actress and singer Dottie Tiyo, and beauty queen Selina Kolae, on the Johannesburg mine dumps, often used as 'beach background' in *Drum* photos. In another series of photos from the *Drum* archives in their commemorative publication, *The Fifties People of South Africa*, Themba appears, playing around and posing for pictures with several different women.[8] In three of the pictures, he is kissing different women, and in one he is clowning around with two others, with a note attached to his back reading, 'Not Now the Mrs is Around Phone 351240'. The latter is obviously a joke, and many of the photos were taken at very light-hearted moments, but they do confirm the claims that Themba was loved by many, and had many occasions for loving.

One of the cultural icons of the 1950s was beauty queen Dolly Rathebe, who achieved fame both on stage as a musician and on screen as an actress. Themba's article 'Dolly and Her Men', published in the January 1957 issue of *Drum*, claimed he was 'one of the men in Dolly's romantic life'.[9] In a different image published in *The Fifties People of South Africa*, Can appears locked in a passionate kiss with Dolly Rathebe.[10]

No other journalist from the 1950s' generation wrote as comprehensively and passionately about Dolly Rathebe as Themba did in a series of articles, now republished as a single piece, 'The Life and Love of Dolly Rathebe', in *The World of Can Themba*. The wide-ranging essay includes subheadings such as 'Dolly and Her Men', 'Dolly in Films', 'Dolly in Jo'burg's White Night-Clubs', 'Dolly from Place to Place with African Jazz', as well as 'Queen of Song'. Describing Dolly's musical prowess, Themba says, 'She used the stage as if every square inch belonged to her; as if she were a boxer in a ring and her art depended on her ability to prove that she had a life lease on it.'[11] On the matter of Dolly and her men, Themba writes: 'Her love affairs of this period were like wisps of smoke. One moment thick and meaningful, the next moment gone and forgotten.'[12] He closed the third instalment of his series of tributes to Dolly with the following words: 'People have called her all sorts of names, those who thought they were entitled to cast the first stone. But somehow none of these things stuck. Out of the mire has emerged a queen, on the compost heap has grown a flower to perfume the township air … If she has been a she-devil, that's because she's a helluva woman!'[13]

In the story 'Requiem for Sophiatown', Themba reveals that at one point Dolly sang the blues to him: 'I didn't ask her. She just sidled over to me on the couch and broke into a song. It was delicious.'[14] The story that Themba relates here sounds like a replay of the scene in the film *Come Back, Africa*, where he plays a cameo role alongside Bloke Modisane and Lewis Nkosi. In a set-up that depicts a shebeen, venerated musician Miriam Makeba breaks into song, and everyone sings and dances along. Themba appears as his usual self – constantly puffing on a cigarette and moving rhythmically to the song, even though he does not quite break into his famous clockwork dance, described earlier.

In another instance mentioned earlier, on the occasion of the official opening of Themba's House of Truth, Dolly graced the event with a special performance. It is unimaginable that a superstar of Dolly Rathebe's stature would bother rendering a live performance at the opening of a one-and-a-half-roomed bachelor apartment unless for very special reasons. Can and Dolly had a close relationship, irrespective of whether there was a romantic association or not.

Another beauty with whom Themba was rumoured to have had a relationship was Juby Mayet, a cover girl and one of the very few women journalists who worked for *Drum* magazine in the late 1950s to early 1960s. Mayet joined the stable in 1958, and worked closely with Themba, who was by then the associate editor of *Drum* and the news editor of the *Golden City Post*.

Mayet understandably idolised Themba, her senior and mentor, whom she described as the inimitable 'Can von Themba'. She went on to write, 'Now there was a guy an aspiring young writer could admire, could love, even, as in that special way I loved him.'[15] This is further corroborated by her assertion in the interview she gave me in 2015, that her love for him was platonic; she spelled out that she had nothing but respect for Can Themba.[16] There was mutual admiration between the two, as evidenced by Mayet's homage published in *The Classic* in 1968. Themba treated her like a little sister, and even called her 'Kid'.

Mayet told me the story of how she ended up sharing a bed with Themba. One night, Juby, a 'Malay'[17] girl from a middle-class family in the suburb of Vrededorp, found herself in Sophiatown, and had no choice but to sleep over at Bob Gosani's place (Gosani was a photographer at *Drum*). The only trouble, she was to learn from Bob's wife, was that she had to share the only available stretcher with a man – Can Themba. Concerned about her safety, but left with no options as she could not even dream of travelling to Vrededorp that late at night, she agreed to share the bed with her male colleague. 'My God, I'm going to sleep next to Can Themba, am I going to be safe?' she wondered. She awoke the following morning totally untouched, except by the bedbugs.

Themba's most documented romantic relationship is an affair he had with Jean Hart, a British émigré who came to South Africa to join her husband, Malcolm Hart, in 1957. Malcolm had arrived in the country earlier that year and was already part of liberal circles in Johannesburg. He struck up a close friendship with Bloke Modisane, who introduced him to his circle of friends and colleagues at *Drum* magazine. They defiantly went to shebeens and attended racially mixed parties in the townships as well as the white suburbs. Upon Jean's arrival, a party to welcome her was organised at Ma-Bloke's place (Modisane's mother and herself a shebeen queen) in Sophiatown. It was at this party that Jean first laid eyes on Can Themba, and their initial conversation was hardly conducive for romance. Apparently he walked up to her and declared up front, 'Before we begin, just remember there are twelve million of us and three million of you, and if we kill one of you and die ourselves there are still enough of us to carry on. That's how you must remember your position in South Africa.'[18]

She elaborates in her interview with Mike Nicol: 'This was a bit heavy, especially from him, because he turned out to be quite the opposite. I fell in love with him and we had an affair eventually … Apart from that introduction though, he turned out to be a most gentle and tolerant and humane person, not a politico at all.'[19]

Jean's interpretation was that he was saying that they could be jolly and have fun together, but they could never forget the reality of being a black and a white person in a racist South Africa. 'It was a rather hysterical, over-elaborate way of describing it, but I think that was what the intention was. We can now be friends, but …'[20]

Can and Jean had one of the most sizzling and dramatic affairs of the 1950s, which became the subject of several books, films and plays. According to Sylvester Stein, their relationship became a socio-political allegory reflecting the absurdity of the discriminatory laws of the time. 'I never did get at the full truth until eventually a total of four different books based on that daring story appeared. As it happened, one of them was a novel of my own.'[21] The lovers were well aware of the threat posed by the security police, and either thought theirs was a worthwhile cause, or valued their love for each other more than they feared the prospects of arrest and jail.

Apart from the threat posed by the apartheid Immorality Act prohibiting romantic and sexual relationships between blacks and whites, as well as the brutality of law enforcement officers – who could beat Themba to the end of his wits – there was the little matter of Jean being a married woman. Almost fifty years later, when I asked Mayet about the affair during our interview, she still felt uncomfortable talking about it, probably because of the element of adultery. Her most expansive comment about what was a well-known relationship was: 'We had suspicions, there were some of us who had inklings of it, but it was his private life and we felt it wasn't our place to ask questions or to discuss it or anything.'[22]

The story of Jean and Malcolm Hart and their troubled relationship is germane here. When she came to South Africa to join her husband, they had been married for about three years. Even before meeting Can, Jean had never been fully committed to her marriage. Her husband was aware of this, but was determined to forge ahead. In my interview with him in January 2020, Malcolm suggested that he had suffered in the relationship partly because his wife was more experienced than he was in matters of the heart.

They first met in 1950 as students at St Martin's School of Art in Charing Cross Road, London. Jean came from a working-class background and was highly political. She had joined the institution from East Ham Grammar School for Girls, where she had studied after winning a scholarship. 'She was one of the first generation of working-class East Enders to pick up a decent education and, almost inevitably, a confirmed belief in Marxism.'[23]

Malcolm was in his second year when the 'strikingly attractive' Jean, who had 'everyone's eye', arrived to do her first year at the art school. Because of her beauty and vocal talent, she was the centre of attention. The two students shared a passion for blues. Jean had a guitar, taught Malcolm some chords, and they started singing together. They became popular entertainers on campus and entered into a relationship.

Malcolm started showing signs of insecurity as early as their student days. Because of her popularity, Jean got along with anyone who professed to love her. This left Malcolm feeling somewhat inadequate and constantly suspicious of any interactions Jean had with other men. Malcolm thought that marriage might be a solution: 'Despite my despair over each of her short-lived affairs, real or imagined, I'm determined to marry her, sure that things will be different when we're husband and wife. Things will be as they ought to be.'[24]

Their wedding was set for January 1954 at Wandsworth Town Hall. It was a bitterly cold day, an omen of what was to unfold. Jean woke up on the morning of the wedding and announced that she could not go ahead with it. Malcolm was furious: 'I'm angry as hell thinking of all our promises, the arrangements we've made, the people we'd invited. I threaten her with worse than death if she walks away. Later that morning we married. The wedding photograph, a grey picture, looks more like a public execution than a wedding.'[25] Despite having forced matters along, Malcom's victory was short-lived. Ten minutes into the reception, frustrated and miserable, Jean threw her wedding ring at Malcolm and fled, leaving the wedding guests astonished and the groom embarrassed.

They later talked things over, with Jean remorseful at having embarrassed Malcolm in front of his family. Malcolm had already had the difficult task of convincing his family to accept Jean, as he came from a Jewish family and his family would have preferred him to marry a Jewish woman. His family had, in fact, emigrated to South Africa in 1952, following an encounter with a South African

Jewish family whose son they had accommodated in England during a school visit. They wanted Malcolm to move to South Africa with them, but, after a short visit in 1954, his first-hand experience of the racism prevalent in the country made him reluctant to emigrate. However, following the spectacle of his dramatic wedding, and keen to relocate to avoid military conscription at home, he reconsidered his position. No doubt attempting to compensate for the humiliation she had caused him, Jean agreed to move to South Africa.

This was a victory for Malcolm, but only for a brief time, as much worse was to follow. Jean had been exposed to the cultural dynamism of South Africa through music before she had ever set foot in the country. On his return from his first visit to South Africa, Malcolm had brought back a number of vinyl records by African artists, including the original Solomon Linda composition 'Mbube', popularly known as 'The Lion Sleeps Tonight'. Malcolm and Jean learned the songs and were able to sing the lyrics in the original African languages. Jean, who was a good dancer, also learned kwela dance steps to go with the music. However, Jean's appreciation of South African music did not blind her to the racism in the country, or its racist laws. Apartheid was under rapid construction, and law after law was being promulgated to further entrench racial divides. As a staunch communist with a working-class background, she saw this as a matter of concern.

Arriving in South Africa, then descending into grand apartheid, Jean tried to fight the system, questioning the rampant inequalities that whites around her and the broader society took for granted. Her husband had a job in the corporate sector and, at social gatherings, Jean would confront his colleagues about how they treated their fellow black citizens. She was miserable, unable to enjoy anything South Africa had to offer.

This all changed when Malcolm took her to the Bantu Men's Social Centre, where he was giving guitar lessons. The club was partly a response to the Bantu Education Act, which deliberately lowered the standard of education for black South Africans. The ANC found innovative methods of schooling, organising what were called cultural clubs or 'education shebeens' in the townships as replacements for the formal classroom, which offered rapidly degrading content. In November 1955, Bloke Modisane published an article in *Drum* describing the cultural clubs as follows: 'Education shebeens! Yes, that's what they are calling the Cultural Clubs set up by the A.N.C. to train 8,000 African children who cannot and will not attend Bantu Education schools. Education shebeens – where the children can furtively get some of the "strong drink" of knowledge.'[26]

During his previous visit, Malcolm had been recruited by Nelson Mandela from the ANC to contribute to the alternative cultural schools; on his return, he offered guitar lessons at the centre. There was an immediate change in Jean's mood: 'She smiles for the first time in a week. Not only does she see Africans, she sees a room full of working-class folk she can identify with.'[27]

A graduate with two degrees from art school, Jean found that using art as a teaching method came naturally to her. She joined her husband and other volunteers in finding innovative ways of teaching and thus subverting the objectives of the apartheid government's education policies.

She made a good impression as a dancer, and endeared herself to her new black friends as she jiggled her hips and performed rhythmic kwela moves as expertly as an African woman. She was both a marvel and a wonder to watch, so much so that Stein had the idea to take their repertoire to the streets of Sophiatown. The street performance was covered in *Drum* magazine, and accompanied by a picture of the British man and his wife in full swing.

In identifying with Africans, Jean seems to have become a little too comfortable, because within no time she left her husband for Can Themba. Malcolm had suspicions that Jean had had extramarital affairs before, but this was the first time she had actually packed her bags and gone to stay with a lover. That lover happened to be someone Malcolm admired and considered a friend, with whom he had shared drinks and attended parties after they had been introduced to each other by Modisane. 'I'm hurting, my ego bent out of shape, not knowing how to deal with this grand social embarrassment. With Jean gone, my life is in limbo.'[28] Malcolm's agony was compounded by the security police, who visited him and seemed to know all about his movements in political circles, his activities at the Bantu Men's Social Centre and his wife abandoning him. Worse, they knew of her violation of the Immorality Act in having a sexual relationship with a black man: 'Flying in the face of the law, she's living dangerously somewhere in a White Johannesburg suburb with our friend Can Themba.'[29]

Meanwhile, Jean and Can were hopping from one nest to another, trying to find a safe haven for their cross-racial romance, something hardly permissible in apartheid South Africa, with its Group Areas and Immorality Acts set in legislative stone. 'So we had an affair and we lived together under those circumstances, at friends' houses and so on,' Jean told Nicol.[30] There were practical difficulties: members of the black community were prohibited from living in or visiting white-designated areas after certain hours, while whites were not allowed to visit townships except for purposes of collecting or dropping off their employees (mostly domestic workers and nannies). These racially based prohibitions presented a fresh set of humiliations: Jean reported how after parties, she and other white liberals had to write letters for their black friends giving them permission to be in a white suburb for 'work'.

Love across the colour bar also meant sleeping with one eye open, and this apparently bothered Can a great deal. In reflecting on their relationship, Jean also told Nicol that 'Can, who was very analytical as well as being fun, thought things through and I think saw that you couldn't indulge in love and friendship without constantly remembering that those things were going to get distorted by the environment. It was a great pain to him because he was a very open, loving, amiable man.'[31]

Nevertheless, for the black intelligentsia, bringing white guests and lovers to the shebeens in the townships at the height of laws such as the Immorality Act and the Group Areas Act was, it could be argued, a way of subverting the system.

This we learn from Themba's 'Crepuscule', where the narrator takes his white girlfriend, Janet, to a shebeen. But while this creates a sensation among the patrons, it is not necessarily a comfortable one. Seeing that the narrator has arrived with a white guest, two men are rushed off their chairs to make comfortable space for the cross-racial couple. Here we see the narrator's stature being elevated above that of his usual drinking buddies, to the extent of being addressed as 'Mr Themba', a departure from the norm. Although the story purports to be fiction, this kind of awkwardness must have been something the couple had to negotiate in the recreational spaces of the township.

Meanwhile Malcolm had come to realise that there was nothing for him in a racist South Africa that had also robbed him of his shaky marriage, and he decided to return to Britain. It was at this stage that he realised that even though Jean had left him for another man, he still cared for her. They made an appointment to meet so he could inform her about his plans to return home. Here he learned that she had also been contemplating leaving South African shores with her lover. She could not bear the prevalent racism in the country, and the security police were watching her like a hawk, both because of her involvement in political activities, as well as her illegal relationship with Themba. The only hindrance, she shared, was that despite the promise London offered of a much freer society, where no ridiculous race laws would prohibit their relationship, her African boyfriend did not want to leave South Africa.

Can Themba 'felt his place, come what may, to be in Sophiatown'.[32] No amount of persuasion could change Can's mind. Jean was disappointed that Can would not go with her; Can was disappointed that Jean was prepared to leave without him. As for Malcolm, during our interview, and with the benefit of hindsight, he claimed to have been 'sympathetic to their feelings for each other'. He believed that Can and Jean were a good match; he found Can to be a 'brave and smart intellectual', and Jean possessed similar traits.

As Can was determined to stay in the land of his birth, while Jean wanted to leave, she asked Malcom if they could travel back home together. He readily agreed and, on 31 December 1957, the two set out on their journey, hitchhiking and using ground transport to cross the African continent on their way home. This marked the end of a dramatic cross-racial romantic affair between Can Themba and his English lover.

7

Drumming up a Storm

Anthony Sampson, a young English man who had come out to edit Drum *in the beginning of the fifties, had gathered around him an exciting bunch of young writers who considered it, or at least gave the impression of considering it, a mark of great honour to get into trouble with the authorities as often as possible while in pursuit of fact or photograph. In their work they were alive, go-getting, full of nervous energy, very wry, ironic, and they brought to South African journalism a new vitality which none of the white writers had seemed capable of achieving.*

Lewis Nkosi — *Writing Home* (2016), 248

In his journalism work, Can Themba caused quite a storm. He followed in the footsteps of Henry Nxumalo, who was on his way to achieving legendary status for his investigative journalism. The byline 'Mr Drum' was initially conceived as a gimmick to attract the attention of readers. Used first by Nxumalo, 'Mr Drum' soon become a legendary character as Nxumalo embarked on dangerous assignments in his investigations.

One of the first major stories of investigative journalism that appeared under the 'Mr Drum' name was the Bethal farm saga, which exposed massive abuse of labourers. Nxumalo went to the farm under the guise of searching for employment, and worked on the farm for two weeks, thus uncovering a thrilling and scandalous story. However, during those two weeks, his life was at risk, as the working conditions were the definition of modern-day slavery, and he had no way of returning to Johannesburg. Back in the newsroom, the editorial team was getting anxious, and photographer Jürgen Schadeberg was sent to investigate and rescue Nxumalo if possible.

Schadeberg drove for over two hours to get to the small country town of Bethal in what was then the Eastern Transvaal. Once there, he set out to find the Sonneblom farm where Nxumalo was supposedly working as a farm labourer. He noticed Nxumalo among the labourers working on the potato fields under the guard of a man on horseback, carrying a whip. Giving an account of the rescue mission, Schadeberg reports: 'I opened the door of the passenger seat and pressed the hooter, which gave a miserably squeaky sound. I saw that Henry had dropped his basket and had started to run towards me. My heart was racing. Henry stumbled into the car as I put my foot on the gas and the Austin jumped up and down the rough dirt road, engine straining.'[1]

The Bethal story (March 1952) became the biggest news story of the year, and the circulation of *Drum* magazine increased exponentially. From that moment, the Mr Drum exposés were carefully planned as periodic stories. Nxumalo was the daring journalist who originated the stories, and he carried out this task until his transfer to *Golden City Post*. Themba had to fill his shoes. According to Bloke Modisane: 'In 1955 Henry Nxumalo was transferred to *Golden City Post* in his appointment as news editor, and Can Temba [*sic*], next in seniority, was appointed associate editor of *Drum* magazine.'[2]

Themba took to the mammoth task of becoming the voice of Mr Drum like a duck to water. Some of the stories he handled might well have been ordinary, but because he had a certain aura, simple incidents that would barely make it into print under normal circumstances ended up becoming sensational.

One of the more memorable investigative stories he was involved in was the church exposé. This landed in Themba's lap by default after Modisane had bungled it a number of times. Modisane had been selected to carry out Mr Drum's top assignment of the year – one that involved going to services at white churches as a litmus test for their commitment to non-racialism and Christian values.

After several attempts, it was becoming clear that Modisane did not have what it took to elicit a sufficiently dramatic story. The editor at the time, Sylvester Stein, wrote that 'Bloke simply didn't have the raw guts, he'd wilted at the very thought of offending the bourgeoisie, let alone having them boot him out. He felt safer outside. In the end we had to trail off with no story.'[3] After Modisane failed to live up to expectations, an alternative had to be found. 'Can Themba was invited to join me in the assignment, and he immediately proved luckier than I was, his personality invited more violent reaction, in one church, than I had managed in mine,' reported Modisane in his autobiography, *Blame Me on History*.[4] Themba also had a jittery start, failing to show up for the first church visit to which he had been assigned. However, he would soon redeem himself.

The *Drum* team visited several churches over a period of a few weeks and, while Themba was purged like the devil incarnate from many, others welcomed and invited him in; on at least one occasion he was welcomed by the police. In his story 'Brothers in Christ', Themba gave his account of one such a visit: 'It just so happened that it was Nagmaal (Communion) and my fancy was caught by the ritual. When the collection saucers came round I prepared to give my little coin, but the official passed me. As they sang the last hymn, I rose quietly and tiptoed out.'[5] As he stepped out of the church, he was greeted outside by plain-clothed policemen led by none other than his nemesis, the notorious Major Spengler, head of the Special Branch (security police). Spengler was the kind of police chief who did not stay at the police station, but went out to find his targets on his own. He knew by name almost all the 'troublemakers' in Johannesburg.

Other visits were more dramatic, leaving Themba with bruises and losing a few millilitres of blood. In my interview with Peter Magubane, he related one such story. 'We went to a church here in Johannesburg – it was an Afrikaner church. We just walked in like ordinary people coming to church to worship. The minister, as we walked in, he was preaching, then he changed and looked towards us pointing the finger. He said, "Daar is 'n duiwel, daar is 'n duiwel tussen ons midde!" [There is a devil, there is a devil in our midst!] They all looked back and saw Can Themba and I walking in. All hell broke loose. We ran out of the church. Can Themba could not run fast so they caught up with him and *moered* him.'[6]

During one visit to the Seventh Day Adventist church, Themba was manhandled by the members of the church who had anticipated his visit. 'I was suddenly yanked off my feet and rushed down the steps. A big, hefty man, without even stopping to ask me to leave the church, twisted my arm behind my back and together with two others bundled me over to a waiting car,' reported Themba.[7] Schadeberg was there to witness it all. During our interview, he gave his account of the moment: 'They grabbed Can, dragged him and pushed him into a car, and then they noticed Sylvester Stein and said "there's another one" and grabbed Sylvester Steyn and dragged him into a car. Then they saw me, "there's another one", and I started running – you see I had been taking pictures all the time. I was running through town and there were about half a dozen young men with Bibles in their hands chasing me.'[8]

Themba was arrested together with his editor, Stein. Once again, he ended up in front of his nemesis – Major Spengler – and was taken to Marshall Square police station and charged with trespassing. His white editor was not charged for the 'crime' they committed together – the crime of going to church. The church story was so dramatic that everybody spoke about it, and *Drum*'s competitor, the *Rand Daily Mail*, reported on it extensively. The journalists themselves became the news, and by the time *Drum*, which appeared only monthly, published their own story, it was no longer newsworthy.

Themba developed a knack for going down to the 'grassroots' level in far-flung communities to come up with intriguing stories of ordinary people. In 1956, when Lewis Nkosi first arrived at *Drum*, among his earliest recollections are of Themba wearing a suit covered with mud after his visit to a remote rural area, where he had been investigating a story. The lanky scribe would soon be known to Nkosi and many others for his habit of chewing on a matchstick or pin (which would sometimes disappear into his mouth). Nkosi recalls:

> From the conversations I gathered that Can Themba, then *Drum*'s associate editor, had recently come back from the interior of the country where he had investigated the plight of political leaders restricted to security camps by the South African Government on the grounds that they constituted a threat to peace and security. During the writing of the story, Can Themba, being in his melodramatic mood, dubbed the restriction areas 'South Africa's concentration camps'. From then on what had seemed a mildly interesting story assumed a scandal of international proportions. Top-notch Fleet Street correspondents flew into the country in search of what they supposed were Nazi-type 'concentration camps' and it can only be imagined how embarrassed and angry the South African government became.[9]

The place that Themba had just visited on this occasion was Frenchdale, located on the outskirts of Mafeking (now Mahikeng), in what is today known as North West Province. The focus of his interviews was a man called Alcott Gwentshe. His was an extraordinary story. Gwentshe was born in Tsomo, a rural village in the Transkei region of the present-day Eastern Cape. He went to Queenstown for his schooling, and worked in different places around the Cape Province, including Cape Town, before opening a business in East London. Gwentshe was a colourful character: a politician, musician, sports enthusiast and charismatic socialite.

He was politically active as the leader of the ANC Youth League in the Cape, and it was for this 'crime' that the Native Commissioner instructed him to leave for Johannesburg at a day's notice. He was then taken via Nelspruit to Bushbuckridge, a remote rural area that he had never been to before, where he did not know anybody, and where the language spoken bore little resemblance to his native Xhosa.

It was at this point that Gwentshe's dramatic story took further twists and turns. In every place he was sent to, and in spite of the difficulties of his circumstances, he would make friends, start a music band, join a soccer club, and became a popular figure in the community. The response of the apartheid government was to keep removing him from whatever community he had just acquainted himself with, and banish him to yet another remote corner of the country.

Themba had this to say about the Bushbuckridge episode of Gwentshe's banishment: 'At Bushbuckridge he was taken to the Native Commissioner's office. The Native Commissioner allocated him a house near the forest and there he stayed for nine months. When he came there he was broke – "stone broke. I tell you, sir." – worse still, he did not know Shangaan, the staple language of the people around there.'[10]

Gwentshe found himself in a sleepy village, unable even to fend for himself. He wrote to the ANC asking for support, and got assistance from leaders like Z. K. Matthews, and was thus able to survive for a while. He even joined a local soccer club, but what made a major difference was the arrival of his saxophone, sent to him by his wife in the Cape. With the arrival of the musical instrument, Gwentshe joined hands with some locals to start a group called the Bushbuckridge Band. But even this was frowned upon by the apartheid government, which sent its agents around searching for information, trying to establish which local people he had contact with. They intimidated those who were known to have spoken to him to such an extent that some were too terrified to speak to him ever again. For his 'friendliness' with the local people, Gwentshe was served with a yet another banishment order, which took him to another obscure corner of the country – Frenchdale in the Mafeking district.

The conditions in Frenchdale were even more appalling, and Gwentshe made a point of registering this with the authorities. The place was virtually a desert, and he was not allowed to visit Mafeking, where he stood at least a small chance of getting a job and interacting with people. Never to be discouraged, Gwentshe took to his horn again, formed a band, and started playing at functions in Mafeking and its surrounds. They were hired to play at parties, dances and similar functions.

In February 1956, the band played at a reception for the new Barolong chief, Kebalepile Montsioa. The function was graced by the Native Commissioner and other government officials. Gwentshe was arrested and held in custody on the spot for violating his banishment conditions – which required him to stay in Frenchdale and forbade him to venture into the bigger town of Mafeking.

It was this case that attracted Themba's interest, and he travelled all the way to Frenchdale to hear Gwentshe tell of his experiences. This was also how South Africa and the world got to know about this modern 'concentration camp', thanks to Themba's sharp nose for stories.

What is fascinating is the manner in which Themba presented the story. As Nkosi noted, the title was sensationalist enough to raise the concern of international human rights bodies. The headline screamed, 'Banned to the bush' and the subheader read, 'At Frenchdale, Mafeking, the government has a Concentration Camp for its political offenders'. The story opens with a blast: 'South Africa has a "concentration camp" for political offenders and people whose presence in other places has been considered "inimical to peace and good order." The camp was discovered by *Drum* ace reporter Can Themba.'[11]

The choice of words is provocative without distorting the facts. As Nkosi pointed out, by drawing parallels between the situation in Frenchdale and the concentration camps of the Holocaust in Germany so soon after the Second World War, Themba drew the attention of the whole world. While these apartheid isolation areas were not concentration camps of the kind established in Germany and Poland during the war, their existence as places of banishment violated human rights, and Themba wanted them seen as such.

Gwentshe took the matter to court, and ANC and South African Communist Party heavyweight advocate Joe Slovo came all the way from Johannesburg to represent him – in a case that he ultimately won. However, winning a case against the apartheid government was only ever a temporary reprieve, and Gwentshe's troubles continued.

Nevertheless, during his visit, Themba interviewed a number of other 'detainees' in the concentration camps, providing them with a mouthpiece to express their bitterness and share their stories with broader audiences. The chief journalist (what might today be referred to as a 'spin doctor') for the Department of Labour, Dr T. S. van Rooyen, tried to dismiss Themba's assertions, arguing that it was technically incorrect to refer to Frenchdale as a 'concentration camp'. Although there was an element of truth to this, the horse had already bolted. The human rights violations of Frenchdale and similar places of banishment had been exposed to the whole world. The eyes of the global community had been opened to some of the more under-reported atrocities of apartheid South Africa.

When he chose to focus on urban issues, Themba was equally ruthless and scathing in criticising the government. In April 1957, he co-wrote a story with Todd Matshikiza about the Treason Trial and the bus boycott of that year. The story, dubbed 'A Country Marching into Trouble', was written in a similarly sensational and alarmist tone, and demonstrates Themba's political insights. In this story, he and Matshikiza tried to 'psychoanalyse' the South African condition, suggesting remedial actions for the country before it plunged itself into further crisis, referred to as 'the biggest trouble she's ever seen'.[12]

They focused on ordinary people affected by the situation: the 'average boycotter of buses'. They insisted that readers examine what this 'average' person was dreaming of: 'a warm, happy, comfortable future for himself and his kids, where he doesn't get bullied around for passes, where schools are open to all, where jobs are open to all, you can be sure.'[13]

The authors did not just paint a gloomy picture, but used language sure to provoke the apartheid government, writing that South Africa was becoming 'madder and madder'. The introduction to the article was equally sensational: 'In the last few months the Treason Trial arrests and the great bus boycott have helped to hop up political tempers in South Africa until we have suddenly arrived at a dangerous point on the road, with even more dangerous corners ahead. It's a time of crisis and a time to have a look around properly.'[14]

This was a follow-up to an article Themba had written the previous month, in which he was equally scathing and sensational. This was titled 'World's Longest Walk to Work', in which he analysed the meaning of the bus boycott slogan 'Azikwelwa!': 'For all its fierce passion and aggressive power, this slogan of the bus boycott in Johannesburg and Pretoria is in the Passive Voice. No one uses the active voice form of "Ningazikhweli!" (Don't board them) and "Angizikhweli!" (I don't board them).'[15] In his interpretation, the passive voice form was an expression of the suffering and frustration of the people whose voices were being muffled.

Among the accompanying images, the editorial team chose a picture of a boy with a cast on his leg, and captioned it: 'This young boy on crutches hobbled over the nine miles for painful hours.' This article demonstrates the conflict between Themba's literary training and vocation as a journalist. Much of what he writes in this piece could be termed literary or syntactical analysis rather than reportage. In typical Can Themba style, he drops in a quotation from George Orwell's seminal novel *1984*, which made for a profound and troubling warning, even if not too many realised the depth of its meaning at the time. 'Be careful now, "Big Brother is watching you," prophesied George Orwell in his book "1984." It's 1957 in South Africa, but already the big brotherly watchers are on the job. Non-White organisations, political, semi-political and non-political, are carefully being watched by the paternalistic authorities. There are special detectives, spies and secret agents everywhere.'[16]

South Africa was well on the way to becoming a police state. 'Big Brother' was watching every move, and, with the Sharpeville massacre, the Rivonia Trial and the ban on political organisations looming, things were about to get a lot worse.

In another article on the 'Treason Arrests', Themba asks pertinent questions about the logic of putting behind bars those leaders calling for non-violent resistance, who had the ability and authority to reason with agitated communities. He wondered if arresting these 'responsible leaders' would not leave a vacuum that might allow 'more reckless characters' to take over.[17]

It is also worth mentioning Themba's coverage of the women's rebellion against the pass laws in Zeerust. The story of women's resistance against the pass laws in South Africa has attained legendary status, but it is often limited to the 1956 march on the Union Buildings in Pretoria. Less known but equally intriguing is the story of rural women who resisted the pass laws in the area of Zeerust. The May 1958 issue of *Drum* ran an article titled 'Zeerust: The Women's Battle', written by Themba, who was accompanied by photographer Peter Magubane.

In my interview with Magubane, he related the story of how they assimilated with the community while investigating the story ahead of the appearance of the Zeerust women in court. There was a heavy police presence and the media was barred from the area. 'Journalists were banned from entering Zeerust, but *Drum* did not believe in being banned. It did not believe in being told what to do, so the editor said to us, to me and Can Themba, you go to Zeerust and see what you can do there,' he said. The pair from Johannesburg visited the area and pretended to be locals. But first, the photographer had to capture the moment in his lenses:

> I decided to buy half a loaf of bread, scooped the inside and put my camera inside there. I pretended to be eating my bread whilst I'm taking pictures. When I realised that this gimmick will soon be realised, I went and bought a pint of milk. I took out the milk and put my camera in the milk carton – with my cable release from my pocket, I took pictures. *Drum* magazine was the only newspaper that had the trial yaseZeerust.[18]

The duo also crossed the border and interviewed many South African women who had fled the Union to Bechuanaland (now Botswana) because they were unwilling to carry passes. The subheader read, 'The Story of the Refugees Who Have Fled the Union for Bechuanaland', and the main picture showed the 'gate of escape' – the border gate of Bechuanaland and South Africa. Themba wrote that most of these women sneaked into

Bechuanaland at night. He described the escapees as 'modern [V]oortrekkers, black, bitter, beaten'.[19]

Many of the refugees Themba interviewed asked to be anonymous, as they had relatives on the other side of the border and hoped to return to South Africa some day. He visited various villages in Bechuanaland, where he held 'press conferences' with the refugees. He kept count of the South Africans who had taken asylum in different villages in Bechuanaland: 'In Lobatsi live 90 of them. About 60 have found work. In Ramoutsa, near the border at Zeerust, live more than 700 of them.' These women described their ill-treatment at the hands of security police and their collaborators after they refused to carry passes, as well as thrilling stories of escape from the Union. 'I have had to hide in the fields and the hills many times like an animal. We decided to flee from the Union rather than have passes,' related one interviewee, who chose to remain anonymous.[20]

When the government tried to enforce the pass laws, they worked through the chiefs. When those chiefs objected to the extension of pass laws to women, they were forcefully removed from their positions, and new chiefs hand-picked by the government were installed. This was followed by clashes between chiefs sympathetic to the government and their followers, and the supporters of the dethroned chiefs, together with those who opposed the pass laws. This led to widespread violence, characterised by faction fights. One interviewee questioned the very logic of the war that was being waged against women: 'What war is this that fights women! What law is this that when our chief who is not our chief, and his beat-up men, have no more respect for the huts of their fellowmen, beat up their women.'[21]

Themba wrote that the greatest concentration of refugees was in Ramoutsa, where the young and enlightened Chief Kgosi seemed to be doing his best to accommodate the women and provide for their well-being. He was even allocating plots to them, but the number of South African refugees was rapidly escalating. Themba wrote, 'There are about 720 of them, and every day more and more are dodging in.'[22] Many of the women Themba interviewed were despondent, but were resolute in their opposition to carrying passes.

The accompanying pictures in the article showed the fleeing women with babies tightly strapped to their backs. One in particular, sitting with her child and seemingly unfazed by the intrusive photographer, refused to speak, and to Themba, her silence spoke volumes. The caption for the picture read, 'Holding her baby, this woman listened dejectedly, saying nothing, when a group of refugees talked about their troubles at an impromptu meeting at Lobatsi.'[23] It has been more than 60 years since Themba visited Bechuanaland to investigate this story, and the descendants of these women are probably permanent residents of today's Botswana. Such stories of the marginalised and the neglected became characteristic of Themba's journalism.

Themba was also a daring investigative newshound in his own backyard. He was famous as a frequenter of shebeens, the supposedly illegal 'drinking houses' or establishments that arose in the townships because racial segregation forbade black South Africans from entering bars or pubs, or drinking Western liquor. In a comprehensive investigative piece entitled 'Let the People Drink', published in *The World of Can Themba*, Themba gives an in-depth analysis of the drinking culture in the townships. He wrote that there were mainly two types of shebeens: the respectable ones; and those that do not exactly care about their clientele. Among the respectable ones, he lists Little Heaven and The Sanctuary in Sophiatown, The Greenhouse in Newclare, The Kind Lady and The Gardens in Western Township, The Basement in Orlando, and Paradise in George Goch. He felt that these made you feel at home, and the atmosphere was friendly and sociable. However, there are those that he believed were there just out to make money and did not show much care for the customers. He described these shebeens in the following words: 'They are dirty, and crowded, and hostile. The shebeen queen is always hurrying you to drink quickly, and swearing at somebody or other. "You b-s act as if you've licences to drink!" She sells everything, brandy, gin, beer and skokiaan, hops, hoenene, Barberton, pineapple, and even more violent concoctions. It is in these that "doping" takes place.'[24]

Such comparisons could only flow from the pen of an author who was a frequent visitor to these establishments. But Themba was also interested, both as a journalist and a patron, in how shebeen owners obtained illicit liquor. Given the prying eyes of the hostile apartheid government apparatchiks, and the many reported raids by the security police, how did these operations keep the booze flowing?

According to David B. Coplan, some of Sophiatown's iconic shebeens, including Aunt Babe's, The House on the Telegraph Hill, and the Back o' the Moon in particular, became 'genuine nightclubs where the elite of the African business, sporting, entertainment, and underworlds came to talk, listen, and dance to recordings of the latest American jazz'.[25] If an illegal trade centre for alcohol had become as prominent as Coplan describes here, there must have been a well co-ordinated and successfully operating system to procure European liquor.

One of the ways through which the shebeen owners obtained the white man's liquor was by sending white people who were not very well off to the beer halls to 'run' and buy alcohol for them. Sometimes these white 'runners' were given small change or alcohol in lieu of payment. This was a familiar practice, as described by Nkosi: 'The liquor "runners" were white people who bought large stocks from bottle stores and resold to shebeen queens at a profit.'[26]

Themba was not satisfied with this kind of rudimentary understanding; he required first-hand experience of the illicit liquor trade. Curious journalist that he was, he embarked on an investigative journey to establish the covert transactions involved in this trade. He later reflected on his experiences in 'Let the People Drink'. Expressing his interest in investigating, Themba says: 'I wanted to find out where all this liquor comes from. This was tough because nobody wants to talk. Not only from fear of the police, but because the shebeens don't want to give away their "holes" – the sources of their supplies.'[27]

In his quest to find out where the liquor came from, Themba had to go undercover. A friend arranged for him to travel in a van delivering illicit liquor. Themba met the 'boys' in town, and he sat with the driver and his friend, separated by a bunch of flowers that was meant to be part of the disguise for the illicit liquor. Everything was done covertly, and even though the driver did not know his passenger had ulterior motives, Themba was not told where they were going and whom they were meeting. He could only observe that he was in the Vereeniging area on the basis of the car registrations that he saw. In the end, he could chalk up the experience, but information was much harder to come by – one of his less successful expeditions as an investigative journalist.

Undercover assignments and exposés or not, by the end of 1957, life started oozing out of the magazine. First came the devastating murder, by unknown thugs, of Henry Nxumalo on New Year's Eve in 1957, while he was investigating an illegal abortion ring. Nxumalo's death marked the beginning of the end of the 'Fabulous Decade', and the end of *Drum* in this particularly racy and provocative form. In 1958, editor Sylvester Stein left the magazine owing to a conflict with the proprietor (see Chapter 8). Over roughly the same period, Themba's fellow journalists – Ezekiel Mphahlele, Arthur Maimane, Bloke Modisane – left the magazine in quick succession.

Stein said, 'We all suddenly took off within a year or so of this as if on a signal, fleeing South Africa, abandoning *Drum* and leaving virtually only Can and Casey remaining on the spot, loyal to their country and their work on the magazine.'[28]

The scattering of the *Drum* generation, many of whom were forced into exile, is a sad history by any account. The alienation and trauma they experienced led to broken homes, alcoholism and premature deaths.

As the exodus began, Can Themba, the mainstay of the magazine, once again had to hold the fort. Each time an editor left, Themba, as the second in command at the magazine, had to keep the editorial seat warm, ensuring that the magazine – then selling 200 000 copies across the continent – remained in production while waiting for a new editor to be recruited.

In December 1958, after steering the ship for nine months, Themba had to make way for the new editor, Tom Hopkinson, parachuted in all the way from Britain. Hopkinson was the new sheriff in town, and things were about to change.

8

Destruction and Demise

I have heard much, have read much more, of the Will to Live; stories of fantastic retreats from the brink of death at moments when all hope was lost ... But the Will to Die intrigues me more ... I have often wondered if there is not some mesmeric power that fate employs to engage some men deliberately, with macabre relishment, to seek their destruction and to plunge into it.

Can Themba — *The Will to Die* (1985 [1972]), 62

It was Sylvester Stein who poignantly described Can Themba as having 'died of a broken heart'.[1] While the autopsy on Themba's body revealed that he had died of coronary thrombosis, regardless of the official cause of death, the lifeless body that was carried out of that room in Manzini had begun dying many years before. The 8th of September 1967 marked the culmination of a downward spiral in a destructive journey that had begun when he joined *Drum* in 1953 – perhaps even before then.

The apartheid government had systematically driven him out the classroom, and, as a journalist in the line of duty, his mind was battered both by police brutality and Bible-thumping Christians. As Lewis Nkosi puts it, 'Back in the office they wrote up these grim stories of farm labour brutalities, police torture and township riots in a cool sober prose in which they permitted themselves the luxury of a laugh.'[2]

It was against this backdrop that Themba had to find a moment to live, to cope with the suffering of being black in apartheid South Africa, ways of relaxing and dealing with stress.

His own writings, reflections by his friends and colleagues from this period, as well as the anecdotes shared by some of his companions in the interviews reveal many elements that very likely contributed to his personal destruction. There is a shift over time in Themba's writing, from the perspective of an observer presenting his opinions (as he does in his journalistic piece 'Let the People Drink') to essays and stories where he becomes the subject of his own narrative, and candidly describes his own relationship with alcohol. The trajectory he himself describes – reliance on alcohol even as his health deteriorated – echoes the dominant views of other writers when they tell the story of Can Themba.

Nkosi captures this aspect of Themba's lifestyle succinctly in his tribute 'The Late Can Themba: An Appreciation', where he describes Themba as having espoused a 'suicidal kind of living that was bound to destroy his life at a relatively young age'.[3]

There was a constellation of social, emotional and political factors that conspired against Themba, and drove him towards the bottle as a coping mechanism. When Jean Hart unceremoniously left South African shores with her previously rejected husband in December 1957, she left behind a broken-hearted journalist lover in South Africa. Although Themba tells the story of his affair with Hart in 'Crepuscule', the impact of the break-up is something that we learn about from other sources. Nkosi, amongst others, wrote of Themba's devastation after Hart left the country: 'The only time I've seen Can Themba's nerve nearly snap was when he was in love with a beautiful young English woman at a time when she was about to leave the country. He was himself trapped – and it seemed forever – in the land of apartheid. At that time I had a glimpse into someone's suffering and I don't care to see it again.'[4]

Jean's departure from South Africa was not the end of the strong connection that Themba felt he had with her. He expected to hear from her, and was extremely worried when he did not. According to Stein, 'Can seemed to be anxious about a letter from a girlfriend that after several weeks had still not materialised.'[5] As he wondered if in fact a letter had been written, or, if written, ever posted, his anxiety worsened, and those around him began to worry about Themba's state of mind. His desperation seemed uncharacteristic, given that he was well known for his 'devil-may-take-the-hindlegs kind of attitude', as Nkosi wrote in his tribute to Themba.[6]

In the same eulogy, Nkosi seems to suggest that this very attitude was merely a facade; behind it, lay deep heartache. The forced parting from Hart exposed Themba's vulnerabilities, and he took to excessive alcohol to numb the pain and disguise his own anguish. This is what Nkosi called a 'prodigious reliance on alcohol as a drug'.[7] To add substance to Nkosi's claim here, Stein cited a conversation between Themba and his protégé, Casey Motsisi, with whom he spent substantial time in the shebeens at a time when many of their peers in literature and journalism were leaving the country: 'But look man, Casey J., before we go on, I've built important decisions on this letter. It will tell me whether life is worth living or not, or whether to sensibly stick to liquor.'[8]

Themba never received the expected letter, and it looks like he kept his word – he went on drowning his troubles in alcohol. Nkosi's assertion that Themba was devastated by Hart's departure is corroborated by the above extract as reported by Stein, and by Nadine Gordimer, who witnessed the after-effects of the doomed affair. Gordimer describes Themba's suffering and how he took to alcohol with even more fervour during this period: 'So yes, Can suffered very badly from the end of that affair and whenever he suffered he always turned to the bottle. He got to the stage where he couldn't work anymore. You should have seen the condition he was in in those days, often in this house. You just didn't know what to do with him. It was tragic to see someone of his intellect, wit and charm so wasted.'[9]

Jean's departure with her husband Malcolm was followed by the brutal murder of Themba's colleague and close friend, Henry Nxumalo, that very same evening. A number of books, including Gordimer's *Occasion for Loving*, have been written about the affair between Can and Jean. In the film *Drum*, by Zola Maseko, the death of Nxumalo is the central story, but it also features Can and Jean's affair.

Themba was robustly attached to both *Drum* magazine and South Africa, but, by the late 1950s, he was the last remaining senior member of the pantheon of writers from the illustrious 'Fabulous Decade', as described by Nkosi in his essay of the same title.[10] His sidekick, Motsisi, managed to stick with his mentor, but they were just about the only ones who remained from the pantheon of '*Drum* Boys'. Many of his companions, those who arrived before him and those who joined the magazine later, including Ezekiel Mphahlele, Arthur Maimane, Bloke Modisane and Nkosi, left the country while Themba was still trying to churn out a living in South Africa as the pressure to go into exile grew stronger.

It was only after all of his companions had left, after he lost his job at *Drum*, after his lover returned to Britain, and after his second stint in teaching ended, that Themba finally resorted to exile.

In Swaziland, Themba worked as a teacher while also writing for different publications in South Africa and abroad. In 1966, he was banned under the Suppression of Communism Amendment Act of 1965, which prohibited him from being published or even quoted in South Africa. This must have been the last straw for anyone plying their trade as a scribe; writers write to be read, and Themba was deprived of this basic right.

By this time, Themba was drinking to excess, an element prevalent in most of his self-reflective writings of the 1960s, such as 'The Will to Die', 'Bottom of the Bottle' and 'The Last Shebeen'.

Alcoholism is often cited, no doubt plausibly, as the main contributing factor to his demise at the relatively young age of 43; unfortunately, this has become the dominant narrative whenever his life is written about.

These issues are worth exploring as only 14 years earlier, in his first interview with *Drum* magazine, Themba claimed to be a teetotaller. Nevertheless, in a very short space of time he underwent major changes and upheavals in his life. The content of his writing, his analysis of issues, and the perspectives of those surrounding him at the time are all crucial in analysing Themba's personal circumstances. These elements illustrate that more than one factor contributed to his destruction and early demise.

Certainly excessive alcohol consumption has been cited as the primary factor that robbed Themba of life. In his own writings, Themba seems to romanticise his drinking and acknowledges its excessive nature. There is an element of intellectual apathy among those researchers who accept his alcoholism without due consideration of the factors that led to it. We cannot be content with the simple assertion that he was just an alcoholic without interrogating the reports that when he joined *Drum* in 1953, he was apparently a teetotaller; yet in a matter of only 14 years he died of medical conditions supposedly brought on by alcohol abuse. This conundrum is explored further below.

The period leading up to the dismissal of Themba from *Drum*, his going into exile and his ultimate demise can be best understood in the context of the parallel destruction of many associated with the magazine during the same period. Whatever happened at *Drum* did not affect Themba alone; he and his colleagues all battled to cope with the ongoing atrocities in broader South African society. It was just that each person found different means of coping.

It is also important to remember that Themba was part of a generation, a cohort of writers, who not only made history in the South African literary and journalism landscapes, but also in the shebeens, the illegal drinking taverns that were such a prominent feature of township social and cultural life. Drinking became part of a certain subculture at *Drum*, with Themba standing out as the main instigator. This drinking came with certain risk-taking behaviour, perhaps sometimes just for the thrill of it. This sense of communality (or collective victimhood) at *Drum* is well captured by Nkosi: 'A *Drum* man took sex and alcohol in his stride, or was supposed to, and stayed in the front line of danger so long as there was danger to be endured. Of course, the *Drum* style was more implicit than prescribed, but no less paramount in one's life for all that.'[11]

The brutal murder of Nxumalo in December 1957 seemed to be an isolated incident, but, viewed retrospectively, it signalled the beginning of the destruction of a generation. Many of the *Drum* writers were to be dispersed across the world, or to die early deaths. In his book *Who Killed Mr Drum?*, Stein used Nxumalo's death as an entry point, but goes on to lament the tragic lives and premature deaths of several of the '*Drum* Boys', including Themba's in 1967. Strangely enough, the rest of the *Drum* writers who died young did not, as might have been expected given the risks of their lifestyles, perish in a similar fashion to Nxumalo, dying at a knife's edge at the hands of ruthless thugs. Yet, their deaths were equally tragic.

Nxumalo's death was followed by that of Nat Nakasa in 1965, who was presumed to have committed suicide in New York. The reasons proffered for the apparent suicide are that Nakasa was depressed at the time, as going into exile had not been his first choice. This presumption has been brought into question in recent years, as Ryan Brown's biography of Nakasa, *A Native of Nowhere*, raises a number of other possibilities, including that he might have been killed.[12] He fell to his death from the apartment of his friend and benefactor Jack Thompson. Thompson worked for the Farfield Foundation, which had provided Nakasa with the scholarship to the United States, and which turned out to be a conduit for the Central Intelligence Agency (CIA). This raises alarm bells, especially when we discover that Nakasa fell from the apartment of a CIA agent, and his file remained classified for more than forty years after his death. It is possible that Nakasa had discovered the CIA connection to his being in America, the country in which he had sought refuge, and started asking questions: this might have led to a confrontation, possibly resulting in him flying off a New York skyscraper. For now, however, this can only be a matter for speculation. Nevertheless, Nxumalo and Nakasa's deaths had a direct impact on Themba, who wrote moving tributes to them.

As an exodus of journalists left *Drum* and streamed out of the country, Themba and a few others, most notably Motsisi, remained at the magazine and in the country. Themba had to keep things running even as he also contributed to several other publications. There was the perennial problem of insufficient salaries, which reportedly never increased – employees often challenged the editors and the proprietor on this matter. Because the monthly salary was so minuscule, Motsisi used to refer to it as the 'monthly mockery'.

The person who was at more or less the same level as Themba in terms of qualifications and experience, and who probably shared the same frustrations with him, was Mphahlele, the fiction editor at the magazine. Mphahlele held an Honours degree in English and, like Themba, he came to *Drum* with teaching experience. After joining *Drum* magazine in 1955, he held various senior positions, including those of political reporter, subeditor and fiction editor. The movement between the different positions did not, however, instigate any upward progression in his salary. Mphahlele gives his account of the salary situation:

> We were paid just miserably on *Drum*. I remember I was being paid £43 a month to start with. And I had an Honours in English. I said to [Cecil] Eprile when I joined that the pay was low for my qualifications. He said that it wasn't my academic qualifications that were important here but experience in journalism, and as I was just starting I had to be on the same scale as the other reporters. I had no choice so I took it on.[13]

By the time he left *Drum* in 1957, after two years of serving in relatively senior positions, Mphahlele was still getting the same salary of £43 a month. He goes on to say that 'when Can Themba was assistant editor he wasn't getting anything for that position'.[14] The question of salary was obviously troublesome, but it was not the only thing that bothered Themba as a reporter and associate editor.

Before Themba was ultimately fired from *Drum*, he had been subjected to disciplinary action that had impacted on his finances and status as the associate editor. According to Tom Hopkinson, Themba and Bob Gosani were sent on an assignment to Kimberley, travelling in the company car. On their way they drove through Potchefstroom, where they were arrested for possession of liquor and drunkenness. According to Themba and his companion, they were arrested for their kindness. Their version of events is that as they were driving through Potchefstroom, a Woolworths store was gutted by fire, and their journalistic instinct dictated that they stop and take pictures.

However, their humanity superseded the journalistic instinct, so they assisted a helpless white man instead. This man was rescuing some bottles of alcohol in a building next to Woolworths, and being the good natives that they were, they decided to assist the white man. In turn, the white man was so grateful that he offered them six bottles of brandy. They drank only five of the six bottles, but they were not really drunk. This act of kindness got them into trouble with other white men.

Writing about this incident, Hopkinson says: 'They denied that they were drunk at the time, and clearly felt it an injustice that their efforts to help one white man should have landed them in trouble with other whites – first with the cops, now with the editor.'[15]

Following this incident, Hopkinson decided that Can's salary was to be reduced, and his title of associate editor revoked. What this meant is that he would continue carrying out the duties of an assistant editor, but he would not be paid accordingly, nor would he be formally recognised as such. Furthermore, 'Can was to be told that any incident of the kind in future would mean immediate dismissal'.[16] It would appear that Can was the lucky one; as a freelancer, Gosani was dismissed on the spot.

It was a matter of time before the same happened to Themba. Notwithstanding other contributing factors, there is no doubt that alcohol abuse ultimately played a role in both Gosani and Themba losing their jobs at *Drum* magazine.

In conversations I had with Nkosi, he indicated, albeit casually, that he and his peers had to face atrocities during their reporting, and these incidents stayed in their subconscious minds long after they had witnessed them. Consuming copious amounts of alcohol helped them to shift from the mental images that haunted them, and provided them a bit of escapism from the atrocities to which they bore witness on a daily basis.

This sounds like a valid argument to account for the drinking culture prevalent at *Drum*, but it leaves one wondering why Mphahlele was never affected in the same way. It is true that Mphahlele worked for only two years at *Drum*, and did not spend much time as a reporter during that period. He was largely office-based as a subeditor and fiction editor, and was not usually on the ground with the other reporters, who were exposed to the appalling realities of the hard news they investigated.

Nonetheless, regardless of the validity of Nkosi's argument as a justification for the excessive drinking culture at *Drum*, or among the journalism fraternity at large, this account here brings to the fore another possibility. The following passage from Themba's reflections in 'Kwashiorkor' gives some insight into the psychic travails of a reporter back then: 'My life, a reporter's life, is rather full and hectic, and I am so vortically cast about in the whirlpools of Johannesburg that no single thought, no single experience, however profound, can stay with me for long. A week, two weeks, or less, and the picture of the kwashiorkor baby was jarred out of me, or perhaps lost into the limbo where the psyche hides unpleasant dreams.'[17]

Apart from the rigours of reporting hard news, Themba was also bothered by editorial interference from Jim Bailey, who extended his hand beyond the role of proprietor of the magazine. It would seem that Themba's life as associate editor was even more frustrating than when he was a reporter. He had been given a title that only presented illusions of editorial mandate; he was effectively running the magazine, but had virtually no decision-making powers.

On one occasion, he and his editor, Stein, decided on the cover of a forthcoming edition. They had chosen a picture of two women tennis players, one white and the other black, kissing each other in a display of good sportsmanship. This image was meant to demonstrate that the world was moving on, that racial prejudice was as backward and irrelevant as the entire apartheid system. This plan was thwarted by Bailey, who thought it might cause unnecessary political trouble. The South African government was sure to view such an image as offensive, so Themba had the unenviable task of removing it. At the time, Stein was visiting Lesotho. Upon returning and finding out what had happened, he resigned immediately and left South Africa in 1957; 'and for nine months the paper was without an editor'.[18] After Stein's resignation, Themba was one of the three senior journalists who alternated in editing it. The others were Jürgen Schadeberg and Humphrey Tyler. With *Drum* being a magazine for black people, it is easy to guess that the primary responsibility for getting the magazine out fell on Themba's shoulders.

As his experienced colleagues left *Drum* and the country, Themba remained as the only senior black journalist, and even though his working relationship with Stein was often acrimonious, it did occur to the latter that Themba deserved more than he received. He was performing the editor's duties, and, for all practical purposes, he was the editor, even though as a black man he could only rise to the level of associate editor. According to Stein: 'He was the heart of the paper. Perhaps he thought underneath that he was the one who deserved to be editor and perhaps underneath I thought the same, and if he couldn't he might as well spend his time as he liked. All to be attributed to frustration with the system.'[19]

This honest reflection by Stein reveals the frustration that Themba probably suffered on a daily basis. He knew that no matter how educated or experienced he was, and no matter how well he did his job, he would never gain the recognition of being editor of *Drum* magazine, nor would he get any salary increase – simply because he was black. This scenario must have reminded him of the similar frustrations that drove him out of the teaching profession. It seems understandable that when he was confronted by the same demons in a different environment, something was bound to give.

At least Stein understood and empathised with Themba; this was not to be the case with his future editor. Towards the end of 1958, Stein was replaced by Tom Hopkinson, a respected journalist and novelist, but a man with a different management approach. He laid down the law, which made conflict with Themba inevitable, as Can was unlikely to comply with any rules that got between him and his drink. Hopkinson was a stickler, and would also not tolerate unaccounted-for absenteeism from work, something for which Themba was notorious. After Hopkinson had given Themba several warnings, he had to do the seemingly inevitable in his eyes. Stein gave an account of this incident: 'Tom Hopkinson after warning Can about his lateness, his unexplained and lengthy absences, his lack of discipline – as his other editors had – after warning him and warning him, had warned him yet again, as his other editors had, and finally he'd given him "one last, final warning" and after that the sack! As none of us had.'[20]

Stein went on to describe the sacking of Themba as leaving the magazine an empty shell, with its soul and its crew now spread around the world. Hopkinson took the decision to fire Themba despite being warned by Bailey that he should not fire anyone from the newspaper.[21] Themba, in particular, as the most senior black staff member, was seen, as Stein described him, as the heart of the paper and the intellectual powerhouse behind *Drum*. This was admittedly not an easy decision for Hopkinson, who relates the incident as follows: 'At the beginning of February, I sacked Can Themba. This was for me a real disaster, not only from the loss of an assistant editor, on whose knowledge of the South African background, quick wit, and what was quite often cool judgements, I had depended very much for the past year – but as a sign of my own failure.'[22]

What prompted the sacking was Can's notorious absenteeism from work. He had gone to Lesotho for a week. During the same week, Hopkinson was ill for two days, meaning that neither the editor nor his deputy were available during the crucial production week. On his return, Themba explained that their car had broken down in Lesotho, and he had had no way of informing anyone. Furious, Hopkinson claimed that he had not known about the trip to the neighbouring kingdom. Themba reminded him:

> 'But you did, chief.' Can pointed to the calendar hanging on my wall. 'Don't you remember my coming in here a couple of weeks back and telling you I wanted to take a week-end off before long?'
>
> 'Well, yes – I do remember that.'[23]

The damage was too severe, egos too bruised and the working relationship was broken beyond repair. The guillotine fell on Themba's neck.

Themba's departure from *Drum* marked the end of an era, a rapid progression towards the end of the 'Fabulous Decade'. The loss of his job, his colleagues and his lover all contributed to his destruction. The apartheid government was also becoming increasingly vicious in dealing with those who contradicted its policies. It was no surprise that Themba leaned more and more towards drink.

Sinking to the Bottom of the Bottle

Alcohol consumption was part of Can Themba's lifestyle, and it is undeniable that it played a fundamental role in his destruction. It is also true that he was first and foremost a writer, and a distinguished one at that.

In almost every text that interrogates the life and works of Themba, these dichotomies seem to be the most dominant binaries of his life. In fact, because he became known in the public domain as a writer and journalist, with his alcoholism a problem that followed thereafter, the received narrative is that the latter came to dominate his story – and its link to his demise frames it as the 'winner'. For this reason, Themba's phenomenal drinking, which, as noted, he romanticised both in speech and in writing, seems to overshadow his great writing talent, to the annoyance of his offspring and all those who appreciate his work.

At the 2013 Can Themba Memorial Lecture, Yvonne Themba bemoaned the over-emphasis on her father's drinking. Her view was that the lecture revealed an important aspect of her father's positive legacy, one that was more constructive and that should prevail over the dominant narrative of Themba as an alcoholic.

Earlier, in her tribute to her father published in the information booklet published for the launch of *The Suit* stage play in 1993, Yvonne quips, while acknowledging her father's drinking: 'I have also been told about his tendency to imbibe with the same gusto as he displayed when he worked. PHEW! I was beginning to worry that I had a saint for a father!'[24]

This statement, when checked against her later comments, simultaneously bemoans and acknowledges her father's excessive drinking. On these occasions, she neither denied her father's alcoholism, nor did she suggest that his drinking should not be spoken of. Instead, she noted that the focus had been on his drinking at the expense of his vocation, and this had led to neglect of his legacy as a teacher, writer and journalist.

A cursory look at the works that offer criticism of the life or works of Themba shows that alcoholism often features alongside analysis or accounts of his impeccable erudition as a writer, journalist and philosopher, if not forming a large part of his story. For instance, one of the most comprehensive academic studies of Themba's works is provided by Mari Snyman in her Master's thesis, 'Can Themba:

The Life of a Shebeen Intellectual'.[25] As the title shows, Themba's intellectual contribution as a writer and journalist is acknowledged; but folded into this is his association with the shebeen, which speaks to the more destructive aspects of his life.

This kind of critical treatment occurs largely because Themba himself wrote extensively about the drinking culture in Sophiatown, with himself as a main protagonist. His nostalgic writing about the boozy days of Sophiatown, which seem to have followed him all the way to Swaziland, borders on romanticisation.

This is corroborated by different critics; whether they are writing about him, his companions of the *Drum* generation, or 1950s' South Africa, the name of Can Themba is often associated with drinking. In a text like Brown's *A Native of Nowhere*, for instance, Themba is described as leading the charge in promoting the culture of drinking in the newsroom, and particularly in inducting new reporters into it.

One of the most startling revelations germane to Themba's alcoholism is the claim he made in his first *Drum* interview with Henry Nxumalo – that he did not drink. It might not have been much of a shocker at the time, but since Themba's drinking at *Drum* became so legendary, the claim that he did not drink before joining the magazine needs interrogation. The article in which he made this claim was accompanied by the maiden picture of Themba published in *Drum*, taken by Schadeberg in 1952. Schadeberg describes the moment (informing Themba that he had won the short story prize) as follows: 'On a stoep with a red polished floor we found a scholarly looking man sitting in a dilapidated rocking chair. He was wearing horn-rimmed spectacles, a white well-ironed shirt and a conservative dark-blue tie. Can was surprised to see us and expressed great pleasure when Henry told him the good news.'[26]

In the subsequent article, penned by Nxumalo, Themba says, 'As for hobbies, I have none other than my reading and writing. I don't drink but smoke heavily ...' Schadeberg's witness to this claim, and his meeting with Themba before he began drinking, provides interesting clues.[27] Schadeberg corroborated the claim made by Themba in his memoir, in my interview with him in 2018, as well as in an interview with Snyman, where he said: 'He only started drinking once he started with *Drum*. There was very much a drinking culture during that period, and there were a number of people at *Drum* who encouraged the drinking. It was illegal for black people to drink, so it was something to fight the system.'[28]

This assertion by Schadeberg does more than just endorse Themba's claim in his interview with Nxumalo. It also alludes to the pervasive drinking culture at *Drum*, which, this suggests, predates Themba joining the magazine as a scribe. It is well documented that Nxumalo was already legendary for his drinking.

The drinking culture was accepted and even condoned by the seniors at *Drum* magazine. This was revealed by Schadeberg in our interview, when he said that one of the most popular games among the *Drum* writers was the Cardinal Puff, which involved participants drinking copious shots of alcohol in quick succession. Themba and many other *Drum* journalists participated enthusiastically in this game.[29] Loosening up with alcohol became a form of therapy after a long day of work. Schadeberg further reveals that drinking was actually condoned by the bosses, as he argues: 'I found it difficult to understand that both Jim and Tony, and now Sylvester, it seemed, tolerated and even encouraged this drinking behaviour. The argument that most of our black writers were intellectual geniuses on a higher plane and therefore their eccentric, erratic behaviour was almost to be expected, even acceptable, made no sense to me. Can now often disappeared for several days at a time.'[30]

What we also learn from this is that the *Drum* journalists used drinking as a means to subvert unjust apartheid laws. Black people were by law not allowed to drink so-called European liquor, which made them both curious and rebellious, and deepened their thirst for alcohol.

In his piece 'Let the People Drink', Themba challenges these laws and mocks them for their ridiculousness: 'Prohibition has been proved impossible. There is too great a thirst for drink among the unentitled. And too great a thirst for money among the bottle-store keepers. And prohibition is asking for too much from the police.'[31]

In one of his later stories, 'The Last Shebeen', Themba ends with a strong injunction: 'Let the Law just say nix, and we'll be foraging.'[32]

Whether Themba's drinking was perpetuated by the desire to defy apartheid laws, a coping mechanism while reporting gruesome stories, kicking against the frustrations of underpayment, or purely self-destructive is a matter of opinion. What is certain is that all these factors conspired against a troubled genius, whose life was cut short with potentially his best work still ahead.

Themba wrote frankly about the dominant role of drinking in his life, and his attempts to recruit his colleagues to this lifestyle. There is a darker side to his mentorship of younger writers and journalists; as an influential figure at *Drum*, he influenced younger reporters such as Nat Nakasa, Stanley Motjuwadi and Casey Motsisi, amongst others. Many of them followed Themba as he hopped from one Sophiatown shebeen to the next.

By Themba's own admission, in his tribute to Nakasa, 'The Boy with the Tennis Racket', on Nakasa's first day in Sophiatown, Themba took him to the room where he would stay for 'three minutes, five minutes?' before taking him to a shebeen in Edith Street.[33] Nakasa himself had given an account of his own experiences of carousing with Themba, and their overt drinking escapades in the shebeens of Sophiatown, as well as drinking sessions in the houses of white liberals in Johannesburg.

In his biography of Nakasa, Brown describes Themba as the chief architect of the rackety shebeen life and drinking culture. The following excerpt illustrates this view: 'But the *DRUM* staff did their best to introduce new writers to their social scene, and Can led the charge. A man of crackling, constant energy, the former high school teacher put little stake in sobriety – or the people who practised it.'[34]

Brown further details how Themba often called new reporters at *Drum* during working hours, and asked them for a favour. It is easy to predict that that favour involved them buying alcohol for him – but it was not exactly that straightforward. It is said that he would thrust an empty Coke bottle into the hands of the unsuspecting and inexperienced reporter, point him in the direction of the nearest shebeen, and say, 'Bring me a Can Themba Coke,' adding that 'They'll know what I mean'. It was clear that all the local shebeens knew the ingredients of the 'Can Themba Coke': a bottle of Coke dashed with a generous dose of brandy.

Juby Mayet gave me a detailed account of a similar experience. However, she had never been sent to buy what she called the 'Can Themba Special'. According to her, no one was allowed to touch Themba's 'Coke': 'In my innocence, I thought it was Coke and one day we were chatting, walking around there, discussing whatever. I took the bottle and took a couple of gulps and I said, "Hell, this Coke tastes weird." It was the first time in my life I tasted brandy and Coke – that was the "Can von Themba Special".'[35]

This almost casual attitude to alcohol in the workplace, along with drinking games, suggests that hard drinking was very much part of the *Drum* lifestyle, not only outside the office but even within it, according to Schadeberg. No one raised an eyebrow at Themba's generosity in recruiting younger colleagues to this lifestyle, insisting that they trawl the Sophiatown shebeens with him. Among others was Nkosi, who went on to be a legend for his own drinking capacity. In 'The Fabulous Decade', Nkosi gives a detailed account of how Themba introduced him to shebeen life. Nkosi, who by his own account was a teetotaller who had no ambitions of joining the drinking culture at *Drum*, had just arrived from Natal. One of the first questions that Themba asked was whether the boy from Natal drank. When the answer was negative, Themba was disappointed, but seemed determined to change the status quo. This after bemoaning the 'bad choices' that the proprietor of *Drum*, Jim Bailey, had made in bringing a teetotaller who would 'corrupt their morals'. Here is Nkosi's account: 'He then reassured the august company that nothing was lost yet; he vowed to break me in before the month was over. This was to consist generally of taking me on the rounds of Johannesburg shebeens or speakeasies, that twilight underground world of urban African life where all classes met, united only by the need for European alcohol, the consumption of which they were prohibited.'[36]

Nkosi resisted Themba's overtures for over a month, and, perhaps realising that resistance was futile, he took to drink under a different tutelage barely three months later. His pride, of course, lies in the fact that someone other than Themba managed to break him. Nkosi does not tell who the person was, and one would not be surprised that it was Nkosi himself who decided to take his first drink. Nevertheless, Nkosi was satisfied that he had won his own resistance struggle; he was determined that it was not going to be Themba who was going to start him drinking. He regarded Themba as 'someone I presumed to be waging a war against my morals'.[37]

Themba had mastered the art of drinking in shebeens to the extent that when he blacked out, he had a strategy to deal with tsotsis who might try to pickpocket him. Taban Lo Liyong quipped:

> And, since every thief knows that travellers thought their socks were the safest places for hiding their monies, the thief normally went for the shoe and what was inside. Can Themba had therefore promised

> himself that awake, dozing, sleeping, should he feel a touch on his shoes, then the other foot was to administer a sprawling kick. So when Lewis was first employed, and they had repaired to their favourite shebeen, the moment Can Themba took his first nap, a colleague asked Nkosi to remove the shoes for shining. Lewis did. And Can Themba let out his reflex action. In no time Lewis was on the floor at the farthest end of the room.'[38]

Harry Mashabela was another young scribe who recalled Themba taking him to a watering hole: 'On yet another occasion, he took me to Basotholand, a Dube village shebeen, not far from his home. We settled down with a haja (half-bottle). It hit us so heavily that we lost each other in the course of the evening.'[39]

Such jocular drinking stories, and humorous teasing of teetotallers to 'corrupt' them in the newsroom, not only reveal the almost approving attitude to heavy alcohol consumption among the *Drum* cohort, including senior staff; they also stand in stark contrast to Themba's later painful self-awareness of the negative impact of alcohol, not only on his life, but also on the lives of the young people who looked up to him. In the 'Bottom of the Bottle,' he comments:

> The table was spired with bottles of brandy, gin, beer, and we were at the stage of high discourse, much like the majestic demons in the burning pit.
>
> For a moment, as I looked at those young men around me, the luxury of a mild flood of conscience swept over me. They had all at one time or another had visions: to escape their environment; to oppose and overcome their context; to evade and out-distance their destiny, by hard work and sacrifice, by education and native ability, by snatching from the table of occupation some of the chance crumbs of the high-chaired culture. Lord, it struck me, what a treasury of talent I have here in front of me. Must they bury their lives with mine like this under a load of Sophiatown bottles?[40]

While only monikers are mentioned here, perhaps made up in the interests of protecting the identities of the personalities behind these characters, we know of young people who were close to Themba, and who lived lives that resembled his chaotic path. Nakasa, a younger colleague and subordinate of Themba's, fell or jumped from a window in

New York in 1965, dying two years before Themba. Motsisi, Themba's sidekick, who stayed at *Drum* for as long as Themba was there, and was devastated when Themba was fired, died in 1977, exactly ten years after Themba's death, and in similar conditions. As Stein put it, 'He died in hospital, as predicted, and of the effects of drink on his overburdened frame, as predicted, while still in his early forties.'[41]

The point is not just to recite the roll-call of the demise of the '*Drum* Boys', but to note the element of submission, an atmosphere of hopelessness, in which Themba seems to have resigned himself to the life of alcoholism. While he asks whether his young acolytes should go down the same destructive path he is following, he invokes the dreams they may be abandoning, the 'visions' of overcoming their current circumstances. The implication is that he has chosen his path, and that there is no turning back for him. However, he regrets the idea that these young men might bury themselves alongside him under 'a load of Sophiatown bottles'.

Another piece in which Themba seems to be very much aware of the corroding effects of alcohol is 'The Will to Die'. Typical of Themba's writing, the story is autobiography thinly veiled as fiction – if naming the first-person narrator Philip 'Foxy' Matauoane qualifies it as fiction. Here we have a first-person narrative in which the author tells of a fellow teacher and colleague, Philip, whose profile is strikingly similar to that of the author. He is a graduate of the University of Fort Hare who majored in English, and trained to be a teacher, significant resemblances he shares with Themba.

In this particular story, we gain insight into the suffering of a man trying to wash away his troubles with alcohol and whose health is fast deteriorating. He lays bare his feelings for everyone to see, as the following extract demonstrates: 'Superficially it hurt him to cause us so much trouble, but something deep down in him did not allow him to really care. He went on drinking hard. His health was beginning to crack under it. Now, he met every problem with a gurgling answer of the bottle.'[42]

The deep pain that Themba suffered is revealed, for instance, in the following extracts from various of his writings:

> I knew that they were excited by me when I said: 'Why should one believe in anything, when one could live – live, gentlemen, at 212 degrees Fahrenheit? The trouble is, gentlemen, for me, human

> nature stinks; but that is all the material we have to work with.' They said these things I said. But never with my own deep sense of doubt, the sleepless, tossing suspicion that often made me itch in the very heat of my enthusiasm.[43]

> As I brood over these things, I, with my insouciant attitude to matters of weight, I feel a sickly despair which the most potent bottle of brandy cannot wash away. What can I do?[44]

> But I keep having a stupid feeling that somehow, Philip 'Foxy' Matauoane would have felt: 'This is as it should be.' Some folks live the obsession of death.[45]

It is clear that 'insouciant' front or not, Themba was a troubled soul. The anguish he experienced could not be hidden from himself even as he tried to put forward a brave face among his friends. The first excerpt above, from 'The Bottom of the Bottle', reveals his self-doubt, something to which his friends and protégés were not privy. This honest self-reflection offers a glimpse of Themba's vulnerabilities and pain.

The second excerpt, also from 'The Bottom of the Bottle', confirms Themba's use of alcohol as a means of attempting to erase his troubles, yet not even 'the most potent bottle of brandy' is able to wash them away. The final excerpt given here, from 'The Will to Die', is one of the last pieces that Themba wrote before his passing. It subsequently became the title of his first collection of short stories, which was published posthumously in 1972. This particular story is suffused with a sense of despairing surrender. Foxy's obsession with death is that of the author's.

In a foreshadowing of the future, Hopkinson relates a telling incident. On a Monday, after a week in which they had produced the latest edition of the magazine, Themba and the rest of the staff who reported to him did not show up for work. Infuriated by this incident, which happened within weeks of his arrival, Hopkinson decided to go to their houses and force them to come to work. He started at Themba's place; this is how he described the scene after he had knocked hard on the door for a long time: 'At last a face at the window, and a girl let us in. Can, lying across rather than in bed, was in a sleep from which no shakings or shoutings could recall him. Once his eyes rolled up, and it seemed that the dying man might recover consciousness, but a second later he had slid back into the pit.'[46]

This was, in a sense, baptism by alcohol for Hopkinson, as he also ended up in a shebeen to cool off his frustrations. He was with Schadeberg and Butch, who ended up passing out.[47] Hopkinson writes: 'All I had achieved by my ill-tempered expedition was that the one member of the staff who had been partly sober when we set out, was now as drunk as the rest.'[48] Schadeberg did not see any easy resolution, as Hopkinson seemed very impatient and did not try to understand the people that he worked with. The same criticisms of Hopkinson were made by his boss, Bailey, and other contemporaries such as Nkosi and Jean Hart, according to the interviews in Mike Nicol's *A Good-Looking Corpse*.

Themba's pattern of drowning his frustrations in booze, with destructive consequences, is all too common in alcoholics and other addicts. In his essay 'Self-Destructive Behavior: Slow Dying', Samuel Klagsbrun says: 'Of the many forms of slow deaths that professionals meet, certainly alcoholism and drug abuse stand out as major examples of slow suicide ... The issues involved in blatant continuing self-destructive behaviour in the face of clear evidence of self-damage beg for attention. Certainly the problem of massive denial that is "I can overcome anything" plays a role in the personality of such patients.'[49]

Colleagues, friends and lovers acknowledged Themba's alcoholism with varying degrees of fatalism. In her interview with Nicol, Jean Hart said: 'As you would know he was an alcoholic and that I think is where he buried that clarity of vision of what was possible in the society in which he was living. I think it was true of Can that he drank to stop hurting. He drank most of the time.'[50]

In addition, and no doubt related to his excessive alcohol consumption, Themba was plagued by chronic stomach ulcers – stories of him suffering ulcers surface as early as the 1950s, before he was fired from *Drum*. In a fictional depiction of Themba as 'Pan' in Mphahlele's *The Wanderers*, he is constantly mentioned as suffering from the pangs of ulcers, induced by alcohol. As Mphahlele left *Drum* in 1957, the possibilities are that he either witnessed Can's suffering in person, or he was told about it.

Themba was technically a sick man, but one who relied on self-medication to treat his ailment, creating a vicious circle by turning to the bottle to ease the physical pain, of which drinking was the root cause. Keorapetse Kgositsile knew Themba in the 1950s, even though he did not work for *Drum*. In our 2013 interview, he demonstrated how Themba could not walk upright in the mornings, hunching over in response to the pain in his abdomen, until he got his *'regmakertjie'* (fixer-upper). Then he would become lively again:

> One time Can Themba came from covering some story in Lesotho, and he walked into Whitey's, almost bent over with pain, and wanting a drink ... At some point Casey decided to pour him a drink, almost filled up his glass with brandy. And Can went tha-tha-tha [sound demonstrating gulping down], and then f-f-f [exhaling and straightening up with relief]. So it seemed like, this thing is okay for him. We didn't realise that it was not healing, it was numbing the pain. But the destruction of the liver continued.[51]

Nkosi also mentions Themba's ulcers in his essay: 'He tossed the entire contents of a large glass of brandy down his throat, smote his chest and grimaced while the alcohol burned its way down his ulcerous stomach'.[52]

These eye-witness accounts emphasise Themba's reliance on alcohol, not only to wipe away the troubles of the day, but to numb the physical pain caused by his stomach ulcers. This is what led colleagues and friends like Kgositsile to accept that Themba was better off with his drink than without.

It is clear from these accounts that Themba had become a full-blown alcoholic during his years at *Drum*, and this eventually became a marker of his will to die. There was the emotional pain that he suffered, perpetuated by the daily experience of being black in a racially stratified South Africa, where even the most learned had to bear the indignities of unfair working conditions. As Themba said in 'Requiem for Sophiatown', 'Christian Brotherhood must be real. Democracy must actually be the rule of the people: not of a white hobo over a black MA.'[53] Then he had physical pain to contend with, a result of his reliance on alcohol as a coping mechanism. Towards the end of his life, it became clear that Can Themba was a troubled genius whose life was set on an irreversibly destructive path. His will to die was unwavering.

9

The Road to Swaziland: A Kind of Suicide

> *Must we lose all our best people to other countries? Teachers, lawyers, doctors, writers – all troop the ant-road to the north. Obviously, South Africa is left the poorer, and one would have thought this country just can't afford the loss.*
>
> Can Themba — *Drum* (June 1960), 59

The words above are taken from Can Themba's piece on Alfred Hutchinson's memoir of his escape from South Africa into exile, *Road to Ghana.* In reviewing it, typically, Themba injects his voice and opinions about the effects of exile and the brain drain it was causing.[1]

Themba fought to remain, staying on at *Drum* until Tom Hopkinson fired him in 1959. Even then, he remained in South Africa, watching his contemporaries stream out of the country in droves. Many of his colleagues left the country long before he did. Ezekiel Mphahlele left in 1957, Arthur Maimane in 1958, Bloke Modisane in 1959, Todd Matshikiza in 1960, and Lewis Nkosi in 1961. When Themba finally went into exile in 1962, of the illustrious 1950s' pantheon of *Drum* writers, he left behind only Casey Motsisi and Nat Nakasa, who was writing for the *Rand Daily Mail* and preparing to launch his magazine, *The Classic.* Nakasa was to leave South Africa on a one-way exit permit in 1964.

A strong case can be made that by going to Swaziland, Themba was conceding defeat; and, like his other colleagues, he did not survive the exile experience. He was already on course for destruction, and going into exile did not reverse or even halt his downward spiral. While he did not wish to leave South Africa, the apartheid government made it impossible for him to stay, no matter how much he tried to hang on. In 'Requiem for Sophiatown', he asks a rhetorical question: 'What about our African intellectuals who leave the country just when we need them the most?'[2]

This question, which Themba never followed up with further argument, is doubtlessly key in reflecting his sentiments on exile. He believed in supporting the development of his country and fostering change from within. This view is reflected in an interview he did for an American TV documentary, *Changing World*, where he repudiated apartheid 'because ... it does not allow a man to have an opportunity to contribute to the development of South Africa, and he is prepared to throw in everything he's got to make this country a viable country, a beautiful country'. He went on to say, 'I want a co-operation, a communication between different sets of people – even if they are different for whatever reason they are different, I'd like us to live together.' Throughout the interview, Themba emphasised co-operation between black and white people so that they could organise a common destiny for each other as South Africans.[3]

This argument is in line with Mphahlele's reasoning for coming back to live in apartheid South Africa, after many years in exile. Mphahlele returned to South Africa in 1978 despite warnings against that decision from his peers in the literary fraternity, as well as those in the liberation movement. Dennis Brutus, among others, wrote an impassioned plea to Mphahlele, showing him the harm his decision could potentially cause the liberation movement. Themba, on the other hand, tried to hold on to South Africa for as long as he could, putting forward strong motivations for doing so. In the fictional representation from my play *The House of Truth*, inspired partly by the above quotation from 'Requiem for Sophiatown', Themba says: 'In happier times, we philosophised about those African intellectuals who leave the country just when they are needed the most. I made it clear that the last thing I want is to go into exile. I regard exile as the ultimate assault on the human soul. But right now I don't see myself being part of this bigoted society.'[4]

Indeed, Themba crossed the border in 1962. In a video-recorded interview conducted with Themba's widow in 2013, Anne (who passed on in 2014) indicated that her late husband had left South Africa for the sole purpose of writing a book once in exile. He could not do so under the circumstances of the time in South Africa. Swaziland as the destination of choice for exile is a curious one, especially when many South African exiles at the time travelled beyond the southern African region, some going as far afield as Europe and the Americas. After I posed this question to Mrs Themba, her reply was simply that Swaziland resonated with her husband's surname. The name 'Themba' is of Nguni origins, and could fit with any of the Nguni languages, including Zulu, Xhosa, Swati and Ndebele. In southern African countries outside South Africa, the Nguni languages are spoken mainly in Swaziland and Zimbabwe.

This supports the notion that Themba did not want to leave South Africa in the first place, and that he still wanted to be culturally connected to the country, as there is a strong cultural interface between Swaziland and South Africa, even if the political boundaries dictate otherwise. In a written message prepared ahead of the performance of Themba's most famous story, 'The Suit', in 1993, Mrs Themba quotes her husband motivating for his destination of choice for exile: 'The best way out will be to emigrate to one of the protectorates, where I will be as free as air to write the book; and we shall live off the royalties of the book.'[5]

Themba found himself a teaching job at the Swaziland Trade School, also known as the Swaziland College of Technology, a tertiary institution where he held the post of English lecturer. One of his colleagues and closest friends, Swazi journalist Parks Mangena, had fond memories of the days they stayed in the government houses for lecturers. With the help of Father Angelo Ciccone, a Catholic priest, Themba later got another job as a teacher at the St Joseph's Catholic Mission School in Umzimpofu, just outside Manzini. He remained there until his demise in September 1967, following his banishment in South Africa under the Suppression of Communism Amendment Act of 1965 a year earlier.

Finding himself exiled across the fence from his home country, Themba had no choice but to fashion life the only way he knew how. He taught, he wrote and he drank just as he had been doing in South Africa. He hosted parties like he had done at his House of Truth in Sophiatown. Lindiwe Mabuza shared her memories of attending a party hosted by Themba: she got invited through her uncle, George Nxumalo, a brother to Themba's late friend and colleague at *Drum* magazine, Henry Nxumalo. She said Themba was 'a celebrity and a fun person to be with'. It was a privilege to be invited to his house in Mbabane, and everyone would relish the occasion: 'People would come from all corners of Swaziland for a function of that magnitude at his house, the who's who's from Swaziland, from South Africa, [they were] there that night. I had gone with George Nxumalo and his wife Beauty.'[6]

It was not only through the parties he hosted that Themba tried to create a 'normal' life similar to the one he had lived in South Africa. The bars were also his stomping grounds, though in Swaziland they were not illegal shebeens. According to Mbulelo Mzamane, Themba used to spend a lot of time at the George Hotel, one of his favourite watering holes in Manzini. The George was only one of them; according to Mangena, there was also a 'Can Themba corner' at the Central Hotel, their favourite drinking spot in Mbabane.

So, while the countries might have changed, the drinking culture remained the same. This is implied in one of Themba's final published pieces, 'The Last Shebeen', about a shebeen he discovered in Umsunduza township, half a mile outside Mbabane. He quips, 'Trust Can Themba to find a shebeen in the Kalahari if there is one.' Themba goes on to say: 'It's probably the only shebeen in the whole of Swaziland. Of course, it's only a piccanin three-quarter affair, but already I'm on tick there for those Sundays when the Law says we can't carry liquor out.'[7]

If Themba was an alcoholic before he left South Africa, exile offered no reprieve. In fact, his 'will to die' might have been even stronger, with alcoholism his chosen form of slow suicide. Having left South Africa, his South African problems crossed the border with him. His banishment is mentioned as if in passing, whereas it must have delivered one of the most crushing blows to any writer: it meant, among other things, that his words could not be published, quoted or circulated in any form, imposing a permanent silence on a man who lived for words. Themba, who had serious reservations about communism and had written a column in the *Golden City Post* titled 'This is Why I Am Not a Communist', was ironically declared a 'Statutory Communist' in 1966.[8] The impact of such a step by the South African government must have been devastating to Themba, a writer who had gone into exile with the sole intent of writing a book. The writer was deprived of his right to publish. He could never go home. He died a year later.

Sylvester Stein gave an overview of the various factors he believed contributed to Themba's frustrations:

> Can too died in a foreign land – the British Protectorate of Swaziland – and in pallid obscurity, enduring his last few years of life quite unlike the old one. Here again an official and respectable cause of mortality is pinned up on the bulletin board, coronary thrombosis; yet gossip had it that he tumbled off a lorry on a drunken spree, breaking his head and bringing on a heart attack. Yes, no, well – yes, perhaps the official verdict was right, strictly right, *for whatever the actual mode of his going, he surely died of a broken heart* [my emphasis].[9]

It should be noted that the troubles that Themba had had with the Transvaal Education Department had never before been mentioned. While Stein omitted this very important element in his catalogue of Themba's miseries, he was not too far off the mark in general: 'Can had needed to absorb a number of hard knocks – the girl he had loved was gone and he could not follow her, all his colleagues had run off, the life was leaking out of the magazine and he'd been banished from his milieu, his House of Truth and all Sophiatown. Casey too, as his sidekick, suffered from the side-effects of Can's depressions.'[10]

The passing of Themba has also become something of a legend, leading to speculation and a variety of accounts of his death. The divergent views about the life of a man who passed away half a century ago further complicate any attempt to establish factual accuracy of some aspects of Themba's life story. The period of his life in Swaziland, in particular, as he edged closer to his demise, is a hard nut to crack, as he did not write as prolifically as he had in earlier years, which gave room for various rumours to circulate about his life and death.

What has been unclear for a very long time are the whereabouts of his family when he died. In fact, his family is barely mentioned, to the extent that Obed Musi could claim, as mentioned earlier, never to have met anyone related to Themba.

When Themba first crossed the border into Swaziland to eke out a living free from apartheid restrictions, he left his wife and young daughter behind. They later followed, and the family lived together in Mbabane. However, as indicated in the opening chapter, once

Themba found a teaching post at St Joseph's Catholic Mission School, he rented a flat in Manzini, a town not too far from Mbabane. He only joined his growing family in Mbabane on weekends. Regarding this, Anne Themba said: 'I was running the first UNICEF-sponsored nursery school in a township in Mbabane, when Can was transferred to St Joseph's Mission in Umzimpofu, five kilometres outside Manzini. Can, therefore, came to Mbabane over weekends.'[11]

This should answer many lingering questions about Themba's living arrangements in Swaziland, especially regarding the reason he was alone when he died.

The differing accounts of his death make it all the more difficult to be sure of how his lifeless body was discovered on 9 September 1967, a day after he had passed on. Pitika Ntuli's account is probably the most accurate, for even though Themba's door was never opened, his precision in terms of detail, including what day of the week it was, is convincing. Ntuli said that when he visited Themba it was on a Friday and, indeed, 8 September 1967 was a Friday.

A perhaps more apocryphal account comes from legendary poet Don Mattera, who was not in Swaziland during Themba's exile and passing, but had known him while living in Sophiatown. According to Mattera, he envied the manner in which Themba shuffled off this mortal coil, because his exit nurtured living creatures on earth. His claim is that Themba died peacefully in his sleep, and was not discovered immediately. When he was finally found, birds of prey had arrived first and feasted on his eyes. What was stretchered out of his dwelling was a body with pecked-out eyes.[12] While a horrifically gory image, this version does not necessarily contradict the first one.

Mattera's account of events has never been suggested by any other interviewee, but it appears in a poem 'Till No One' by the poet and artist Wopko Jensma, himself a mysterious character whose disappearance in 1993 is still unaccounted for. In his book of poetry, illustrated by his own woodcuts, Jensma pays homage to Can Themba. The last stanza of the poem reads:

In the morning they found him
Cold as a stone
Sparrows pecking his eyes[13]

It is probable that Jensma used poetic licence in imagining the condition in which Themba's body was found. This, however, could mislead readers not privy to the exact facts. Another element with the potential to mislead is that Jensma's poem places Themba's death in Sophiatown. Such inaccuracies render his account defective and unreliable as a source, no matter how compelling as art.

While Themba's passing on 8 September 1967 might have been the culmination of the slippery slope he had been sliding down since joining *Drum*, the converse is also true that his death was the beginning of a process of reconstructing his life. To end this chapter, let me invoke the words of the late South African Nobel laureate for literature, Nadine Gordimer. Concluding her eulogy to Themba, she said: 'Can Themba will never be dead, for us: South African literature, South African readers of his writings, the stirring flash of enlightenment, and the vivid pleasures of his interpretation of our world, along with his.'[14]

PART III

The 'Intellectual Tsotsi'

10

Black Englishman or Detribalised African? A Quest for Shared Identities

We spoke English and Afrikaans in the house because we were both from 'detribalised' family backgrounds – blacks whose first language was Afrikaans. We were not the stereotypical religious family, walking to church on Sundays together with their children. Can professed to be atheist and I am a hard-core Anglican. I still sing in the church choir to this date. We never clashed because we respected each other's beliefs.

Anne Themba — Can Themba Memorial
Lecture pamphlet (June 2013)

As we grapple with the question, 'Who was Can Themba?', an important related question arises: 'Who did Can Themba think he was?'

Can Themba's life was cut so brutally short, leaving these fundamental questions lingering and a lot more unaccomplished. So much for Themba's life trajectory, and the demise hastened (as for so many of his peers) by the fate that sited him in South Africa at a time when burgeoning creativity was being stifled by the rapid evolution of grand apartheid; and by a full-blown addiction. Because the glamour and drama of the *Drum* days, and the tragic whiff of doomed love and self-destruction via the bottle, have so often been the focus of studies of his life and writing, a thorough scrutiny of his self-identity and the complexities of his location in context has been lacking, along with detailed investigation of his politics and his intellectual legacy.

It is at times easy to describe what one is not, but a more difficult task is to describe what one is or stands for. The pertinent questions germane to Can Themba's identity are whether he fell into the category disparagingly referred to at the time as a 'Black Englishman', or if he fitted the definition of a 'detribalised African'. These two categories are obviously subject to interpretation, and are not mutually exclusive; the same individual can possess elements of each. While Anne Themba, in the above epigraph, might have proclaimed quite proudly that she and her husband were a detribalised family, citing as proof the issues of language and modern tolerance of their divergent attitudes towards religion, the counterclaim could be made that in their process of detribalisation, they had lost their cultural doctrines, including their native languages.

The so-called Black Englishmen of Can Themba's era were a cohort ridiculed for aspiring to be something they were not. This antagonistic attitude unfortunately often extended to those Africans who had received Western education and excelled in certain aspects of foreign cultures while remaining loyal to African values.

It is from the strong views expressed by Govan Mbeki, political activist and father of the former president of South Africa, Thabo Mbeki, that we learn about attitudes towards so-called Black Englishmen prevalent at the time. In Daniel Massey's *Under Protest: The Rise of Student Resistance at the University of Fort Hare*, Govan Mbeki is quoted as speaking disparagingly about this group: 'We were not happy about the fact that when we came there most students had majored in ethics, in English, in logic, things like that. We said it was wrong. Fort Hare was producing black Englishmen ...'[1]

When Can Themba went to Fort Hare in 1945, the institution had been in existence for almost three decades and, with the political situation across the country becoming more volatile, student militancy was on the increase. Fort Hare's identity was changing from a missionary institution into a political hothouse. Student revolutionaries believed that the association of the new elite with the English language, for instance, was not merely a choice of a form of communication; it encapsulated an entire range of attitudes towards African identity, culture and values.

This concern about the expropriation of black intellectuals and their assimilation into Western cultures became a central tenet in efforts to revolt against the system, and the concept of 'Black Englishmen' was rejected outright. Debate about the absorption of black intellectuals into what H. I. E. Dhlomo described as 'Victorian colonial mentalities'[2] was prevalent in the generation of 'New Africans' immediately preceding Themba's time at university.

This was one reason why Mbeki Senior did not send his son, Thabo, to Fort Hare, according to the younger Mbeki's biographer, Mark Gevisser. Themba arrived at Fort Hare a few years after Mbeki's generation; majoring in English, he fell into this supposedly assimilated and resented category.

What is pertinent to this discussion is Gevisser's description of how Themba's generation of 'New Africans' grappled with the assertions that they were 'Black Englishmen', real or suspected. Gevisser suggests that they were conscious of these dynamics and forged their own identities:

> But it would be a grave error to conclude on this evidence that men like Modisane and Nakasa had turned a full circle back to the 'Black Englishman' pathologies of their grandparents, or ... that they had forgotten where they came from. For the very best among them were willing to look inside themselves as well; to acknowledge the damage that had been done to their souls and the very specific ways their personal needs and desires had intersected with South Africa's historical reality.[3]

While Nat Nakasa and Bloke Modisane were Themba's friends and colleagues, there is nevertheless a distinct difference between their respective identity constructions. The commitment of all three to resisting tribal notions is indisputable, but there are noticeable inconsistencies as to what identities they chose. In other words, it is easier to distinguish what Nakasa and Modisane opposed than to define what they stood for. By contrast, Themba's commitment to formulating new identities and asserting his own identity is evident through both his lived experience and his writings. He did not seek acceptance in the 'colonial world'. His stance was not just one of resistance to being bracketed as a 'Black Englishman'; he was determined to forge a new identity, to define himself according to his own terms.

Their opposition to the expropriation of black minds into Western culture did not mean that Themba and his peers supported a tribally rooted society. They were equally opposed to tribalism (not to be confused with ethnicity); and, aware that the apartheid government relied on and heightened tribal differences as primary tools in its divide-and-rule tactics,[4] they resisted attempts to turn Fort Hare into a tribal enclave for Xhosa people. Someone like Kaiser

Matanzima, for instance, went to Fort Hare fully aware that he was being groomed to lead the Thembu people of the Transkei as a form of narrow and tribally rooted nationalism.

Many of these young intellectuals had to find ways of creating an equilibrium that would ensure the preservation of their cultural values, while at the same time embracing the more constructive aspects of Western civilisation. Themba belonged to the generation that followed in the footsteps of early African intellectuals such as Pixley ka Isaka Seme, Sol T. Plaatje and Tiyo Soga, who had received missionary educations, but made it their business to reject cultural subjugation and dominance by the same colonial Western powers. At the same time, they embraced certain elements of Western culture, including religion and education. They did not, in a metaphorical sense, throw the baby out with the bathwater. They were also not apologetic about the fact that they were the products of Western missionary education (those mentioned above, and indeed most early-twentieth-century African intellectuals, had either received their schooling in missionary institutions or studied in Europe and the Americas, if not both). Nevertheless, no matter how much they excelled in the skills taught by the West, most of them identified with and remained committed to African values.

The African intellectual community was generally held in high esteem; its members became very influential figures in their communities. One result was that they were great assets to missionaries and colonial administrators. They served as intermediaries between their African communities and Western missionaries and other colonial instruments, translating the Bible into indigenous African languages, and helping to convert indigenous African communities to Christianity, as well as more broadly encouraging more Africans to embrace the trappings of Western civilisation. They believed there were elements worth expropriating from Western cultures, but with the intention of adapting them to suit the African context. In this regard, Ntongela Masilela argues: 'Although profoundly appreciative of the education imparted by the missionaries, the New African intellectuals who had been educated under its auspices came to resent and eventually resisted their process of acculturization into Europeanism and Eurocentism, which in effect was white domination and hegemony, while embracing European modernity with the intent of transforming it into African modernity.'[5]

In other words, this generation of African intellectuals favoured a hybrid approach: adopting elements of European cultures and combining them with intrinsic African values (as Themba himself was to do in his manipulation of the English language, and his delight in locating Shakespeare in the African world).

Can Themba and Tribal Discourse

Can Themba came from the culturally mixed community of Marabastad and was not a tribal man. There was no rural constituency to which he was connected, and he had no obligation to serve as a treasure trove of traditional African values. He built his audience mainly as a scribe at *Drum*, and this was the platform he used to share his views and perspectives. The question remains as to what kind of values he espoused and imparted to his readers.

His wife, Anne, as we have seen, described both their backgrounds as 'detribalised'. The very word presupposes the existence of a tribal discourse, or subscription to tribal identity. It is often presumed, quite incorrectly, that all Africans belong to tribal structures or groups. The apartheid government relied on tribal divisions to divide and rule the black population. Part of this strategy was to glorify a kind of tribalism in which one tribe saw itself as superior to the others. This meant that tribes became suspicious of each other as competitors, or even foes, while tolerating or accepting the colonial or apartheid masters.

According to Ezekiel (later Es'kia) Mphahlele, the idea of creating and maintaining these tribal divisions, including in the cities, was perpetuated by the government, which considered a united movement of Africans to be dangerous. It was in this context that Mphahlele disputed so-called Bantu culture, arguing: 'They concocted the idea of "Bantu culture", by which the content of our education was to be determined. By "Bantu culture" they really meant "tribal customs". We, on the other hand, never recognised tribal culture. We believe in African culture that cuts across artificial boundaries. African culture has roots going down several centuries deep. No one can wish it away, unless we ourselves deny it. At the deepest spiritual level African culture unifies the whole continent.'[6]

The migrant labour system also relied on the creation of a romantic picture of tribal communities, in which only stronger and younger black workers serving white businesses, primarily in the mines, were welcome in the cities. The remainder were expected to live in the remote rural reserves, enacting a kind of imaginary pastoral idyll. Even the literature of the time followed this trend of idealising the simple rural and tribal life versus the rough and corrupting cities – the founding of *Drum* itself was based on exactly these misconceptions.

Some early African intellectuals bought into these motifs of rural nostalgia and vilification of the urban space. R. R. R. Dhlomo, in his very short novel *An African Tragedy*, encouraged tribalism, if not downright xenophobia, by blaming all social ills on life in the city of Johannesburg.[7] In his text, the venereal diseases to which migrants in Johannesburg were exposed were essentially blamed on the Blantyre – the term for the Malawian immigrants who came to Johannesburg for jobs in the mines. Further, in a sinister prefiguring of the recurring spates of xenophobia-related conflicts in South Africa, Africans from across the Limpopo River were blamed for stealing jobs from the locals.

This suggests one of the major departure points between the African intelligentsia of Themba's era and some of their predecessors. Themba and his contemporaries, notably Modisane, Mphahlele and Nakasa, were unapologetic in rejecting tribalism and declaring their opposition to tribal doctrines. This is a perennial feature in their narratives and is echoed in the following extract from Themba's story 'Kwashiorkor': 'He only knew that this feverish life had to be lived, and identity became so large that a man sounded ridiculous for boasting he was a Mopedi or a Mosotho or a Xhosa or a Zulu – nobody seemed to care. You were just an African *here*, and somewhere *there* was a white man: two different types of humans that impinged, now and then – indeed often – but painfully.'[8]

The role of African intellectuals in bringing oppressed races together dates back many years, with some key moments being 1906, when Pixley ka Isaka Seme delivered the 'Regeneration of Africa' speech at Columbia University in New York, and the formation of the South African National Native Congress in 1912: both were demonstrations of this determination to unite beyond tribal divisions.

Themba was a thoroughly urban creature, and this played an important role in his identity, as reflected in both his literary and journalistic output. He and his contemporaries, many of whom came from rural backgrounds, embraced the city as their natural home and environment. The often rosy pictures they painted of life in Johannesburg – and specifically Sophiatown, where most of them lived – bordered on romanticisation. They insisted on celebrating Sophiatown, even with its social ills, speaking out against state forces determined to destroy the area in the name of 'slum clearance'.

The majority of Sophiatown dwellers – certainly those whose voices have reverberated through the ages – did not consider themselves to be tribal subjects. If anything, they considered themselves post-tribal. Rebelling against forces that sought to confine them to particular social categories – tribal, linguistic, racial – they saw themselves as free men and women confined only by apartheid rules, which they sought to break at every opportunity.

Themba himself preferred to look at the positive; he was less interested in what baggage Africans were shedding than in their efforts to carve new images and identities for themselves. In 'Crepuscule' he argues that 'detribalisation, modernisation, adaptation, acculturation, call it what you like, has to tear its way into their psychological pattern, brute-like'.[9] This aggressive charge against established patterns speaks of a determination to veer away from the well-beaten track and tread new paths.

Themba was not alone in these endeavours. Mphahlele was one of the major agents of this approach. He was born in Pietersburg and spoke Sepedi fluently. He later moved to Marabastad and Sophiatown, both Themba's neighbourhoods and townships housing multiple communities, and he absorbed an urban consciousness. Like Themba, Mphahlele acknowledged the existence of the tribe, but believed that national identity surpassed all that. With regard to tribalism and national identity, in his essay 'The Role of an African Writer' Mphahlele argues: 'National Identity should free us from tribalism. Ethnicity is a neutral concept: a fact of history. We were born into ethnic groups. But tribalism refers to an attitude, a nasty one that imagines one ethnic group above all others by right.'[10]

Themba was equally adamant in rejecting tribalism or anything that smacked of it. One of the age-old traditions in many African societies is the institution of lobolo in cases of marriage. Traditionally a presentation of cattle to the family of the bride by the groom and his family, it is a form of reimbursement to the bride's family for raising and educating a girl or young woman who will now join another family and 'work' for them. The cattle that are presented have resonant practical and symbolic significance in this exchange, as explained by philosophers such as Reverend John S. Mbiti.[11] However, as the twentieth century advanced, cattle were replaced by cash in lobolo transactions, which became exactly that – transactions that reduced the process to the exchanging or buying of goods. This is no doubt why Themba opposed the practice, which he referred to as 'that hard dying custom'.[12] He made it clear to his wife that lobolo should never be asked or paid for his children; Anne Themba faithfully followed this instruction in the case of their two daughters.

It is also important to note that while Can Themba did not conform to traditional tribal practices, he was equally firm in rejecting some elements of Western civilisation. Even though he attended a Catholic school, and identified as Anglican at Fort Hare, once he left university, he no longer associated with Christianity as a form of religious practice, even though his writings regularly referenced the Bible.

As Anne Themba alluded in the epigraph to this chapter, Can Themba was a confessed atheist, even when surrounded by staunch Christians, including his own wife. According to Harry Mashabela, 'Christianity, he [Themba] once observed angrily in a discussion over a shebeen drink, is a cruel travesty.'[13] However, as a liberal parent who did not want to impose his views on his family, he urged his wife to allow their children to make their own religious choices by ensuring they were not baptised before they were able to make conscious decisions independently. As a result, Morongwa Themba clearly remembers her christening at about age 14, an occasion on which she towered above the other children because she was so much older than them. As fate would have it, both his daughters followed in the footsteps of their mother in embracing the Christian religion.

There is a certain irony to the fact that Themba's last job took him full circle: he ended up teaching at a Catholic school. Here he refused to join the rest of the school in their daily prayers. Nevertheless, according to Simon Maziya, his student at St Joseph's, Themba often told them to go and pray for their sins: 'I don't remember, you see, worshipping with Mr Can Themba, or he was too busy, or he would say, "You go and pray for your sins" and he would not go there, so I wouldn't say he was not a Christian, [or] he was a heathen.

I will not say that, but I don't remember, you see, going to church and praying with my, my teacher [laughs].'[14]

One might claim that it was the Church that had the last laugh: Themba was buried with full Catholic rites in the graveyard at St Joseph's Mission (see Chapter 16).

The Puzzle of Can Themba's Language

Tribal identity is strongly tied to vernacular or indigenous language. It is widely reported that Can Themba did not speak any African language. If this is true, it is both ironic and puzzling, given his standing as one of the greatest chroniclers of township life.

The question that arises is whether he actually could not speak these languages, or whether he refused to speak them. The former is highly unlikely because of the environment in which he grew up and worked. The dominant languages in Marabastad and Attridgeville, the two areas in which Themba was raised, included Sepedi, Setswana, English and Afrikaans, with some sprinklings of Zulu and Shangaan. Themba is officially known to have spoken only two of these languages: English and Afrikaans. Likewise, as a high-school student in Pietersburg, he would have been exposed to three indigenous languages – Sepedi, Shangaan and Ndebele, with the first being more common. So once again it might be expected that he would acquire at least one of the languages commonly spoken in the area. This, however, does not seem to be the case. The only language other than English and Afrikaans he was known to speak at times was tsotsitaal, an urban street patois spoken by gangsters and comprised of various indigenous African languages injected with a dose of Afrikaans. This could, of course, have been a survival strategy, given the menacing presence of tsotsis in the townships; or, according to Muxe Nkondo, one of Themba's typical tactics for crossing social and class divides.[15]

Nevertheless, a few of his stories and poems contain Xhosa phrases, where words such as 'Thixo' (God), 'mama' (mother) and 'tata' (father) are used.

His analysis of the bus boycott slogan 'Azikwelwa!', as discussed in Chapter 7, shows intimate understanding of the grammatical formulations and various meanings connected to the phrase. Similarly, on an assignment to Bechuanaland with Peter Magubane, he attended community meetings addressed in Setswana, and interviewed a number of Setswana-speaking people. His ensuing reportage uses Setswana words such as 'Pula!' and idiomatic expressions such as 'dinako di maswe' (times are tarnished).

In 1958, Themba wrote an article for the East Africa edition of *Drum* titled 'The Ban on Congress', in which he argued that the banning of some sections of the ANC was 'likely to serve only extremism, to deprive the people of the responsible and stabilising influence of Congress in some areas'. He moved on to the question of language, warning that 'people who are not Congressites now speak Congress language, think of all forms of protest through a Congress heart'. About greetings in the various African languages, he wrote: 'Africans – tribal Africans mostly – like greeting: Thama Kgosi – Hail my lord – in the Northern Transvaal; Molo – (Good) morning – in Xhosaland; *Sa'ubona* – we greet you – in Zululand. But now, in the politically-charged lingua franca, they all greet each other with the thumbs-up sign and the thunderous *'Africa!'* with the standard reply, *'Iyabuya!'* – She'll come back.'[16]

All this suggests that while he might have refused to speak or did not have confidence in speaking these languages, he was certainly able to use them as tools for communication.

Eye-witness, or rather ear-witness, accounts by Themba's friends nevertheless corroborate that he spoke no African languages in their hearing. Keorapetse Kgositsile stated in our interview that he never heard Themba speaking any of southern Africa's indigenous languages. Kgositsile's assertions, which were later confirmed by Parks Mangena, are also borne out by Obed Musi, a former colleague and friend of Themba: 'I don't think there was ever an occasion when Can spoke a single line in an African language. He either spoke English or township lingo. The reason was probably because Can's surname was actually Tembe, a Shangaan name, and he had his roots in Pretoria.'[17]

While Musi knew Themba quite intimately, his statement is unfortunately replete with inaccuracies. Evidence shows that as far back as his high-school days, Themba never spelled his surname differently, as suggested by Musi. The Themba surname has Nguni origins and could be associated with any of the following language groups: Ndebele, Shangaan, Swati, Xhosa or Zulu. Themba was not known to have spoken any of these languages. Similarly, there is no evidence to suggest that he was Shangaan – not that there is anything wrong with identifying as such – and Musi's claims about his Shangaan background remain unsubstantiated.

When there is no empirical evidence to associate an individual with a particular language or ethnic group, official documents in which these specific details may have been required offer clarity. In his 1944 application for admission into the South African Native College, Themba lists English Higher Grade and Afrikaans Lower Grade as the only language subjects that he took in his final year in high school. According to his student records from Fort Hare, Themba consistently gave his race or tribal background as Zulu, and his home language as Afrikaans. It is obviously a matter of scholarly interest to investigate the reasons Themba might have had for listing Afrikaans, of all other languages that were spoken in Marabastad, as his home language. In South Africa, Afrikaans is a language usually spoken as a mother tongue by whites who regard themselves as Afrikaner in identity, and sometimes by black and mixed-race people previously classified as coloured under apartheid. We will probably never know why it was spoken in the Themba home; it is worth noting that none of the five siblings were called by African names, which could suggest the linguistic leanings of their parents.

We also know that Themba studied and lived at the University of Fort Hare from 1945 to 1947, and again from 1950 to 1951. Fort Hare is located in an area dominated by Xhosa speakers. But not even the experience of staying there prompted him to acquire any proficiency in the regional language. In his poem 'The Ciskeian Maid', he alludes to his inability to speak the same 'tongue' as his beloved. Yet, when the situation demanded, the narrator in the poem strings together a few 'half-words' to describe his passion:

> I told thee then the wild tale of my love
> But because I tripped on the Xhosa tongue
> And the tales beyond words, I told thee half-
> Words on which thou shall so passionately cling.[18]

Given that language is one of the fundamental elements that distinguish one tribe from another, it is possible that his resistance to acquiring or speaking local languages might have been part of a deliberate rejection of tribalism.

One anecdote shared by Yvonne, Themba's youngest daughter, recounts a moment when, allegedly, a young Sesotho-speaking woman was crossing the Swaziland border to Mozambique with a European foreigner. The story goes that the woman could not speak a word of English, and Can was concerned that she might be crossing the border against her will – a case of human trafficking. At that moment, Themba was said to have expressed himself in pure Sesotho, trying to ascertain if she knew that she was about to cross the border to another country. This is not completely implausible, because Sesotho shares the same language group as Sepedi and Setswana, languages spoken in Polokwane and Pretoria respectively, places in which Themba spent significant time during his youth. Furthermore, Themba had indeed visited Lesotho, where the language is dominant.

It is clear that the construction of Themba's identity or identities was deliberate and complex. It is easier to identify the elements he rejected than to enclose his preferences into a single confined space or ideology. The definition that probably comes closest to reflecting his identity was coined by Lewis Nkosi in 'The Fabulous Decade', where he describes Themba as a 'romantic nihilist'.[19]

A Quest for Shared Identities

Can Themba came to maturity and established himself as a voice to be reckoned with at the same time that apartheid was formally entrenched and extending its reach. As a fresh graduate from the University of Fort Hare, Themba effectively became part of the new black elite. His going to Johannesburg, living in Sophiatown and becoming part of the first generation of the historic '*Drum* Boys' placed him in the precarious position of navigating the reality of his blackness in an oppressive state.

His generation added another layer to the so-called New African phenomenon, but, like the generations before them, they confronted challenges that were brought about by the realities of being black and Western-educated in a white world that did not fully welcome them, and a black world that did not fully accept them. They belonged to both communities, yet were tolerated only uneasily or reluctantly, if not downright resented. Some members of the white community, the police in particular, felt threatened by their progress in life, and made it their mission to remind them that they remained black and inferior, while members of their own black communities felt that they represented Western and modern white values that had a corrupting influence in black societies.

This is what led to the new black elite being called 'the situations', described by Bloke Modisane as 'something not belonging to either'; fence-sitters who stood a chance to benefit from either side, but also ran the risk of falling onto the wrong side. Modisane goes on to describe the 'situation' as follows: 'The educated African is resented equally by the blacks because he speaks English, which is one of the symbols of white supremacy, he is resentfully called the Situation, something not belonging to either, but tactfully situated between white oppression and black rebellion.'[20]

The African intelligentsia became 'situations' without necessarily embracing white values or espousing the ideals of their white liberal friends. They earned the label by virtue of their perceived position 'on the fence' and were therefore labelled and classified as such by their own African communities, as well as elements of the white community, to which they were close by virtue of education and class.

Although there are several factors that led to this kind of categorisation, the fundamental differentiating factor was education. It was through education that 'New Africans' got better-paid jobs, spoke the language of the white man, and therefore could attend parties and events organised by white liberals – they could even occasionally have a taste of consensual carnal exchange across the colour bar.

In the years prior to the introduction of apartheid as an official system of governance in 1948 in South Africa, the government elevated educated Africans within their own communities. They were given special privileges, such as permission to buy bottled liquor and the relaxation of certain laws regarding official documentation. However, with the coming of grand apartheid came blanket oppression. In his essay 'A Question of Identity', Lewis Nkosi speaks of the levelling effect of apartheid, wherein the entire black population had to endure the effects of apartheid equally. The black intelligentsia was no longer spared, but suffered alongside the uneducated:

> During the rule of the United Party, which was dominated by English-speaking white South Africans, educated Africans, mostly

> teachers, were exempted from the humiliation of carrying 'passes' or identity documents, which they would be asked to produce at street corners of the city by an official Tom, Dick and Harry. However, the subsequent Boer administrations have discarded any such discretion, and once again the life of the educated class is as insecure as those of the illiterate and semi-literate masses of our people.[21]

Nevertheless, the social distinctions remained within communities. Since the establishment of mission stations and schools, there was a visible demarcation between educated blacks and those who were either non-literate or not educated according to Western standards. This subject is interrogated in great detail in Zakes Mda's seminal novel, *The Heart of Redness*, where the Xhosa people are divided according to the binary of 'Believers' and 'Unbelievers'.[22] In this hierarchy, educated blacks occupied the upper echelons of black society, even though they remained lower than the lowest white. One result was class hostility within the black population. It was in this context that the black intelligentsia were resented by sections of both black and white communities.

The view that they were 'Black Englishmen' was perpetuated by the perception that they aspired to emulate the life of whites by befriending them and attending their parties. In his paper 'Can Themba, Storyteller and Journalist of the 1950s', Michael Chapman expands on this:

> They were over-enamoured with the fads of Western culture, they were regarded as curiosities by a paternalistic white-liberal intelligentsia, and were isolated from any purposeful mass-based activity. Accordingly, Themba's own substance and style are … denuded of experiential necessity and seen as ideologically 'unhealthy.' As the u-Clever of Sophiatown, who claimed to speak no African language, and whose education in English Literature at Fort Hare had seemed to manifest itself in the frustration of his writing tales of intrigue, violence and wish fulfilment, Themba is typified as an alienated 'situation.'[23]

One can argue that this generation of African intelligentsia lived a dual lifestyle: one that related to their people in the townships, and another that was suitable for their white liberal friends.

Figure 1. Can Themba read widely, including *Drum*'s competitors such as *The Star*. (Photograph by Jürgen Schadeberg.)

Figure 2. In this 1948 University of Fort Hare picture, Can Themba *(3rd row from bottom, 11th from left)* is seen alongside his Beda Hall housemates, including Alfred Hutchinson *(top row, 4th from right)*, Godfrey Pitje *(3rd row, 8th from left)*, Ntsu Mokhehle *(2nd row, 1st on right)* Lionel Ngakane *(1st row, 3rd from left)*, and Nthato Motlana *(3rd row, 2nd to the right of Themba)*. (Private collection, Daniel Massey; photographer unknown.)

Figure 3. Can Themba *(left)* receiving the first prize from Henry Nxumalo for the inaugural *Drum* short story competition. (Photograph by Jürgen Schadeberg.)

Figure 4. Can Themba with his right-hand man, Casey Motsisi, celebrating the first anniversary of *Africa!* magazine, where they served as editor and assistant editor, respectively. (From Jürgen Schadeberg, ed., *The Fifties People of South Africa*; Bailey's African Photo Archives, 1987; photographer unknown.)

Figure 5. Can Themba as a 28-year-old teacher in his room in Sophiatown, before he started working as a journalist. (Photograph by Jürgen Schadeberg.)

Figure 6. Can, the family man, seen here with his wife, Anne, and their eldest daughter, Morongwa. (Private collection, Themba family; photographer unknown.)

Figure 7. Elizabeth Maizzie Maphisa was a nurse with whom Can Themba had a son. (Private collection, Linda Maphisa; photographer unknown.)

Figure 8. Juby Mayet was one of Can Themba's protégés in the newsroom. (Photograph by Jürgen Schadeberg.)

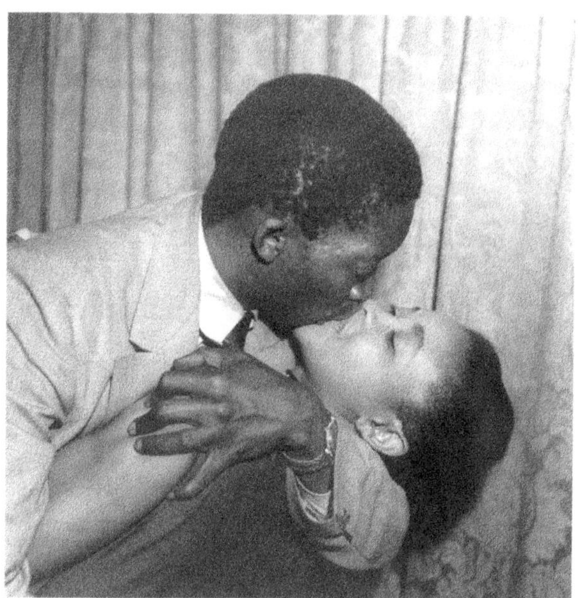

Figure 9. Can Themba wrote extensively about Dolly Rathebe and 'her men' and, according to *Drum* magazine, he was one of the men in her romantic life. (*Drum* Photographer/BAHA/Africa Media Online.)

Figure 10. A moment of fun in the newsroom. (Photograph by Jürgen Schadeberg.)

Figure 11. *Drum* journalists Can Themba and Arthur Maimane often hung out with actresses and beauty queens like Dottie Tiyo and Selina Kolae, as seen in this picture. (*Drum* Photographer/BAHA/Africa Media Online.)

Figure 12. When he joined the newsroom, Can Themba was always smartly dressed and wore a tie – Jürgen Schadeberg said he seemed out of place. (*Drum* Photographer/BAHA/Africa Media Online.)

Figure 13. Sol Rachilo remembers Can Themba as a teacher with an intuitive gift for imparting knowledge. (Photograph by Jürgen Schadeberg.)

Figure 14. *From left:* Henry Nxumalo, Es'kia Mphahlele, Casey Motsisi, Can Themba, Jerry Ntsipe, Arthur Maimane *(wearing hat, with cigarette)*, Victor Xashimba, Dan Chocho and Bob Gosani *(standing, with camera)*, Kenneth Mtetwa and Benson Dyantyi *(on floor, left and right)* were all part of the cohort that turned *Drum* magazine into an iconic publication. (Photograph by Jürgen Schadeberg.)

Figure 15. Can Themba was known for his penchant for debate in the newsroom and shebeens, as well as in his House of Truth. (*Drum* Photographer/BAHA/Africa Media Online.)

Figure 16. *From left to right:* Robert Resha, Patrick Molaoa and Nelson Mandela arriving at the Drill Hall in Johannesburg for the 1956 Treason Trial. Can Themba had conducted a mock trial in which he found Resha guilty of treason the day before Resha was arrested for high treason. (Photograph by Peter Magubane; courtesy of BAHA/ Africa Media Online.)

Figure 17. Can Themba as the associate editor of *Drum* magazine in the 1950s. (Photograph by Jürgen Schadeberg, Sylvester Stein Collection.)

Figure 18. Can Themba was bundled out of a Seventh Day Adventist church during his investigation of whether white churches would admit a black worshipper. (Photograph by Jürgen Schadeberg.)

Figure 19. Can Themba and Bob Gosani were arrested in Potchefstroom for possession of liquor while travelling in a company car. According to Can, they were arrested for kindness as they were helping a white man rescue bottles of alcohol from a raging fire. (Photograph by Jürgen Schadeberg.)

Figure 20. Can Themba with Parks Mangena in what they called the 'Can Themba corner' at the Central Hotel in Mbabane, Swaziland. (Private collection, Parks Mangena; photographer unknown.)

Figure 21. Although Can Themba was not a tsotsi in the criminal and conventional sense, at times he dressed like a tsotsi and spoke tsotitaal. (Photograph by Jürgen Schadeberg.)

So, on the one hand, Themba was a journalist famed for his ability to capture in words the heartbeat of township life, a connoisseur of shebeens, a man who dodged the police and provided poetry to tsotsis. At the same time, he and his peers, including Modisane, Nakasa, Nkosi and others, would attend social gatherings organised by progressive whites such as Nadine Gordimer and Helen Suzman.

In her biography of Nat Nakasa, author Ryan Brown tells the story of how Nakasa, while attending a party organised by Francie Suzman (daughter of anti-apartheid MP Helen Suzman), gave himself a tour of the house. Later, Nkosi found him sleeping in the main bedroom. When Nkosi asked his friend for an explanation, Nakasa's response was that he wanted to see how the other half lived.[24] This statement shows that even when cultural figures such as Nakasa immersed themselves in the lifestyles of white liberals, they remained acutely aware of their differences and critical of the system and the roles, deliberate or not, of their white counterparts, even as they attempted to build bridges between races.

Their criticisms came at different stages of their personal journeys and in different forms. Jean Hart claimed that Can 'kept the real, objective complexities in front of him, as a kind of barrier, because that was one way of being honest with himself'.[25] It may be argued that Themba's outspokenness about matters of race was his way of coping with the status quo. Hart went on: 'Can … would say [it] outright. He would say, You and I can never be real lovers, you and I can never be real friends, because our power-base is unequal. Bloke would avoid it and say, We love one another, there's nothing society can do to us.'[26]

Bloke Modisane, who in his book *Blame Me on History* appears to be bitter about his own social collusion, initially appeared to be docile, almost naive concerning the racial dynamics of his time. Jean Hart felt that Modisane was insincere; that he tried to suppress his opinions for the sake of belonging. In his autobiography, Modisane confirmed these assertions; he confessed to having done things to impress or spite his supposed detractors. In his book, he tells the story of how he bought some Russian caviar at an exorbitant price, simply for the sake of ensuring that he was not thought of as an unsophisticated and uncivilised African. The worst was that he did not particularly like caviar, but his act of buying what he confessed to be a pretentious luxury was 'a bourgeois symbol of social affectation and palatal sophistication'.[27] Modisane's bitterness reveals him to be probably the angriest among his peers. He does not seem to have enjoyed the parties to which he was invited: 'I am instead insulted with multiracial tea parties where we wear our different racial masks and become synthetically polite to each other, in a kind of masquerade where Africans are being educated into an acceptance of their inferior position.'[28]

Themba, his remarkable ability to straddle the fault lines between social strata notwithstanding, had no such issues with making his true feelings and opinions known. As Hart pointed out above, he could be blunt, even harsh, in acknowledging the reality of racial differences in a racist society. Tom Hopkinson was also on the receiving end of Themba's frank views on identity politics. In one of their engagements, which bordered on confrontation, Themba put Hopkinson in a corner, trying to force him to be unequivocal about the side he would take in a racial war rather than assume the nebulous stance often taken by white liberals – which Themba found patronising. Hopkinson reports that Themba asked:

> 'When the shooting war starts – which side will you be on then, black or white? Because one day the whites will start it for sure.'
>
> I made no answer, but Can pressed. 'Which side will you be on?'
>
> 'Depends on who starts it, what the issues are, and where I'm standing at the time.'
>
> Can snorted and went out. Our talk had been unsatisfactory to him as it had to me.[29]

As well as the clarity of his views, this reveals Themba's appetite for debate. He was willing to tackle anyone. In his short story 'Crepuscule', Can Themba, the narrator, who is also a character in the story, presents his case to the tsotsis of Sophiatown after they side with his erstwhile girlfriend, Baby, who reported him to the police for having an affair with another woman – who happened to be white. The tsotsis initially side with Baby, but change their minds after Can explains that going out with a white woman is in fact a revolutionary act of retaliation by a black man – unlike others who freely procured their black sisters for white men.

His capacity to relate to everyone and anyone is eloquently articulated by Musi: 'Can could talk to a professor in the morning, a beauty queen at lunch-time and a gangster in the afternoon. And have everyone laughing and eating out of his hand.'[30]

This illustrates that while every individual possesses multiple identities, Themba's identity ethos was particularly sophisticated and flexible. Where we are fortunate in trying to trace the construction of Themba's identity is the time and context in which he lived, in which he and peers like Modisane and Nakasa deliberately analysed and reflected on their situation in their historical moment. Even more useful, they wrote about each other, giving opinions and insights about themselves and their peers.

In *Blame Me on History*, for instance, Modisane refers to both Themba and Nakasa; likewise, Nakasa talks about his relationship with Themba in a number of published pieces. It is perhaps in Themba's tribute to Nat Nakasa, 'The Boy with the Tennis Racket', that we get the most intimate glimpse of the author's sincere views about his contemporaries:

> The bitterest commentary on the South African is typified by Nat. All those South Africans who wanted to be loyal, hard-working, intelligent citizens of the country are crowded out. They don't want to bleach themselves, but they want to participate and contribute to the wonder that that country can become. They don't want to be fossilised into tribal inventions that are no more real to them than they would be to their forefathers.
>
> Nat's was such a voice. Sobukwe's is that of protest and resistance. Casey Motsisi's that of derisive laughter. Bloke Modisane's that of implacable hatred. Ezekiel Mphahlele's that of intellectual contempt. Nimrod Mkele's that of patient explanation to be patient. Mine, that of self-corrosive cynicism. But Nat told us: 'There must be humans on the other side of the fence; it's only we haven't learned how to talk.'[31]

The above excerpt does more than provide snapshots of the various individual characters; it also gives context and clarity to their identity journeys. When Themba wrote this piece after the passing of Nakasa in 1965, he was exiled in Swaziland, just as Nakasa had been exiled in the United States. One might have expected his piece to be filled with anger and frustration, given that, like him, Nakasa had been forced to leave the land of his birth. Instead, Themba's piece is a nostalgic one that journeys down memory lane, recapturing his first encounter with Nat and reflecting on their lives in Sophiatown. The first paragraph cited alludes to their refusal to be reduced to tribal subjects, while simultaneously rejecting the idea of being turned into white ('bleached') subjects. While they believed in and shared the broad quest for identities beyond tribal and ethnic confines, on an individual level their differences were notable. These differences have been astutely and concisely captured by Themba, who, in this excerpt, lists prominent black South African intellectuals who shared common backgrounds and yet differed widely ideologically.

Themba knew each of the personalities he listed, and shows acute understanding of their characters and what they stood for in society. Robert Sobukwe, his peer at Fort Hare, went on to become a prominent politician and the founding president of the Pan Africanist Congress; Motsisi was once Themba's student and worked for *Drum* magazine before becoming a legendary journalist in his own right; Nimrod Mkele, who won the *Drum* short story competition after Themba, was one of the most educated journalists at the magazine; and Nakasa, Modisane and Mphahlele were all Themba's colleagues at *Drum*. Themba shows that these men, as members of the new black elite of the 1950s, were by no means a homogeneous group: their individual traits, personalities and ideologies were integral in defining their identity paths.

It is perhaps Nakasa who presented the sharpest conundrums on the question of identity in this generation. He came from a middle-class family in Natal. Unlike Themba, he was linguistically grounded in a 'tribal' language: he spoke Zulu at home and cut his teeth in journalism writing for a Zulu newspaper. He nevertheless did not associate with any tribal doctrines. He took a conscious decision to ignore the apartheid laws, and to act as if racial discrimination in South Africa was non-existent. He was of the view that the best way to live with the colour bar was to ignore it. This was quite a controversial stance for a black person and an influential public figure living in Johannesburg at the height of apartheid. (He was the first black journalist to have a weekly column in the *Rand Daily Mail.*) He rejected the reality that he was part of the oppressed black population to the extent of refusing to live in the racially demarcated townships. At times, Nakasa would sleep in a watchman's shed in a white suburb or park rather than spend the night in a township.

In his imagined space, what he called the 'fringe country', he lived in a different world, one where there was no racial discrimination, and people lived together in harmony.

The fringe country that Nakasa created existed predominantly in his imagination and on the periphery of the black reality, which was dominated by oppression, poverty and violence. Even in the exclusive suburbs of Johannesburg, if he and his colleagues wanted to attend a social event, their white friends had to write permits explaining their presence – indicating that the 'boy' (a disrepectful term for a black adult employee such as a gardener or waiter) was working late.

If they were spared raids during these gatherings, harassment began the moment they stepped out of the houses. Mphahlele wrote passionately about this: 'When white people invite us blacks to their suburban homes, we are the ones who are exposed to road blocks, to humiliating police orders for us to undress, to assault by white hooligans. This is the metaphor that should illuminate the hazards of reaching out to whites. So blacks have good reason not to try to know whites more intimately.'[32] White liberals might sympathise, but could not share the humiliations to which their black friends were subjected.

Nakasa, on the other hand, had delusions of grandeur: holding on to his dream of a utopian society, he believed that because he was not a political activist, he presented no threat to the apartheid government. He experienced a rude awakening when he was invited to take up a Nieman Fellowship at Harvard: his application for a passport was declined. In an earlier letter, he had assured the Nieman Foundation that 'as I have never been active in politics, except as a journalist, I expect no difficulty in obtaining a passport'. This was not to be, and it left him with no choice but to take a one-way exit permit, something that would make him a 'permanent wanderer' and a 'native of nowhere'.[33]

Themba was one of the first among the *Drum* generation of writers to realise that simply getting on with life while turning a blind eye to racial oppression and suffering was not an option. For decades, if not centuries, the monkey on the backs of every progressive South African had always been racism and discrimination, and the new black elite knew that the dream of an equal society could not be realised until racial discrimination was abolished. They were encouraged by the winds of change that were sweeping across the continent, with Ghana becoming the first country to attain colonial independence in 1957. Many other countries followed soon thereafter.[34] Themba believed that a genuine understanding of black people's material conditions was a precondition for any cross-racial bridge-building in South Africa, and he reminded his acquaintances of this reality maybe a tad too often for their liking.

This was part of his own personal struggle, in which he tried to change one person, one mindset, at a time. This is perhaps another factor that distinguished him from some of his peers. Whereas Nakasa, for example, tried to squeeze himself into the ambit of progressive whites, Themba wanted white liberals to be the ones identifying with him, and he tried to bring his white friends into his own fold. In his story 'Crepuscule', during an evening tour of the township, a thinly disguised Themba requests a head wrap, known as a *doek* and commonly worn by married women in African society, for his white girlfriend: 'So that evening when I said, "Mama, how about a doek for Janet", I was proposing to transform her, despite her colour and her deep blue eyes, into an African girl for the while.'[35]

What can be deduced from Themba's life is that in an unequal society, it is not enough to refuse to be incorporated into different social and racial categories. It is also crucial for the majority to be assertive in carving out their own identities. Themba was a member of the elite who identified fully with the working class, and in his writing (as shown in the discussion of his journalism in Chapter 7) he brings our attention to the mundane, the unnoticed, the marginalised and even the resented.

This write-up in *The Fifties People of South Africa* captures the essence of Can Themba: 'Can's interest lay in people and his magic lay in his understanding of them, black, white, yellow, brown, what cared he?'[36] This Themba makes clear in his monologue in *Come Back, Africa*, where he says: 'I'd like to get people to get at each other, to talk at each other – if I could get to my worst enemy over a bottle of beer, maybe we could get at each other.'[37]

11

A Politico in a Poet

I can't accept apartheid, because from the first principles it does not allow a man to have an opportunity to contribute to the development of South Africa, and he is prepared to throw in everything he's got to make this country a viable country, a beautiful country.

Can Themba — *Changing World*

Discussion of Can Themba's identity ethos will remain incomplete without a critical look at his reflections on socio-political themes and perspectives. But before beginning an analysis of this topic, it is worth speculating, somewhat ruefully, on the perils of projection during the research process.

Many modern commentators with contemporary political awareness are almost desperate to gain clarity on the politics and political ideologies of their subjects and icons, especially if they suspect that this evidence exists, but might be lost in the mists of time. I was no different. I kept coming up blank as I tried to establish whether Themba had been actively involved in politics, as well as to trace his views and perspectives on the subject.

Then came a breakthrough – or so I thought. I was referred to veteran politician and former Robben Island prisoner Ahmed Kathrada, whom I was told was one of very few people alive who knew of my subject's direct political involvement. I believed this would be a turning point in my project on Themba, as information from a man who had spent years on Robben Island with other liberation struggle heroes such as Nelson Mandela and Walter Sisulu, both of whom were resident in Sophiatown during the 1950s, was sure to carry weight. Rumour had it that part of what Kathrada would share with me were startling details of Themba serving as an underground operative of the ANC during the struggle days.

Greatly excited, I finally secured an interview with Kathrada on Thursday, 8 October 2015. Before this date, I had indicated to the struggle stalwart that I was interested in hearing about Themba's political involvement, as Kathrada apparently knew things about Themba's political activism that not many were aware of. My intention was to jostle his mind and ignite memories so that he could share anecdotes about the man who, as was already clear, was a charismatic character.

Needless to say, I was dumbfounded when the response came that Kathrada knew nothing about Themba's politics. I consoled myself that perhaps he did not want to divulge too much information ahead of the formal interview. In the course of our interview, which was video-recorded, I asked the same question three times; the answer was a consistent affirmation that he did not know of any political involvement on Themba's part.

I was shattered, but this 'repudiation' by Kathrada opened my eyes – and not before time – to another factor with the potential to compromise and even derail the credibility of a research project: concerted efforts to refine and even rewrite history for purposes of expediency or, more likely, purposes of modern relevance. This was a reminder to me to keep an open mind and verify sources, and to try to maintain a dialogue between the views and memories of those I was fortunate enough to interview and more formal existing records.

This interest and investment, even, in Themba's political perspective is founded on the presupposition that a writer has a role to play in society, and that this role goes beyond the entertainment value of his or her writing. This is eloquently expressed by Nadine Gordimer in her paper 'The Essential Gesture: Writers and Responsibility', where she says: 'Ours is a period when few can claim absolute value of a writer without reference to a context of responsibilities.'[1]

The 'context of responsibilities' is determined by the socio-economic and political circumstances of a particular historical moment. Gordimer was Themba's contemporary; even though she presented this paper in a very different era, decades after Themba's death, her insistence on the principle of commitment to social values remains relevant.

The act of writing is driven by a purpose, and this purpose is usually indicative of the writer's convictions. It is these that define the socio-political preoccupations of the author. In his essay 'Why I Write', George Orwell articulates this view eloquently: 'Writing a book is a horrible, exhausting struggle, like a long bout of some painful illness. One would never undertake such a thing if one were not driven on by some demon whom one can neither resist nor understand.'[2]

In this respect, writing becomes an act of exorcising those demons that will continue haunting one's conscience for as long as one fails to address them. For the writer, therefore, it is both a necessity and an obligation to articulate their concerns, and the concerns of those around them.

Themba's position is a complex one, partly because he was not only a writer of imaginative literature, but a reporter, columnist and assistant editor of the magazine with the widest circulation on the continent. *Drum* was not only the biggest magazine that had the black masses as its primary target market in South Africa; its reach extended to other English-speaking African countries, and struck a chord across the Atlantic, attracting the attention of the civil rights movement and later the black power movement in America.

As the winner of the very first *Drum* short story competition, Themba later sat as one of the short story competition adjudicators alongside Langston Hughes, the famous African American writer and a leading figure in the historic and internationally acclaimed Harlem Renaissance. Themba was one of the writers from across the African continent included in *An African Treasury*, a landmark 1960 anthology of stories, poems, articles and essays compiled and edited by Hughes. In the introduction, Hughes describes this publication as 'a personal treasury – a selection gathered from several thousands of pages of writing by Africans of color that I have read during the past six years'.[3]

Drum magazine was the window through which Hughes had received a glimpse of the kaleidoscope of African writing. His 'Mr Simple' articles were run as regular columns in *Africa!* magazine, established as an imprint of *Drum* under the editorship of Can Themba. In 1954, *Drum* magazine requested Hughes to serve as one of the judges for its short story competition. This experience is reflected in his introduction to *An African Treasury*: 'My interest in native African writing began when I was asked by the editors of DRUM, a Johannesburg magazine for non-white readers, to become one of the judges for a short story contest for indigenous South African writers. Some of the work that came to me contained pages which moved, surprised, and quite delighted me. I determined to see how much more writing of interest was being produced by black Africans.'[4]

What this meant was that while many South African writers, particularly those from the *Drum* stable, benefited immensely from their association with Hughes, the relationship had reciprocal benefits for him, as he explains above. *Drum* writers, many of whom would later be forced into exile, maintained strong relations with like-minded people and civil movements in Europe and the Americas, in particular. So it came as no surprise that when the apartheid government started banning its opponents, including the more outspoken *Drum* writers, these countries became the destinations of choice for many South African exiles.

Themba was known as a writer who understood and epitomised the African urban world. Given his unerring ability to keep his finger on the pulse of the community he wrote about, the logical question is: if Can Themba was so close to the people, and if, as Michael Chapman argues, he typified the new urban culture, how could he turn a blind eye to their suffering? Is it even possible that any writing chronicling the lived experience of the oppressed majority during this period – whether reportage or imaginative – could be totally devoid of political content?[5]

Themba was first and foremost a writer. He came to *Drum* not to change its ethical conduct or business approach, but to contribute to its growth along an already established path. So, like any other journalist or contributor to a newspaper or magazine, his approach was informed by the values, principles and strategic direction of the magazine.

One of the founding principles of *Drum* magazine was that it would steer clear of politics. It remains a mystery as to how a magazine purporting to represent the interests of the majority black community, who remained oppressed in their own country, could somehow avoid carrying political content. Anthony Sampson explains the conundrum that resulted: '*Drum* originally announced that it would be non-political, and the first issues made no mention of politics … But however much we tried to ignore them, in South Africa all roads led to politics. Political theory affected every moment of our readers' lives: it could have them arrested, jailed, transplanted, even deported.'[6]

This declaration of non-partisanship or, more specifically, the determination to avoid politics nevertheless presumably constituted part of the code of conduct for those writing for *Drum*. Even if some journalists were to try to delve into the political dynamics in their reportage, they risked censorship by the editor or, worse, disciplinary action for dereliction of duty.

In spite of the constraints imposed upon the writers by editorial policies and journalistic ethics (which more broadly maintain – and continue to do so – that reporters ought to remain 'objective'), it is well established that the subjective views, values and perspectives of journalists shape their work, and that these views invariably steer in one political direction or another. This assertion is in line with the claim by Keorapetse Kgositsile, who, in a tribute to Nat Nakasa, made a poignant remark applicable to Themba as well: that in a racist, oppressive and exploitative society, it is impossible for a writer not to be political.

The argument above undermines the recurrent descriptions of Themba being apolitical or a 'political virgin' (to use Stanley Motjuwadi's phrase). Es'kia Mphahlele took Kgositsile's point further. In his reflections on Can Themba, simply titled 'Themba: Rebel Par Excellence', he wrote: 'The rebel par excellence – he was apolitical if we think of institutional or organisational politics. He was cynical about the political being. But the cynic has to be first hyperconscious of, hypersensitive to a reality before he can turn cynical as a protective device.'[7]

Mphahlele reminds us of another dynamic: that to be political does not necessitate holding a membership card of a particular political party. Among the 1950s' generation of *Drum* writers, Mphahlele and Bloke Modisane were among the very few who actually joined political organisations. Mphahlele became a member of the ANC during the drafting of the Freedom Charter in 1955. He writes in *Down Second Avenue*: 'It was later in 1955 that I joined the African National Congress (ANC). I had for some years been torn between it and the All African Convention.'[8] Modisane, meanwhile, had been a member of the ANC Youth League, which he later denounced in favour of the more radical PAC. Infuriated by ANC President-General Dr James Moroka's decision to appoint a separate counsel during a mass political trial, Modisane severed his ties with the organisation. 'I burned my Youth League membership card and retreated into a political wilderness,' he wrote in *Blame Me on History*.[9] Mphahlele demonstrated that membership of a political party did not necessarily translate into political consciousness, or vice versa.

It is this nuance that was missing from an unpublished paper by Sandile Memela, a former journalist turned government spokesperson, who joined the chorus, arguing that Themba was 'apolitical'. However, his argument was based on a single short story, 'The Bottom of the Bottle', in which two ANC politicians try to recruit the narrator (a version of Can himself), and he shows no interest in joining the organisation. Memela's argument seems to be based on a semantic misinterpretation, where being non-partisan is presumed to have the same meaning as apolitical.[10]

These criticisms levelled against Themba seem to stem from the long-held view that the 1950s' *Drum* generation of writers were apolitical, or at least lacked political commitment in their writing. It did not help that the writers themselves, Themba among them, claimed to be apolitical, even as they flouted apartheid regulations every chance they got. Chapman alludes to this: 'Themba's writing frequently presents this problem, which is common in the stories of the decade. Several have been seen in fact as politically naïve or, at least, disdainful of politics.'[11] In fact, according to Paul Gready, the very claim that one is apolitical is itself a political statement: 'Many of the remaining Sophiatown writers claimed to be apolitical. According to Motjuwadi, Themba was as "apolitical as his ever-torn sock … a political virgin," while Themba himself confessed to his "insouciant attitude" to matters of weight. His desire to appear apolitical and his self-corrosive cynicism in a sense became his ideology.'[12]

The criticism made of Themba here has been repeated by many scholars over the years. Mari Snyman refers to his 'Wet Sentimental Sexy' stories (an assessment, in my opinion, based on his earlier writings) in her thesis: 'It has been argued that Can Themba, instead of protesting the inhuman apartheid legislation, the absurd social situation, concentrated on lively, investigative journalism.'[13]

In her work, Snyman grapples with Themba's attitude towards politics, asking whether Themba was indeed 'a political virgin', given his own 'insouciant' words in dismissing the use of literature as a political vehicle, with his alter ego in his story 'Bottom of the Bottle' declaring, 'By this time it was becoming clear to me that I was really fighting something inside that nibbled at my soaked soul. Yet, what the hell! We were cavaliers of the evanescent, romantics who turned the revolt inwards upon our own bruised spirits.'[14] It was perhaps Lewis Nkosi who captured the politics and drinking paradox deftly when talking about Themba in 'The Fabulous Decade'. He wrote: 'Can grinned happily, arms lifted to silence the hubbub. "Anyway, I say to hell with politics and bottoms up to glasses!" He tossed the entire contents of a large glass of brandy down his throat.'[15]

The debate was a contentious one at the time, and has raged ever since. Nkosi was one of the most brutal critics in deriding the obsession of South African writers with politics, sacrificing literary aesthetics on the altar of political expediency in the process. This is perhaps the counterbalance to Gordimer's belief in the social responsibilities of the writer, and the logic of using writing as a form of protest against those in power. Themba's friend and fellow journalist Robert Resha is an example of someone who straddled the two realms before party politics took over in his case.

Resha was in fact one of a number of politicians Themba knew personally. In 'Treason Arrests', which Themba wrote for *Drum* magazine in 1957, he directly addressed political issues, particularly in a subsection provocatively titled 'Who will lead the Congress now?'. But, as always, he was interested in the human and sensational elements: he described how during a rowdy afternoon at a local shebeen with political figures Resha, Tennyson Makiwane and Lionel Morrison, one of them was accused of 'living a dissolute life'. They set up a mock trial, in which Themba acted as the 'magistrate', an echo of Mangosuthu Buthelezi's vivid memories of Themba hosting a mock graduation and acting as the chancellor of the university during their student days (as described in Chapter 2). In the case of the mock trial in Sophiatown, however, in which the accused was found guilty, reality was about to imitate art. The very next day, Themba recounted, three of the participants (Resha, Makiwane and Morrison) in the mock trial were arrested for high treason. Themba described this sequence of events as 'comical farce that had in it foreboding ingredients of upcoming tragedy'.[16]

Nevertheless, as Snyman notes, 'Unlike Mphahlele and Modisane, it has repeatedly been claimed, [Themba] was not outspokenly political. He did not join any liberation movement and did not base his criticism of apartheid on an ideological system. In fact, in a sense his claim to be apolitical and his cynical wit became his ideology.'[17]

Addressing this issue, his former lover, Jean Hart, told Mike Nicol: 'He [Can Themba] would talk about how the reality of being black and white in South Africa tortured relationships. And because he was a poet and not a politico, I think it was constantly a great pain for him, but at the same time he had to recognise it and keep reminding me.'[18]

Here Hart made the firm assertion that Themba was 'a poet, not a politico'. Yet, there is no reason he cannot be seen and read as both; politics and poetry are not binary opposites.

It was certainly not lack of confidence or faith in his own abilities that led Themba to eschew formal or organisational politics, as we can see from the following report in Sampson's book: '"If I went for politics, I would be the most dangerous man in Africa," said Can. "I would be cunning and ruthless and I would stop at nothing. The boys are always imploring me to go into politics. 'We need you, Can,' they say ..."'[19]

Likewise, Tom Hopkinson, in his memoir, testifies to Themba's confidence in stating his views. One of their run-ins involved a confrontation over race relations in South Africa, and the position of liberal whites such as himself. Hopkinson reports that Themba told him in no uncertain terms: 'We don't want someone who supports us when he thinks we're okay, but withdraws his support when we do something un-Western or un-gentlemanly. We've had too much of this patronising liberal attitude – pat us on the head when you think we're going the right way, kick us in the pants when we take a different turning.'[20]

The fact that Themba was not loath to say this to Hopkinson – a white man and his senior at work – is a clear indication that he had no inhibitions about expressing his viewpoints. Testimony by Hart and others corroborate this aspect of Themba's personality and politics. After all, this was a man who had debated with Mandela at the University of Fort Hare,[21] and he was well known as a man of debate among his fellow students, as Mangosuthu Buthelezi told me in our interview.

Themba, who had no false modesty, saw himself as an intellectual giant who could engage on any topic. This is why he had no qualms challenging the 'Lion of the North', as Prime Minister J. G. Strijdom was called at the time, to a verbal duel, according to Nkosi: '"All I want," Can challenged, "all I am suing Strijdom for is a chance to sit down with him over a glass of brandy and talk to him man to man. I reckon I have a few things to tell him. It may very well be that after the umpteenth drink, even with the lowest intelligence, a man may see reason."'[22]

So, although no liberation heroes could give me an explosive scoop on a never-before-known side of Themba as an underground activist, there is indeed documented information that reflects his views and perspectives on politics. His journalistic and imaginative writing, traced over his career, reveals, increasingly explicitly, a growing political consciousness. This is especially true of his later years of journalism, as *Drum* itself began loosening up and was more open to exploring the political landscape.

Can Themba on the Political Condition

The urban world about which Can Themba wrote so compassionately was a racially polarised and highly politicised landscape. Given Themba's deep embedding in the urban black landscape as a journalist, and his voracious reading habits, it is inconceivable that he would have remained ignorant or unaffected by the unfolding sociopolitical upheavals around him.

Moreover, as someone who discreetly attended parties organised by white liberals and had a clandestine romantic affair with a white woman, Themba had first-hand knowledge of the political world of this period and the restrictions it placed on him and other citizens. In 'Crepuscule', his narrator states: 'I do not necessarily want to bed a white woman; I merely insist on my right to want her.'[23]

As *Drum*'s attitude towards political content evolved, so too did Themba's own engagement with political subjects. In the latter years of his career in South Africa, he wrote quite extensively on political events and ideologies, providing sharp analyses of developments on the political scene, proactively giving insights on issues that later became dominant political questions and, in retrospect, historic landmarks in South Africa's long walk to freedom.

The most explicitly political engagement in his imaginative writing is probably found in his 1961 story 'The Bottom of the Bottle', in which he details attempts by ANC leaders to persuade the narrator/character, Can Themba, to join the liberation movement. Although he agrees to join them in the struggle against oppression, it is clear that the said ANC leaders were not convinced by Can's utterances, suspecting that his consent was fuelled more by alcohol than conviction. It seemed their interest in him was prompted by his influence in society; recruiting him to the movement would mean enlisting someone whose voice reached hordes of people through his writings, and who had young people looking up to him and emulating his way of life. This encounter, however, seems to have had a lasting impact on Themba, as the narrator of his story recounts: 'After that, perhaps largely because I paid more attention, I heard more and more *politics*: bitter, heady, virulent stuff. It expressed, in venomous terms, the wrath of a people who had come to the damn-it-all threshold. Also, the despair of a people tied helplessly to an ant-heap: it was savage swearing. What struck me more those days was the great number of ordinary folk who spoke politics [original emphasis].'[24]

What fascinated Themba was how the political condition affected ordinary citizens. He did not dwell much on the dominant political questions; instead he focused on their impact on ordinary people, especially in marginalised communities, and those whose voices were often overlooked by the mainstream media. He sought to demonstrate, often in a discursive manner, how government policies affected the downtrodden, and how the masses responded to these. This was especially true as the growing political ferment spread across the country, including the rural areas. This we see, for instance, in his narrator's words in 'Bottom of the Bottle': 'For the machine that was ploughing up the country could not leave one square inch undisrupted. In Zeerust, Sekhukhuneland, Pondoland, official policies were driving the tribesman to resistance.'[25]

This concern for the condition of ordinary citizens, to the extent of empathising with the victims, became the forte of the *Drum* writers, according to Chapman: 'Most of the writers were concerned with more than just telling a story. They were concerned with what was happening to their people and, in consequence, with moral and social questions. It is this which distinguishes the *Drum* writers from purveyors of pulp fiction.'[26]

One of the most succinct commentaries on Themba's political perspective is captured in Sam Mathe's review of *The House of Truth*, a bioplay of Can Themba penned by myself. Writing about the scene where the unnamed characters from Themba's story 'Bottom of the Bottle' are represented in the play as Mandela and Sisulu, Mathe says: 'Their attempts to recruit him as an ANC member failed, but their belief that he was politically non-committal [is] refuted by the sheer volume of his political reportage which exposed apartheid injustices, including the hypocrisy of white churches, the humiliation of black men during nude parades and brutal prison conditions.'[27]

This transition of *Drum* – from being averse to reporting anything political to tapping into explicitly political subjects – did not come overnight. It was a gradual process, with one of the earliest pieces being Henry Nxumalo's investigative story in Bethal about the farm labourers and the abuse by the farmers (see Chapter 7). According to former *Drum* photographer Jürgen Schadeberg, the story was hatched at the suggestion of Nxumalo during their editorial meeting as the headline for the March 1952 issue, which would be celebrating their first anniversary: 'About 200 kilometres east of Johannesburg was the district of Bethal, a potato and mealie farming area where, in 1947, the Reverend Michael Scott had conducted an investigation into and produced a report on slave conditions on farms. From what Henry said, it appeared that nothing had improved since the Reverend's report about beatings, killings and forced labour conditions. He wanted to investigate further and expose the truth of the current farm labour conditions there.'[28]

This story rattled the cage of the apartheid government as it exposed the abuse suffered by black labourers at the hands of white farmers, and readers were enthralled; a new market had opened up for *Drum*. The editors were still very cautious, and the proprietor in particular was concerned about the imminent financial losses should the magazine be closed down or the government take drastic steps against them. According to Sylvester Stein: 'He's got the wind up, fearing we'd be closed down if we did this one, just as he'd been scared back in 1955, when Henry, Can and I had given the year's big Mr Drum special a different twist from the usual, going more directly political than in former years, with a provocative sports piece demanding that South Africa allow blacks into the Olympic team.'[29]

Fortunately for Stein and his team, the Olympics story garnered significant interest and support, and they continued to explore the issue of politics in sport, including campaigning for the exclusion of South Africa from world football on the basis of its discriminatory policies. Stein reported that one result was that FIFA (International Federation of Association Football) became one of the first world sports bodies to ban South Africa from international competition.

Meanwhile, as part of the 'Mr Drum' team, Themba became increasingly daring, writing stinging commentary and risking his skin as angry Bible-waving young men chased him through the streets for investigating local churches. As can be seen from the discussion of his journalism in Chapter 7, there was no doubt that his reportage was becoming explicitly political, even as he focused on the stories of individuals like Alcott Gwentshe (in his 'concentration camp' exposé) and ordinary rural people like the women of Zeerust, who refused to carry passes. His interest was in the human element, but was no less political for that, as can be seen in his account of the bus boycott, where he painted a picture of stoic and trudging pedestrians and analysed the grammar of their slogan.

When he had the liberty to write his own columns, he was able to tackle political content as he desired. This is best demonstrated in his *Golden City Post* columns, where he commented regularly on pertinent socio-political issues. *Golden City Post* was the sister weekly newspaper of *Drum* magazine. In 1960, following his expulsion from *Drum* in 1959 and a short stint as a teacher at the Central Indian High School, Themba continued working for *Golden City Post* as a columnist, news editor and occasional acting editor.

Here he used his columns to express his political opinions directly and unapologetically; they also demonstrate his sophisticated grasp of national and indeed global political ideologies. In his 'Can Says' column in *Golden City Post*, he published a piece titled 'This is Why I Am Not a Communist'. In it he challenged communists, stating clearly why he does not believe in their ideology: 'What is perhaps even more serious is the apparently "Unhuman" attitude of communism to social problems. It is on the one hand a result of the philosophy that teaches us that the individual counts for little compared with the state. Your human emotions – some of them are the deepest experiences in your life – are said to be illusions – worse still, tricks that a designing upper class has devised to keep you down.'[30]

Themba's criticism of communism demonstrates his deep knowledge of the subject, but also makes his own political stance explicit. His assertions offended many readers who wrote to the newspaper, some of them highly emotional and disgusted. After a torrent of responses, many accusing him of becoming a 'fascist', Themba hit back in a column he titled 'I Am Not a Fascist Either': 'Now it seems that just about every Leftist in town wants to prove that I am a Capitalist, an apostle of Apartheid, and every traitor imaginable since Judas Iscariot … I would like to say while I am not a Communist, I am still less a Fascist. I hate Fascism and Nazism much more than I hate Communism.'[31]

While many of the responses he received came to the defence of communism, many more endorsed or agreed with his critique. According to him, these came from 'ordinary folks' from all over South Africa who happened to think, as he did, that independence of thought was fundamental and priceless for all human beings.

Themba was fully aware that he was choosing the risky path of coming across as an armchair critic refusing to pay allegiance to any particular political creed, though as a daring journalist he was no stranger to political upheaval on the streets. He refused to be bound to a monolithic and zealously followed ideology. In his follow-up column, he defended and further clarified his position: 'So I am an individualist, I admit it. I realise fully no modern state can be run for 24 hours by letting individuals do whatever they like. The problem here is one of organisation, adjustment, evaluation of conflicting tastes, sometimes even curtailment. But not of the destruction of individuality.'[32]

The above extract reveals a certain level of self-awareness as much as it illustrates Themba's political consciousness. On this topic, Kgositsile said that 'if you were looking for the kind of popular political rhetoric from Can Themba, you would never find it. He was not the kind of person to regurgitate preconceived ideas. He was his own man.'[33]

Themba was not only a keen observer of national politics; he had a particular interest in the political condition of the continent. As *Drum* had offices in Kenya, Nigeria and Ghana, covering East and West Africa respectively, some of his articles were written specifically for these communities. When Ghana became the first African country to attain independence from Britain in 1957, Themba rejoiced with the rest of the continent. He penned an ode, 'O Ghana', which read in part:

> Bright with the souls of our fathers,
> Beneath whose shade we live and die,
> Red for the blood of the heroes in the fight,
> Green for the precious farms of our birthright,
> And linked with these the shining golden band
> That marks the richness of our Fatherland.
> We'll live and die for Ghana.
> Our land of hope for ages to come![34]

But as much as Themba had a good grasp on the political condition on the continent, he displayed a certain naivety with regard to the politics of his own country. Even with his knowledge of the workings of the apartheid regime, he harboured ambitions of being allowed to leave the country legally to cover political revolts in other countries on the continent, and to return to publish these. Of course, he did go to the Kingdom of Lesotho from time to time, but to dream of travelling north, to cover resistance against colonial governments, was at best naive, and at worst delusional.

In 1954, Themba wanted to travel to Kenya and Tanzania to cover the developing stories of the uprisings led by the Kenya Land and Freedom Army, popularly known as the Mau Mau, against the British colonial regime. He expected the South African government to grant him a passport to travel to these respective countries to cover what freedom fighters in South Africa could only dream of. In response, the Johannesburg acting Native Commissioner, P. H. Liefeldt, wrote to the Director of Native Labour on 9 July 1954, explaining: 'The above mentioned native who is a reporter on the staff of the magazine "Drum" has applied for a passport to visit Nairobi for the purpose of writing a series of objective articles on the Mau Mau rebellion for "Drum".'

In writing this letter, Liefeldt indicated that Kenyan authorities had no objection to the proposed visit and its purpose. He also made it very clear that the applicant's credentials were beyond reproach. However, he stated that 'a visit by a Union native to the area at the present time may very easily lead to his being influenced in the wrong directions and publication of his findings may sooner or later lead to an embarrassing situation'. The supposed 'embarrassing situation' was not stated explicitly, but it is obvious that such a story could have inspired the oppressed in South Africa into action. The application was ultimately escalated to the Department of Native Affairs, under the ministry of Dr Hendrik Verwoerd. It was rejected outright, as was to be expected.

In 1960, there was a heightened global interest in South African politics, following the Sharpeville massacre in March. One result was that Hopkinson, as the editor of *Drum*, hosted international experts who wanted to engage on political matters. Even though he had fired Themba a year earlier, such was the level of trust Hopkinson had in his former assistant editor that he called on him to advise and give informed political commentary to these international experts. Themba, with his insatiable appetite for debate, was never reluctant to participate in such forums, and Hopkinson continued to rely on his knowledge and expertise as a public intellectual.[35]

Themba's views were not always the most popular, but they were well informed and he could sustain his arguments. Most importantly, he was conscious of his own capabilities and shared his ideas fearlessly. Some of his political ideas are expressed in an interview he did for an American documentary broadcast in June 1965. The interview begins with a narrator saying: 'An African risks his neck in front of the camera by talking frankly and critically to the outside world about conditions in his country. Can Themba speaks for many who have been silenced. We included Mr Themba's statement knowing that he is now safely in Swaziland.'[36] The prelude by the narrator gives the context of the South African political situation, and acknowledges that Themba would not be in a position to speak freely if he had still been in his homeland.

Part of Themba's statement in this documentary appears as the epigraph of this chapter. In the interview, he continues to describe his ideal South Africa, where there is co-operation across colour lines in the interests of building a common destiny. He blames the lack of co-operation on the white regime, maintaining that their impulse when dealing with black people is towards violence: 'It's so difficult to communicate with a white man in a country where we think we belong together and we would like to organise a destiny together, but the white man has got this psychological fear of organising life only on his interest. I want a co-operation, a communication between different sets of people – even if they are different for whatever reason they are different, I'd like us to live together.'[37]

These are the exact same sentiments Themba expresses in *Come Back, Africa*, a film that was secretly shot in South Africa in 1957.

It is quite obvious that the views that Themba expresses in these films had no place in a South Africa that had apartheid as an official policy. He made use of available platforms to express his political views for as long as it was safe to do so, and, in the end, this was no doubt how he earned himself a place in the bad books of the Minister of Justice, B. J. Vorster. In 1966, Themba was listed by Vorster among 45 other individuals as 'Statutory Communists' (his public denunciation of communism notwithstanding), whose works could not be referred to or cited inside South Africa. Although he was already exiled in Swaziland by this time, this was a major blow to the soul of a writer. So much for the charge of being 'apolitical'.

Although Themba's published texts do not feature any known monolithic political views, he certainly was not politically naive. His politics are not separate from his life and his literary output. They are embedded in every piece of his writing. A closer look at Themba's works, as well as the context of his life and times, suggests it is fair to conclude that his politics are deeply embedded in his writings and form the bedrock of his narratives.

12

The People's Intellectual

Although some people may describe him as an intellectual, I don't dismiss that – of course he was – but he wasn't a type of intellectual who was somewhere above people. He was a very approachable down-to-earth person that you could meet and interact with. You know, we had many intellectuals, they are sort of a little above ordinary people like us, so it was not easy, but not with Can. It was easy to interact with him because … although he was described as an intellectual, he was also a people's man.

Ahmed Kathrada — Interview (2015)

One of the leading theorists on African intellectuals, Toyin Falola, posits that 'thinkers may be variously labelled as pragmatist, traditionalist, assimilationist, or Afrocentrist, although the line is not always clear-cut. Some are radical, others are conservative.'[1] Can Themba defies these parameters, as his intellectual architecture cuts across the conventional categories. The closest we can come is to label him a pragmatist, simply because he adapted to different situations and contexts; but this is not always an accurate assessment, as testimonies by people close to him, such as Jean Hart, reveal that he was never afraid of taking unconventional or extreme positions at times.

It might be more useful to consider Themba in the light of Antonio Gramsci's definition of an organic intellectual, and examine the various factors he listed as key. The fundamental elements of Gramsci's definition include position in society; intellectual training; preoccupation with abstract ideas; and fulfilling a public role.[2]

If we take a brief look at Gramsci's components and apply them to Themba, we find that the element of position in society is probably the most challenging. Themba was by law a second-class citizen in the land of his birth because of the apartheid government's aversion to the colour of his skin. Yet, his natural charisma, erudition and role as a mouthpiece of ideas as a journalist for *Drum* gave him a position that enabled him to wield considerable influence.

Themba's editor at *Drum*, Sylvester Stein, strongly believed that Themba was a natural leader: 'Can was a natural chief by force of personality, and intellectually a giant. I put him down as a coming man of Africa.'[3] In his memoir, Stein repeatedly remarked that he believed in Themba, and 'never abandoned the thought that certainly Themba could have been that leader of Africa whose future greatness I had perceived in the auspices'.[4]

Although Stein implied that Themba's demeanour gave the impression that he was of royal blood, specifically a chief, genetically no such a connection existed. The leadership qualities he possessed were not earned in a political arena, nor were they the result of some cultural inheritance.

Themba was a thoroughly modern man, part of a cohort of African intellectuals who, in the middle of the twentieth century, were increasingly establishing themselves as the new black elite in South Africa (as detailed in Chapter 10). Members of this new elite were penetrating political, cultural and intellectual spaces, and driving public discourse.

This was the generation of modern intellectuals who, as Mcebisi Ndletyana argues, 'owe their origins to the spread of Western formal education, which began in some parts of Africa in the sixteenth century'. Ndletyana goes on to say: 'Early African intellectuals were a product of the missionary enterprise and the British civilising mission. They were part of a new middle class that the colonial agents wanted as a buffer between colonial society and the rest of the indigenous population.'[5]

Themba might indeed be a perfect fit with this definition – if not for his resistance to the notion of being used as a buffer between colonialists and the oppressed masses. Instead, he tried to build bridges between the intellectual elite and the ordinary masses, as is demonstrated by his ability to mix with all levels of society: to recite poetry to tsotsis in shebeens and debate with leaders of the calibre of Nelson Mandela, Robert Resha and Rosette Ndziba.

The risk with building bridges is that it requires one to balance precariously between two terrains. Themba nevertheless managed this tightrope act masterfully, compared to many of his colleagues at *Drum*.

He brought literature closer to the people, and, since he was a journalist writing for the most popular publication in Africa, he brought people's stories to the paper in turn. It was through his writings that the residents of Sophiatown, Meadowlands, Alexandra and Dube, among others, saw their lives represented and reflected on paper. He wrote their stories using language they understood and in a manner they could easily visualise. While this epitomises some elements of tsotsi culture, it is also in line with one of the functions of intellectuals as articulated by Ndletyana:

> Intellectuals explain new experiences and ideas in the most accessible and understandable ways to the rest of society … Intellectuals thus provide answers and leadership mainly in the conception and articulation of ideas.[6]

To apply Gramsci's criteria further, Themba's 'preoccupation with abstract ideas' and his 'fulfilling a public role' are easier to discern, as they are embedded in his writings, which cut across genres, and which engage with a wide range of ideas, abstract and otherwise.

Juby Mayet recounts an incident that sheds light on the construction and catholicity of Themba's intellect, what Gramsci might term 'intellectual training'. She claims to have been rather bemused to find Themba, a man widely recognised as having a brilliant mind, reading a comic magazine. When she asked him about this seemingly bizarre choice for an intellectual, Themba told her that it was important to read indiscriminately.

This is perhaps the first lesson to keep: Themba's intellectual capacities were not exclusively gained in a classroom, even though there had been plenty of that, first at Khaiso Secondary School and then at Fort Hare. Instead, he continuously expanded his mental faculties by consuming all kinds of material and life experiences. This tale by Mayet leads us to Essop Patel's words in the preface to *The World of Can Themba*: 'The aspiring black writer is seldom surrounded by volumes of belles-lettres; instead he is in the midst of human conditions and experiences – hunger, misery, deprivation and lurking fear.'[7]

Nevertheless, no matter what Themba's personal circumstances, he read widely and hungrily. Testimonies by those who knew him personally confirm that Themba maintained a close relationship with books throughout his life.

When I interviewed his friend and fellow journalist Parks Mangena in 2017, the latter was still in possession of a book that Themba had presented to him as a gift in 1962. *Lonesome Traveler*, by the American novelist and poet Jack Kerouac, sat comfortably in Mangena's house in Mbabane as one of his most prized possessions. The fact that this book reached Themba, who had never been to America, in the same year it was published can only suggest that he was a committed reader who made an effort to get hold of books.

Themba read not only popular comics and contemporary American poets, but poets and playwrights from the full range of the Western canon. In her address at the Can Themba Memorial Lecture in 2013, Nadine Gordimer argued that Themba read Euripides and Blake, among others, on the principle that 'all human knowledge and art belong to and should be used by the intellects of the world'.[8]

This is confirmed by Jürgen Schadeberg in his memoir, *The Way I See It*. From the first day Themba reported to work, he connected with Anthony Sampson, the editor at the time, on the basis of their shared love of the classics: '"It was the best of times, it was the worst of times," Can said, looking at Tony [Anthony Sampson]. *A Tale of Two Cities* was very popular amongst Sophiatown intellectuals and at *Drum* everybody quoted lines from the book, even more so than from *Knock on Any Door* ... I drank my coffee while Tony and Can carried on debating Shakespeare and Dickens and comparing their work with that of contemporary African writers.'[9]

During our interview in 2013, Don Mattera aptly described Themba as a 'connoisseur of the language', while Gordimer, in her address at the Can Themba Memorial Lecture, referred to him as the 'master of language'.[10] This mastery is evident in Themba's writings. The late Aggrey Klaaste, legendary journalist and distinguished newspaper editor, encapsulated Themba's linguistic abilities and his intellectual disposition thus: 'His English was beautiful, high intellectual, and yet with a swagger of journalistic style that was sheer stimulation and titillation.'[11]

The evolution of Themba's writing style and an analysis of his literary works is provided in Chapter 13, but Klaaste confirms that as his writing matured, it remained lively, dynamic and accessible to those he wrote about, people who were also his primary audience. After the lofty flights of fancy seen in his early poems and stories, his writing was never obscure or abstruse. Although he was a product of missionary education, and had imbibed copious amounts of the works of the English Romantic poets, he consciously chose to localise both his content and language, so he could speak directly to his immediate audience.

While he possessed the hallmarks of a traditional intellectual who displayed his abilities through regular debate, mainly in his House of Truth and in local shebeens, he also distinguished himself through his writing, something that can be preserved for posterity and offers immediate reference for his intellectual output. His determination to transmit knowledge, to nurture young minds inside and outside the classroom, speaks of a man who was a great visionary with a fortitude for the future of the intellectual tradition on the African continent.

These could be early indications of what has become known as the decolonial project, where African intellectuals started to rid themselves of unnecessary colonial elements, and embraced only those that would be constructive in their immediate environment. His joining *Drum* magazine in 1953 was part of this project, given that *Drum* was initially established with misguided perceptions about the reading habits and desires of Africans in urban spaces. He spoke their language and interrogated their living conditions exceedingly well. This is in line with Michel Foucault's thesis in his essay 'Intellectuals and Power', where he opines: 'The role of an intellectual is no longer to sit himself "slightly ahead" or "slightly to one side" so he may speak the silent truth of each and all; it is rather to struggle against those forms of power where he is both instrument and object: in the order of "knowledge," "truth," "consciousness," and "discourse."'[12]

What makes Themba an outstanding intellectual of his generation is probably the manner in which he was able to navigate between different classes of society and relate to all of them without compromising a fraction of his persona. This malleable approach to life reflected itself in his idiom and his prose, which shifted from the esoteric and lofty writing evident in the early stages of his career, to the simple yet evocative literature that he produced as he matured as a writer. It was also the authentic manner in which he and his colleagues captured people's stories in *Drum* that led to the black urban classes (who were initially not tempted to buy the magazine) becoming reliable consumers of the magazine.

If we consider Gramsci's 'preoccupation with abstract ideas' as a criteria for standing as a public intellectual, it is clear that Themba was no ivory-tower scribe or thinker. He was at his best when it came to debate, and he relished such opportunities. He was clearly a dynamic thinker whose intellectual discourse varied from engaging with students in the classroom to engaging junior reporters in the newsroom, to engaging with editors.

As a man of debate, Themba also contributed orally to intellectual growth. Mattera revealed that he was hired to provide private lessons to families; then there were the famous debates at the House of Truth. As revealed by Tom Hopkinson, he also engaged intellectually with right-wing students from the University of Pretoria, and delivered guest lectures at institutions such as the University of the Witwatersrand. Hopkinson admits that Themba delivered one of the best lectures he had ever heard: 'I knew how well Can could talk from having driven him up a couple of times to give lectures to groups of students at the Witwatersrand University. One such talk he had given – delivered mainly over his shoulder as he walked up and down in front of a blackboard – was one of the most brilliant lectures I had ever heard.'[13]

It is unfortunate that Hopkinson does not say more, and sadly the contents of these lectures are not publicly available.

Although it may be argued that an intellectual has no obligation to ensure a positive legacy in a form of community development, Themba's chosen vocation as a public intellectual, which includes his work as a teacher, creative writer, mentor and journalist, meant leaving a considerable legacy in his wake. This legacy is also seen in many of his former students, who have gone on to become intellectuals of note in their own right, and continue to nurture budding intellectuals in turn.

In this sense, Themba fulfils the final element in Gramsci's notion of an intellectual: that of fulfilling a public role. The ease with which he combined the dichotomies of intellectual and 'tsotsiness' entrenched him in the annals of history as one of the prominent thinkers of twentieth-century South Africa.

The Shebeen as a Point of Convergence

Many of the aspects of Can Themba's standing as a public or organic intellectual converged in that place of liquor consumption, the shebeen. Often humble and always illicit, these were places that Themba and his friends would turn into a kind of public forum, where drinking was coupled with debate and intellectual engagement. The shebeen had become, among other things, a point of convergence for people from all walks of life, an entertainment hub for everyone and a favourite environment for initiating good conversation.

The title of Mari Snyman's thesis on Themba refers to him as the 'Shebeen Intellectual'.[14] While not the first to use this label, her work is a reminder that for Themba, shebeens were not mere watering holes; they constituted an intellectual landscape where patrons were free to debate ideas. They were also places that straddled the gap between the masses and the intelligentsia, a convergence important to Themba in his role as a public intellectual. The world came to the shebeens of Johannesburg, and this was where Themba could meet the world. It was Lewis Nkosi who said that in the shebeen one could meet 'teachers, businessmen, clerks, showgirls, payroll robbers, "nice-time" girls and occasionally, even renegade priests'.[15] In Sophiatown in the 1950s, it was literally a place where a tsotsi could engage in conversation with a priest or teacher.

Shebeens represented a prominent element of township life in the African urban world, especially during the politically volatile period of the 1950s and 1960s. The word 'shebeen' itself testifies to its illegality: it is derived from 'sibin', an Irish word for illicit whiskey. The prevalence of shebeen culture was a response to the racially based laws of liquor consumption of the time. Black people were legally prohibited from buying 'Western liquor' from the pubs or bottle stores, and, as alternative mechanisms, they either brewed their own liquor or bought illegally acquired alcohol from the shebeens in the townships, if not both. Ezekiel Mphahlele in *Down Second Avenue*, Modikwe Dikobe in *The Marabi Dance* and Bloke Modisane in *Blame Me on History*, amongst others, write about the illicit liquor trade and shebeens during this period in South African history.

As described in Chapter 8, for Themba and most of his fellow journalists at *Drum*, the shebeen might have been somewhere they could quench their thirst and relax after a long day of covering gruesome stories of starvation, poverty and violence. But shebeen culture offered not just respite; they were places of conviviality, intellectual debate, entertainment, political subversion and even defiance, as places where members of the new black elite could take their white friends and colleagues – breaking the race laws of the time in multiple ways. They fitted Nkondo's definition of the House of Truth as the 'parliament of the streets'.

Along with subversion, the element of conviviality was an important one, according to Obed Musi: 'Can was more of a teacher than journalist, more of an intellectual than a hard scribe, more of a pedagogue, but *he made people feel at home and you enjoyed his company* [my emphasis].'[16]

It was in shebeens that Themba clearly felt at home, and made others feel at home. The noise and bustle of this environment also apparently suited him. Never the reclusive or 'ivory tower' kind of intellectual, according to Keorapetse Kgositsile, he would write even in a crowd: 'Can Themba could be in a place with people drinking, making noise or even fighting if they had to be fighting, and he was always with his notebook, so his jackets were always a little distorted. And he'd just whip out his notebook and write. And the following day he'd just go to the office and set up the typewriter and write what he produced.'[17]

Themba reflected on shebeen culture in his journalism and short stories, but also played a role in entrenching shebeen culture as an integral part of the black urban lifestyle of 1950s Johannesburg. For him, drinking went hand-in-hand with intellectual debate; hence the shebeen was his favourite hang-out spot. Themba was part of a shebeen culture that not only he, but also the rest of his colleagues, including Nkosi, Modisane and Nat Nakasa, recorded. In his generation of scribes, Themba is probably rivalled only by Casey Motsisi in his interest in and understanding of the shebeen culture.

Themba not only frequented shebeens, but recruited new patrons to these establishments. In Chapter 8, we looked at how he insisted his younger peers and mentees accompany him to shebeens. Many of his former colleagues and friends relate tales of being inducted into their first shebeen experience by the man from the House of Truth.

Gordimer revealed that Themba had initiated her into her first shebeen experience. She reminisced at the Can Themba Memorial Lecture: 'Can introduced me to my first-time shebeen in the 1950s. Can had – he said – the honour of naming that shebeen "The House of Truth". But it was something of the truth of African daily

Johannesburg lives.'[18] This, of course, refers to Themba's abode at 111 Ray Street; as we know from Chapter 1, Themba established his apartment – the House of Truth – as a forum for intellectual debate, so it did not meet the definition of a shebeen in the strict sense.

A man of Themba's insatiable appetite for alcohol could hardly carry out such trade; it would be tantamount to leaving a flock of sheep in the care of a wolf. But while Themba himself may not have sold alcohol, his den had all the other attributes of a shebeen – drinking, music and debate combined.

Themba himself writes with droll humour: 'The other day in a shebeen I was caught by members of the liquor squad with a nip of brandy. At the police station I was told I could pay an admission of guilt fine that was £5 for a bottle of brandy or part thereof. The police were very friendly. They told me that a man of my standing ought to apply for a liquor licence, and ought not to be found drinking in shebeens.'[19]

Themba had an impressive track record in introducing white liberals to shebeen life. We already know that he took Jean Hart, his white girlfriend, to do the rounds of the taverns with him. He was also responsible for the maiden shebeen experience of his editor at *Drum*, Sampson, with whom he enjoyed a close relationship. He took his editor to 'Back o' the Moon', a shebeen that was to become one of Themba's favourite watering holes and one of the most legendary in Sophiatown. According to Sampson: 'Can introduced me to Sophiatown. "Come to the Back o' the Moon," he said one evening. "It's a new shebeen I've just discovered. I think you'd be interested."'[20]

Sampson's initiation into shebeen life did not end there. Themba went on to introduce him to the plethora of shebeens that were sprouting in the area. They visited shebeens with names such as 'Going to Church', 'Cabin in the Sky', 'Thirty-Nine Steps' and 'House on the Telegraph Hill'. These names, it is understood, were not always the official names; Themba enjoyed giving names that he thought were most appropriate for the shebeens. There were others, including 'Little Heaven' and 'The Sanctuary in Sophiatown'. Although Sampson believes that the most interesting shebeens were in Sophiatown, Themba pointed out shebeens that were within the city of Johannesburg, some within the shadow of the *Drum* offices.

As has been noted, in all these visits and encounters it was ironically the illegality of shebeens that enabled them to become points of convergence for different classes of society – including tsotsis and intellectuals united by their thirst and their abhorrence of the establishment. The educated elite might have been engineered to create a buffer zone between the white community and the oppressed blacks, yet the shebeen brought them together.

Can Themba epitomised the paradox of the 'intellectual tsotsi', and, as Ahmed Kathrada noted in the epigraph to this chapter, he was not only an intellectual, but also 'a people's man'. His sphere of influence spread across age, gender, class and racial divides, and the shebeen was the forum that enabled him to straddle these complex social strata with ease.

PART IV

Dances with Texts: Writing and Storytelling

13

No Ordinary Storyteller

There's a theory that was associated with T. S. Eliot, where he says the mind that creates is different from the man who suffers. So T. S. Eliot made a distinction between the experience of a writer and what he writes about. Can Themba collapsed that distinction. The man who suffers and the mind that creates is one and the same thing.

Muxe Nkondo — Interview (2015)

The life history of Can Themba is as amorphous as much of his writing, a great deal of which is hard to define in terms of conventional literary genres. Both in his writing and in his lived experience, Themba challenged established conventions and orthodoxies regarding intellectual behaviour, ideologies, reading, writing, life and living.

He was, as Es'kia Mphahlele puts it, 'a rebel par excellence'.[1] In his tribute to his mentor and icon, Harry Mashabela concurs with Mphahlele: 'Can was over-complex. A rebel. A man of the people. A kind of genius. A rascal. Sensible. Nonsensical. All crammed up in one man. And yet he remained something of a legend. As a rebel, he scorned convention, tradition, custom and loathed authority. But as a man of the people, he lived at the very bottom of life, mixing with the lowly and doing precisely what he himself felt was the right thing to do.'[2]

The elements mentioned by Mashabela and Mphahlele are repeated by several people who interacted with Themba. These elements are also palpable in his writing, which is characterised by abundant wit and irony, with a magnetic turn of phrase that captivates the reader.

A close reading of Themba's works reveals that from inside the House of Truth, he wrote his own life history. However, few of his stories fit conventional literary genres, and the volatility of his writing earned Themba both critical praise and rebuke in equal measure.

One eminent scholar who was critical of his works is Muxe Nkondo, who, as a student, encountered Themba during a guest-teaching visit to Orlando High School in Soweto in the late 1950s. While Nkondo was impressed with Themba's lesson, which seems to have stayed with him in perpetuity (as described in Chapter 3), this did not cloud his judgement of *The Will to Die*, about which he wrote a very unflattering review. Part of it read:

> This volume attests to a lack of skill in Can Themba's handling of the short story ... Most of the stories are of dubious merit even on technical grounds. 'Crepuscule', the first story in the book, sets out to probe the black man's perilous sense of cultural negation (a sense of something akin to sterility) in South Africa. But it is loose, if not random, in its structure and lacks the self-containedness and epigrammatic force characteristic of the short story as a genre.[3]

In this review, Nkondo seemed most disappointed by the author's failure to conform to the conventional characteristics of a short story. While Nkondo recognised the positive aspects of the story – he found it 'disturbingly illuminating' – he remained unsatisfied with its fluid nature and departure from orthodoxy.

Nkondo's review demonstrates a general difficulty in locating Themba's work within the ambit of conventional literary genres. It was only later that critics came to realise that the transcendent nature of his writing in fact typified his literary oeuvre. As long as we try to confine Themba's work within a particular orthodoxy, we are unlikely to realise its significance and full potential.

Themba's writing defies structural impositions, not just in terms of structure, but also in the narrative techniques and character portrayals in his works. The ambiguity of form is evident if we look at his entire body of work; with the exception of several stories published in literary journals, particularly in the 1960s, Themba's writings largely straddle different fields and forms. In the majority of his stories, the presence of the author is usually overt, not only through the voice of the narrator (who is often Can himself), but also in the direct expression of his opinions and the reflection of his lived experience.

A few of Themba's stories, including 'Crepuscule', 'Bottom of the Bottle' and 'The Will to Die', illustrate this. In his review, Nkondo chose to focus on 'Crepuscule' – the first story in *The Will to Die*, and one in which a multiplicity of narrative approaches is evident. 'Crepuscule' remains difficult to locate within the more conventional notions of the short story because of its undefined form and structure. In this piece laced with vivid imagery, the author combines narrative and poetic prose with philosophical musing. Although the narrative style seems to suggest that it is fiction, it is widely understood that this particular story is based on Themba's lived experience, and the author, whose first-person narrator is named Can Themba, makes this clear.

In 'Crepuscule', Themba tells the story of himself and his white girlfriend, Janet, who wants to be with him without turning him into an anthropological subject. He brings her to Sophiatown, and, after doing the rounds of the township, they go to sleep in his room. In the middle of the night he wakes her up and, despite her protestations, he insists that they go to her flat in Hillbrow. As fate would have it, they leave just as the police are on their way to raid his home after receiving a tip-off that Themba is committing a crime according to the Immorality Act of 1950 (renamed the Sexual Offences Act in 1957), which barred cross-racial romantic and sexual relationships. It turns out that a jealous ex-girlfriend, Baby, has reported him to the police. Baby is a Xhosa woman, and her reasoning for snitching to the police is to punish Themba for humiliating her for 'a white bitch'. The police hope to catch the couple in bed together, so that there can be no denying their association, but they arrive shortly after Can and Janet have left their love nest in Sophiatown.

As Themba narrates this story, he takes us through the journey and the challenges of a racially stratified South Africa, along with the stereotypes that emerge from discriminatory legislation. Nkondo's comment that Themba uses the story as an excuse for discursive social commentary is perhaps prompted by the following excerpt: 'There are also African nationalists who profess horror at the thought that any self-respecting blackman could desire any white woman. They say that no African could ever so debase himself as to love a white woman. This is highly cultivated and pious lying in the teeth of daily slavering in town and in cinema.'[4]

The narrator here offers an opinion on social issues in a racially stratified society. Themba was fully aware of the political significance of his relationship with Janet, and its broader implications for race relations in South Arica. Here he advances his story from a personal recounting to one that grapples with the racially imposed social structures in South Africa at the time.

While one might be tempted to treat this story as pure memoir, Themba's decision to change the name of his companion (calling her Janet instead of Jean, the name of his lover at the time) suggests that he wanted to cover the story with the thin veil of fiction. Nevertheless, Themba is both the author-narrator and a character present in the story. The overt imposition of the author's voice in this story demonstrates why it is difficult to box Themba's writing into any particular literary genre. Like many of his stories, this one wraps together memoir, social commentary and literary criticism.

The extract below, which follows extensive citation from the opening of Charles Dickens's 1859 *A Tale of Two Cities*, demonstrates both the prevalence of intertextual reference in Themba's work and the way he uses literary criticism to illustrate his views about his society.

> Sometimes I think, for his sense of contrast and his sharp awareness of the pungent flavours of life, only Charles Dickens – or, perhaps, Victor Hugo – could have understood Sophiatown …
>
> It is a crepuscular shadow-life in which we wander as spectres seeking meaning for ourselves. And even the local, little legalities we invent are frowned upon. The whole atmosphere is charged with the whiteman's general disapproval, and where he does not have a law for it, he certainly has a grimace that cows you.[5]

The latter part of the excerpt offers Themba's analysis, after having used Dickens as a gateway for a social commentary. The excerpt also clearly shows the way the author diverts from linear storytelling and gives direct authorial opinions, something that Nkondo is critical of in his article. Yet, in Themba's world, life and literature are intertwined.

This was indeed a distinctive feature of South African writing during the period of the 1950s and 1960s. After the Sharpeville massacre in March 1960, when many writers streamed out of the country into various destinations of exile, autobiography thrived as a genre. The urgent need to reflect on the South African experience was likely too intense for these writers to focus on longer and more imaginative prose works such as novels. Two notable examples of autobiography/memoir arising from these circumstances are Mphahlele's *Down Second Avenue* and Bloke Modisane's *Blame Me on History*, which rank among the most significant reflections of the period by this generation of writers.[6] In his lecture at the American Society of African Culture, published in the March 1963 edition of the *AMSAC Newsletter*, Modisane said:

> It is because the pleasures of living in South Africa are such that Africans develop what is properly described as a 'short term morality'. They have to live from day to day. You don't know if the sun is going to shine tomorrow. Everything you do must be done today. Only today is important. You cannot budget for six months in order to write a novel. The short story, therefore, serves as an urgent, immediate, intense, concentrated form of unburdening yourself.[7]

Even though Modisane was referring to the short story here, the same reasons can be advanced for the popularity of biographical writing. After having published his autobiography, and once he had completed his doctoral thesis at the University of Denver in 1968, Mphahlele reverted to the self-reflective mode, writing a biographical work disguised as fiction. The resulting novel, *The Wanderers*, which features incidents and characters modelled on the lives of those around him during the 1950s, has a character named Pan, and it is easy to discern that this character is modelled on Can Themba.[8] Lewis Nkosi argues: 'South African fiction seems determined to close the gap between the author and his inventions; often the author is his own subject matter, the anguish of his characters essentially his own.'[9]

One distinct feature of many writers of the 1950s is that they were simultaneously their own chroniclers and critics. They did not just report daily incidents in the newspapers that they worked for; they also wrote about their own experiences and critiqued each other's works, with Mphahlele and Nkosi some of the most notable critics from this period. Although Themba is not widely recognised as a literary and cultural critic, his literary criticism precedes that of more established critics like Nkosi, who remains the most prominent chronicler and critic of the '*Drum* Decade'.

Themba's literary criticism is not very well known, probably because it hardly ever took the shape of stand-alone or formal features, in which he wrote a paper explicitly offering literary criticism. He wrote a number of reviews while working for *Drum*, but, interestingly, the magazine seems to have needed his expertise even after relieving him of his duties. In June 1960, the magazine published his review of Alfred Hutchinson's book, *Road to Ghana*, titled 'The Man Who Took the Lonely Road to Ghana'. Hutchinson had been Themba's housemate in Beda Hall at the University of Fort Hare; later, they later both worked at the Central Indian High School in Fordsburg. Themba described Hutchinson's book as 'the intellectualised, poetised expression of the ordinary man's desire for release'.[10] In the July edition of the same year, *Drum* ran his review of Noni Jabavu's *Drawn in Colour*, simply titled 'How Different is the North'. Born in Middledrift in the Cape Colony, Jabavu left South Africa at the age of 13 and had been living in England for almost three decades. About her book, Themba wrote, 'It is told by a girl who writes English like an angel, truly knows and feels the quaint sincerity of rural African life, although, in a subtle sense, she is no more of us. That makes her a critic of us worth listening to.'[11]

Themba also wrote the preface to *Darkness and Light: An Anthology of African Writing*, inspired by the independence of the Gold Coast in 1957.[12] After the book was made available in South Africa in 1959, Themba penned a review published in the *Drum* issue of May 1959, simply titled, 'Here It Is at Last'.[13]

In these pieces, Themba makes some poignant observations that would later be echoed by other social commentators. In his review of *Darkness and Light*, he says: 'Here, Africans are creating out of English a language of their own: a language that thinks in actions, using words that dart back and forth on quick moving feet, virile, earthy, garrulous.'[14] This assertion would later become part of the discourse on language spearheaded by Ngũgĩ wa Thiong'o. Ngũgĩ's seminal collection of essays, *Decolonising the Mind: The Politics of Language in African Literature*, is emphatic in its defence of African languages and its dismissal of the hegemony of the English language, especially in African societies.[15]

Meanwhile writers such as Chinua Achebe were adding to this debate. In his paper 'Politics and Politicians of Language in African Literature', as well as in an earlier essay, 'In Defence of English? An Open Letter to Mr Tai Solarin', Achebe seems to echo Themba's philosophy of appropriation and enrichment – Africans creating their own language by infusing the English language with their cultural nuances, imagery and idioms.[16] Achebe claims that writers who choose to express themselves through the medium of the English language do so in order to 'enrich their idiom and imagery by drawing from their own traditional sources'.[17] This demonstrates, amongst other things, that Themba was ahead of his time; he made these observations on language as early as 1958. The debate on language would later resurface at the historic Makerere Conference in 1962, which led to Ngũgĩ denouncing his English first name, James, and choosing to write in his Gĩkũyũ mother tongue.

Themba had strong opinions on the issue of literature and its relation to politics, which would become a contentious matter in the critical reception and treatment of South African literature, especially that produced by black writers. Themba's review of *Darkness and Light* closed with the following lines: 'Much of the literature of protest has been trapped into sacrificing its sincerity for the cause. This does not detract from the justice and vitality of the cause. It does not even suggest that no great literature can come from great causes. But no artist will ever be content to substitute the noise of the war for the music of his soul.'[18]

Here Themba touched on the delicate topic of literature and politics. This was an argument that would resurface in public discourse through the works of Nkosi, amongst others. Nkosi was particularly critical of the overt portrayal of the political condition in literature by black South Africans. In his 1965 essay, 'Fiction by Black South Africans', republished in his posthumous collection, *Writing Home*, he criticises the obsession of South African writers with documentary prose to the extent of neglecting the form.[19] Nkosi would return to this theme repeatedly in his career as one of the leading essayists from the African continent.

Themba, however, while making some poignant observations through sporadic references such as those given here, never lived to articulate a sustained or explicit theory on the relation between literature and the wider world, as has been seen in the discussion of his politics in Chapter 11. This means that Themba's philosophical positioning, including his own biographical background, is reflected throughout his entire body of work. He seldom separated his writing from his lived experience; and the literary material he read and studied was always part of his imagery and lexicon (see Chapter 14 on his use of Shakespeare and other writers of classic works of literature).

In her 2013 lecture paying homage to Themba, Nadine Gordimer described his piece 'Through Shakespeare's Africa' as a 'story-essay-political-philosophy in one'.[20] This is typical: the refusal to be defined by the form of a singular literary genre is a distinct feature of Themba's writing.

Over the years, a number of scholars and social commentators have made differing assertions about Themba's writing. The views expressed by Nkondo in his 1973 article, with regard to the structural formations of Themba's writing, are further enunciated in the works of different scholars, including Themba's peers such as Nkosi and Mphahlele. As discussed further in Chapter 16, some of these positions changed over time. In his article 'Can Themba, Storyteller and Journalist of the 1950s', Michael Chapman observes Mphahlele's change of views regarding Themba's writing:

> And Es'kia Mphahlele's response undergoes interesting modifications in relation to his own changed need for reconstructing a sense of belonging and belief. In 1960, soon after leaving South Africa [he had left in 1957] in anger and disillusionment, Mphahlele could see in *Drum* only a trivialisation of black experience. ('Themba', he said, 'is basically *Drum*: romantic imagery, theatrical characters, Hollywood, with a lace of poetic justice'.) After having returned to South Africa in 1978, thus ending almost twenty years in exile, however, Mphahlele was prepared to say, in 1980, that the world of Can Themba helped to fashion a liveable myth.[21]

Nkondo was another who changed his views. In my interview with Nkondo in 2015, he made an about-turn in his criticism of the structural issues in Themba's writing. He said Themba was first and foremost a 'lyric poet', and should not be confined to particular literary orthodoxies: 'That's why I'm now wiser about Can Themba instead of subjecting him into narrow poetics about the tightness of the image, the organic unity of the image, the tightness of narrative structure, the sense of closure, all the things that we were taught: Can Themba collapsed that.'[22]

In a metaphorical sense, what Nkondo is proposing is the need to view Themba's life from *inside* the House of Truth, as opposed to from the outside, like a tourist who peeps through a tour bus window to view township life, about which they promptly claim expertise. The epigraph at the start of this chapter, in which Nkondo talks about how Themba collapsed the gap between fact and fiction, is articulated in the context of his defiance of literary convention.

During our interview, Nkondo referred to T. S. Eliot's theory about the relationship between the author and their words, which Themba seemed to challenge in his writing. Eliot insists on the distinction between the writer and the story or poem, arguing that the character who appears in the story is very different from the one who is writing. In his 1921 essay, 'Tradition and the Individual Talent', Eliot separates the writer from his writing: 'The mind of the poet is a shred of platinum. It may partly or exclusively operate upon the experience of the man himself; but, the more perfect the artist, the more completely separate in him will be the man who suffers and the mind which creates; the more perfectly will the mind digest and transmute the passions which are its material.'[23]

Eliot's epistemology is related to the metaphysical theory of the connection between the writer and his writing – that they are not necessarily the same. According to this school of thought, the poet or writer is not (necessarily) emotionally involved with the message they deliver; rather, they are the 'medium' through which the message is conveyed. At the same time, it can be argued that what is written in fiction reflects the author's preoccupations. It is their ideas that are shared in the text. They choose a particular story because they feel strongly about it, and would like to communicate an idea pertaining to that particular subject. In this sense, the author is intimately involved in their text both intuitively and emotionally. The extent to which they reflect on lived experience versus their imaginative powers is what determines the form of their writing.

According to Nkondo, Themba defies Eliot's theory, as he collapses the barricades between the author and his or her text. The emphasis of Nkondo's more recent argument is that Themba the storyteller and Themba the person overlapped in most of his narratives. As such,

Nkondo believes that 'The Will to Die' was overtly biographical, in fact a cry for help:

> It's very autobiographical, everything, you know – for example, that short story 'The Will to Die' ... he was such a genius, he turned it into a joke, he almost caressed death, caressed suicide, made it look like a joke, but it was a desperate cry for more and more living space we didn't have. That is why he left for Swaziland, looking for living space because he couldn't make the distinction between the mind that is suffering and the mind that creates.[24]

In this excerpt, Nkondo echoes my sentiments: that in the final analysis, Themba's life is reflected in his writing. Close reading of Themba's works, and an understanding of their multiple forms, demonstrate that he weaves different elements, including his own life story, into his works. This view is further articulated by Chapman:

> Themba the journalist and Themba the imaginative writer become completely intertwined. It is not that he follows Plaatje's author-journalist practice where, as in *Native Life in South Africa* (1916), emotive incidents are used to illustrate the attack on government legislation. Rather, Themba the author becomes caught up in the fascination of the shebeen life, and his journalistic self, which is supposed to be adopting the high moral tone of *Drum*'s crusading mission, is forced reluctantly to extricate itself from the 'ruptures' of the story.[25]

While it is helpful to consider each of Themba's short stories on its own merits, it is also important to observe the platforms on which, and the historical moment and circumstances in which, they were published.

The pieces Themba wrote solely with the intention of publishing in literary journals in the 1960s are most easily categorised as short stories of a fictional nature, although it can be argued that there is an element of truth-telling in any fictional undertaking. One platform on which Themba and many of his contemporaries published their best literary works was Nat Nakasa's *The Classic* magazine.

Since 1961, Nakasa had been trying to establish a literary journal that would publish African writers of merit. The first issue came out in 1963 with financial support from the Farfield Foundation. In its inaugural issue, *The Classic* carried two pieces by Themba, including his seminal short story, 'The Suit'. For literary purists, 'The Suit' provided a much-needed reprieve in Themba's literary oeuvre because of its solid narrative structure. It is undoubtedly Themba's most celebrated work, and continues to make epochal inroads through the process of reproduction, adaptation and intertextuality, as discussed in more detail in Chapter 15. It also demonstrates the subtlety in Themba's storytelling that has sometimes led to misreadings of his texts. In Chapter 11, I addressed the perception and indeed criticism that Themba was apolitical; 'The Suit', as the story that is seen as the pinnacle of his career, is sometimes given as an example of the paucity of political content in this writing. Yet, politics is present from the very first paragraph of the story. That Philemon, upon waking, has to go to the same 'lean-to' used by twenty other people living in the same yard is a biting comment on the conditions under which black people lived in the townships. In other words, Themba employs narrative tools to 'show' as opposed to 'tell' us about socio-economic conditions in the township.

The stories that Themba published in literary journals in the 1960s seem more defined, more focused, more structurally organised and compliant to the dictates of form than his earlier works. Although he might not have been conscious of the commonality in terms of time and publishing platforms among these stories, in his scathing article Nkondo observes their distinct nature in terms of form: 'Possibly the most refreshing pieces – indeed those that can be safely termed "short stories" – are "The Urchin", "The Suit", and "The Dube Train". All three are distinguished by a tightness and unity of structure, which manifests itself in a singleness and unity of theme.'[26]

The stories that Nkondo mentions here were all first published in the 1960s. While this suggests some level of maturity in Themba's writing, it also reveals the role of publishing platforms. 'The Urchin' was submitted to Mphahlele for a contest run by the South African Centre of the International PEN Club. It was subsequently published in *African Writing Today*, edited by Mphahlele and published in 1967, the same year Themba died.[27] Themba also reworked his piece of reportage 'Terror in the Trains', published in *Drum* in October 1957, and reproduced it as 'The Dube Train'. This was first published in its rewritten format in *Modern African Stories* in 1964.[28] In short, although these stories may have been inspired by lived experience, they were written with the clear intention of being published in literary journals, and demonstrate a certain level of maturity in their writing.

The last story mentioned above, 'The Dube Train', while following the classic form of the short story, bears testament to Essop Patel's assertion that Themba had 'the rare quality of fusing raw experiences from his terrain in Sophiatown with incisive imagination'.[29] In the same piece, which was reproduced in the form of a booklet when 'The Suit' was staged for the first time in 1993, Patel also observes: 'Can Themba was no ordinary journalist and story teller. He was a rebel. Can scorned conventions, tradition, customs and authority.'[30]

There is no doubt that Can Themba was in the process of becoming; it is entirely possible that his best stories were yet to be published. His untimely death at the age of 43 deprived readers of the realisation of his full potential – both as a writer and as a social and political observer.

14

Intertextuality and the Making of Mr Shakespeare

Themba's use of Shakespeare to describe aspects of South Africa is different in quality from [Anthony] Sampson's. Despite drawing on the Englishman's analogy, Themba writes a Shakespeare who enters into his service rather than using a 'Shakespearean world to denote [the] position of an audience member.'

Natasha Distiller — *South Africa, Shakespeare, and Post-Colonial Culture* (2005), 171

The ability to draw from and play with the vast library of texts with which Can Themba furnished his mind via his reading and education (especially his immersion in the Western canon of English literature at Fort Hare) was a trademark of his writing, debate and even everyday discussion.

Such intertextuality, a crucial element in literary apprenticeship, can be defined as the connection or influence that different literary texts have on each other, and it is a major feature of Themba's writing. Fittingly, it has become a hallmark of critical and creative interaction with his famous short story 'The Suit' (see Chapter 15).

Shakespeare was clearly the greatest influence in Themba's literary output, but many other texts are evoked in his writing: canonical English poets and novelists, African history and oral tradition, the Bible and more are used to comment on his circumstances or to underline a point. Themba's analysis of daily happenings was often informed by the literature he read.

In a single story – in fact, a single paragraph – Themba gives a roll-call of topics, philosophers and writers who shaped his thinking. The piece was sent to Nat Nakasa in 1964 for publication in *The Classic* magazine, with a note saying he should just call it 'Quoth He'; it is one of the last stories we know of that Themba wrote while in Swaziland. However, it did not see print until the 2006 publication of Themba's collection of stories.[1] (It is not clear why it was not published in Nakasa's magazine, but it was around this time that Nakasa left South Africa on an exit permit to take up a Nieman Fellowship at Harvard University, dying a year later in New York.)

In this particular passage, Themba invoked a cross-section of influential figures: 'But too [many] frivolous moods have caught me these days. French Revolutions, St Bartholomew Massacres, a Borgia here, a Nero there, a Medici or a Shaka or a Machiavel [*sic*], those are peripheries of my imagination. Other ones are Schweitzers, Curries, Socrates, Christs.'[2]

The multitudes of texts, philosophers, historical events and figures to which Themba alludes in this single paragraph illustrate the versatility and broadness of his appetite for reading, which stretches to include the French Revolution, religion, and, closer to home, Shaka and other historical figures. One of his students, the late Mbulelo Mzamane, told me how Themba helped him to understand the French Revolution by teaching him Charles Dickens's *A Tale of Two Cities*.[3] Themba made the recounting of this novel so vivid, 'I thought it was a history book,' said Mzamane.[4] Apparently Themba loved the text so much that he entrenched it in his students; subsequently, even in his old age, Mzamane could still recite the entire first chapter of the book.

The invocation of different texts can be seen in Themba's writing from when he was still a student at Fort Hare. One of the poems he published in *The Fort Harian* in 1951, titled 'They Counsel', echoes both biblical and liturgical phrases. To indicate his deliberate use of intertextuality, Themba puts the last line of his poem in inverted commas:

> They counsel smugly from pulpits
> Joy to seek after my last breath.
> Hell, they ought to counsel themselves
> 'In the midst of life we're in death.'[5]

The closing line is taken from the Book of Common Prayer, and reveals Themba's Catholic and Anglican educational heritage. While he may have styled himself as an atheist, he employs biblical verses in a variety of ways, often as a mocking commentary on current events.

In one of his most quoted pieces of investigative journalism from the *Drum* stable, 'Brothers in Christ', Themba juxtaposes Christian beliefs with the racism he experienced when visiting exclusively white churches.[6] On these occasions, he was often chased away because of the colour of his skin, as described in Chapter 7. He ended his investigative piece with the following quotation from the New Testament, 1 Corinthians 12:13: 'For by one spirit are we all baptised into one body, whether we be bond or free; and have been all made to drink into one Spirit.'[7]

This sardonic use of the Bible is similar to his quirky comment in 'Bottom of the Bottle', where he says, 'Funny, the idea with which they impressed us most is not Justice or Love Thy Neighbour or Liberty.'[8] In these two instances, the Bible is used to critique the racist regime, which presented itself as a proponent of both Christianity and racial segregation – two phenomena that are at opposite moral poles.

Themba regularly referenced well-known texts, the English classics in particular, usually as a form of commentary on present society or current events. This was something his peers and colleagues noted as well: Keorapetse Kgositsile shared that Themba always had a book pulling his jacket pocket askew, something that led to the perception that he had a bottle of alcohol in his pocket.[9] This was corroborated by his wife, Anne, who revealed that their first-born daughter, Morongwa, told her that other 'children used to say Dad carries a nip around in his pocket'. Mrs Themba countered, 'Doesn't this stuff in the nip get finished for him to chuck the thing away?' She confirmed that Can 'used to carry a book in his pocket – you know, his jackets used to be like this, slanting'.[10] Lewis Nkosi, meanwhile, described how Themba 'in one hand carried a huge volume consisting of *The Complete Works of Oscar Wilde*', while dodging traffic.[11]

But Themba did not only express his appreciation of literature by carrying books around; he would memorise long passages from literary works and recite them publicly. Nkosi went on: 'Can Themba was leaning against the jamb of the door, a glass of brandy in one hand and a volume of *Oscar Wilde* in the other; but the book was closed since Can was quoting from memory lines from the "Rubaiyat of Omar Khayyam".'[12]

This kind of recital in life manifested itself in Themba's writing as well. Intertextual evocations of many writers, particularly Shakespeare, were always a fundamental ingredient in the construction of Themba's work, which reflected his intellectual development, his reading habits and the kind of literature he treasured.

Mr Themba and Mr Shakespeare

Ironically, it was not as a journalist and wordsmith at *Drum* that Themba was accorded yet another literary moniker, to go along with 'Poet Laureate of Fort Hare' and 'Sage of Sophiatown'. Instead, it was his return to teaching that earned him the title 'Mr Shakespeare'.

Caught between the frustration of having lost his job, and the prospect of having to serve under the hated Bantu Education Act should he return to teaching in a state school, Themba broadened his options. Returning to his great love – teaching – he found a school that presented prospects of nominal liberties. This was the Central Indian High School in Fordsburg, which was founded as an independent private school in 1955, and supported by the progressive/anti-apartheid Transvaal Indian Congress. Although Central Indian High had no choice but to operate within the confines of the apartheid state, it still managed to defy some of its basic principles. In line with the prescripts of Bantu Education, the school was reserved exclusively for learners of Indian descent, but they hired a multiracial team of teachers.

Some of Themba's old friends, including former journalist and political activist Robert Resha, as well as his former schoolmates from the University of Fort Hare, Duma Nokwe and Dennis Brutus, were now teaching at the school, alongside the likes of Molly Fischer, wife of Bram Fischer and an activist in her own right. Themba joined this formidable team of teachers shortly after leaving *Drum* in 1959.

In his tribute published in *The Classic*, Casey Motsisi writes: 'Can went back to teaching. He taught at an Indian High School in Fordsburg. One day the phone rang. It was Can telling me that he had smelt out a swinging shebeen practically in the shadow of the school.'[13] Casey visited Can, and they had a jolly good moment together.

Abdul Bham, who was one of Themba's students at Central Indian High, has vivid memories of his teacher's excessive consumption of the waters of dizziness, and very fond memories of the teacher he describes as the 'master of English'. He says Themba not only taught English very well, but directed a brilliant performance of one of Shakespeare's plays.[14]

The Shakespearean influence on Themba did not end with his early writings as a student at Fort Hare. Shakespeare remained fundamental to Themba's literary appreciation and the single most influential writer in his life. The playwright's works permeated almost every aspect of Themba's life; he was known to recite the Bard's words at will, and often used them in his analogy of everyday happenings, finding a Shakespearean text to interpret any situation. Fellow teachers and students at the Central Indian High School alike fondly called him 'Mr Shakespeare'.

The Shakespearean influence is a golden thread that runs through Themba's works, although taking different forms over time. In the beginning, it might have been unwitting, lodged in the subconscious part of his creative exploration. However, as he gained confidence in his writing and developed his own voice, Themba became more deliberate in invoking Shakespeare.

This reflection of Shakespeare in Themba's writings is revealed in the language, idiom, rhythms and dramatic plots. These dramatic plots are often driven by the politics of difference, in which a character falls in love with someone from an enemy camp. This kind of evocation is seen in Themba's earliest publications, including poetry and stories that he published as far back as the 1940s (as discussed in Chapter 2), as well as his earlier short stories 'Mob Passion', 'Passionate Stranger' and 'Forbidden Love'.

In his later works like 'The Dube Train', 'The Suit' and 'The Urchin', for instance, we see Themba developing new imagery and a different kind of textual intersection. While in these latter stories Themba assumes his own voice, developing a new idiom rooted in the townships as his contextual environment and reflecting the nuances of his immediate and familiar African environment, the foundations of Shakespearean drama are still discernible. He develops narratives that resonate with the era of Elizabethan drama, but localises them to ensure that they fit within the African setting.

In a story like the widely celebrated 'The Suit', Themba diverges from the gory melodrama of Shakespeare's tragedies, and settles for deeply psychological drama, a clear demonstration of his maturity as a storyteller. As much as the story is not confined to the most palpable Shakespearean drama, the literary devices that Themba employs are reflective of his own development as a writer.

In his essay 'Through Shakespeare's Africa', published in *Requiem for Sophiatown*, Themba is unapologetic about employing Shakespeare as a literary antecedent for his exposition of the South African situation.[15] This becomes an almost consistent practice in his later works.

Can Themba's Exploration of Shakespeare's Politics of Difference

The theme of love between members of clashing clans (as a form of politics of difference), as seen in many of Shakespeare's dramas, is common in Themba's early works. Many of these stories are family- or clan-centred dramas, and often involve members of the feuding groups or warring families falling in love with one other.

The first story to explore this was 'Passionate Stranger', Themba's very first story published in *Drum* magazine. It appeared in March 1953, ahead of his award-winning short story 'Mob Passion'. 'Passionate Stranger' follows the age-old tale of love drama thwarted by rivalry or differences between families. In it, Osbourne Ledwaba is visiting his family in Chebeng with his friend, Reginald Tshayi (aka Reggie), who is from Johannesburg. Reggie's eye is immediately caught by Osbourne's pretty sister, Ellen. He promptly expresses his feelings in these lofty words: 'If my declaration sounds premature and impetuous to you, forgive me. Love is on the wing and, whether I will it or not, I must join its flight. Whether I will it or not, I must love you. Destiny itself has guided my wanderings to this far place that I may lay my troubles in your bosom.'[16]

What is unusual about this declaration is the lyrical manner in which Reggie expresses his feelings, clearly reflecting the influence of Shakespearean sonnets. The phrases used show no evidence of African idiom. This becomes all the more clear as Reggie continues to convince Ellen of his love for her: 'Now I know what true love can mean. Nevermore can the stars whirl and wheel the same, if you do not love me too, Ellen. No more would the moon shed soft silver on the earth, no more would the flowers gladden the heart, the birds untune the sky. Oh nevermore! I reach for your lips, knowing I reach for the sun!'[17]

Following Reggie's declarations, it turns out that Ellen had been stung by the same bug, and the two fall in love. They take their relationship to a higher level, as they spend their 'first storm of passion' in the Ledwabas' living room while Osbourne and his father are away. Later on, under the cover of darkness, Ledwaba Senior catches the two lovers in their tryst under the 'big tree opposite the cattle kraal'.

Here the reference to the 'cattle kraal' imparts the flavour of a setting familiar to a South African audience. This is typical of Themba's developing style: to imbue his narrative with unique imagery that combines florid Shakespearean lyricism with a recognisably South African context. In true *Romeo and Juliet* style, it turns out that Ellen's father has already promised his daughter in marriage to Dikgang, who is from the royal family – just as Juliet's father promised her hand to the aristocrat Paris. The Ledwabas' meeting was in fact to negotiate the bride price, with the chief's council informing the family that the chief did not intend to wrangle over the number of cattle, as he was willing to pay any price for their bride. All he wanted was for his son to marry Ellen.

As in the case of *Romeo and Juliet*, the interests of the families do not always align with the romantic wishes of the individuals concerned. Furthermore, the prestige of the family, especially if it is royalty, complicates matters. Dikgang has been promised marriage to Ellen, and as he is a child of the royal family, matters of this nature are traditionally discussed and arranged among the elders of the respective families.

The drama in Themba's 'Passionate Stranger' does not reach the tragic proportions of *Romeo and Juliet*, in which the lovers end up losing their lives. It is the wisdom of Osbourne in bringing his sister to the negotiations, as well as Ellen's courage in confronting the elders and revealing the truth of her feelings, that turns the plot around. In a scene reminiscent of Desdemona's petition in Shakespeare's *Othello*, where she says, 'My noble father, I do perceive here a double duty,' Ellen presents her case in front of the elders:

> My fathers, I know the woman should be silent and suffer her betters and elders to determine her fate. Still, believe me, this way is the best. You are here to make me a wife to Dikgang. What I think of him is entirely irrelevant. But you must know that I already belong

> to another, not so much from the wilfulness of my rebel heart, but because by the law of man and of God I cannot go to any man as a virgin, but to the man I love.[18]

The revelation of Ellen's feelings for Reggie comes as a shock to both her father and the chief's council. In an almost stereotypical portrayal of fathers in a time when daughters were seen as investments that would generate bride price in the form of cattle when they had to marry, Ledwaba Senior is more concerned about his gains than the interests of his daughter. It is the grey-haired elder, apparently the leader of the chief's council, who responds with due consideration: '"My brothers," he said, "let us not chatter like apes. Let us rather retire to deliberate on how to convince the Chief that we do not encourage this marriage and how to avert a crisis in the tribe. Ledwaba, we shall try to suppress the insult to the Royal House. We say no more, for we know how you suffer. Do you hear?"'[19]

What we find in 'Passionate Stranger' is that not only is the diction and imagery influenced by Shakespeare, but the very plot is reminiscent of Shakespeare's tales of lovers on the opposite side of a divide. By foregrounding the politics of difference, Themba demonstrates that his use of Shakespearean elements in his writing was advancing, from stylistic imitation to a hybrid of classic drama and African idiom and location.

The Shakespearean influence is once again clear in Themba's 'Mob Passion', the winner of *Drum*'s Great African International Short Story Contest, which catapulted its author into the literary and journalistic canons of 1950s' South Africa. 'Mob Passion' is a tragic love story set against the background of the tribal violence that erupted during the early 1950s in Newclare, a township outside Johannesburg. The fighting was largely between Basothos working on the Rand mines (known as the Russians) and members of other tribes (known as the Civil Guards). The Russians had reportedly been terrorising the people of the district, and the Civil Guards formed initially with the purpose of protecting township residents against violence. This soon turned into gang warfare. Themba explores this moment in history through the character of Linga, a Xhosa man who is fluent in Sesotho, and who is in love with Mapula, a Mosotho woman.

Themba's personal aversion to violence is clear, and, through his protagonist, Linga, and in an overtly didactic narrative, he bemoans the situation: 'They butcher one another, and they seem to like it. Where there should be brotherhood and love, there are bitter animosities. Where there should be co-operation in common adversity, there are barriers of hostility, steeling a brother's heart against a brother's misery.'[20]

Themba's exploration of the ironies and absurdities of family or tribally rooted feuds once again draws from a Shakespearean sense of drama in setting up the tragedy that is about to unfold. Themba does not spare the reader; we witness the brutal murder of Linga by a mob of Russians led by Alpheus, his girlfriend's uncle.

As is common in Shakespearean tragedy, the murder in cold blood of one character is washed away with another. In Shakespeare's drama, the assassination of Julius Caesar, for instance, was never the end of the tragedy; instead, it led to several other murders. The elimination of the conspirators culminates with the ironic twist of Brutus's suicide, which he commits by running into his own sword. Although not killed directly by Mark Antony, who stood for Caesar's interests and avenged his killing, Brutus's death by his own sword was a powerful literary device to fulfil the tragic scene. Themba's sense of high drama and tragedy follows this tradition in 'Mob Passion'. The death of Linga alone could not be a lesson, as it could be interpreted as perpetrating the triumph of the belligerent mob. Instead, it is avenged and 'compensated' for by another death: that of Alpheus at the hands of Mapula.

This is the climax of the story, and, in terms of evocative power, it almost undermines the drama of the killing of Linga in front of his girlfriend. In fact, the death of Linga seems more of a catalyst for this moment of bloody revenge: 'With the axe in her hand, Mapula pressed through them until she reached the inner, sparser group. She saw Alpheus spitting upon Linga's battered body. He turned with a guttural cackle – He-he-he! He-he-he! – into the descending axe. It sank into his neck and down he went. She stepped on his chest and pulled out the axe. The blood gushed out all over her face and clothing.'[21]

In this excerpt from the climax of 'Mob Passion', Themba's portrayal of a tragic drama is reminiscent of Shakespeare in its evocative power and vividness. The stark contrast between Alpheus's triumphant laughter and Mapula's quiet rage heightens the tension. There is also the paradoxical fact that Mapula, a woman, has an axe in her hand in the midst of a male-dominated mob – a departure from most Shakespearean tragedies, in which women are often meek or hapless victims. In Themba's narrative, we find a woman acting as executioner, avenging the murder of her lover, even though this means taking the life of her own bloodline.

Macbeth is one of very few Shakespearean dramas in which a woman character is actively involved in executing murder. Mapula's strength of character is suggestive of Lady Macbeth in Shakespeare's canon. One of the most powerful woman characters in Shakespeare's dramas, Lady Macbeth excels at conniving, persuading her husband to kill King Duncan in ambition for the throne, but she is not afraid to get her hands dirty when the situation demands. She not only masterminds the murder, she kills the king's guards and plants the murder weapons on their bodies.

While we have two women with murder weapons in their hands, their objectives and their characters are not necessarily the same. Mapula is driven by the desire to avenge her lover's murder; Lady Macbeth, on the other hand, is driven by her lust for power and her greedy ambition to become queen. Although the two characters are not driven by the same motives, their strength and will is the common trait that they share. In both cases, the two women characters display bravery and determination.

Another story by Themba where the politics of difference is explored using romantic relations between characters is 'Forbidden Love', which, as the title suggests, is about two individuals falling in love in an environment that forbids them from doing so. In this story, published in *Drum* in 1955, Michael Chabakeng, an African man, is in love with Dora Randolph, who comes from a so-called coloured family background. Dora comes from a highly conservative family that is almost hostile to black Africans (the latter concept is difficult to explain given that black people are indigenous to the African continent and do not need qualification).

In this story, Themba also explores the complexity of blackness, in which even black people seem to abhor the colour of their own skin. The so-called coloured South Africans in his story seem to resent their very own image; instead of focusing on the apartheid regime that imposed racial segregation based on shades of colour and ancestry, they seem more concerned with their own differing shades of blackness. Not only are these two characters from different backgrounds in love, but Dora's sister, Louisa, who is even darker-skinned than Michael, is kept away from black Africans as she is part of the Randolph family – which does not want to be associated with 'Africans'.

The family has already suffered the humiliation of having David (known as Davie), Dora's brother, classified as an 'African' (by which the apartheid system meant 'black'). This scenario not only highlights the challenges brought about by racial segregation in apartheid South Africa, it also pokes fun at the ridiculous nature of the system that divided families into different racial groups on the basis of appearance – that one member looked 'more African' than others.

At the centre of this is Dora, who finds herself caught up in a situation that she did not create: 'I feel trapped by a doubly guilty shame. I am ashamed that it is my people who are in the forefront of every move against your people – ashamed of my father whom I love, but who is violent in his hatred of Africans … I am ashamed, in a queer way that I hate, of this secret love of ours.'[22]

Given their circumstances, Michael and Dora have to be discreet about their affair to the extent of sitting separately when watching the same film in the cinema. It so happens that Michael is not even supposed to watch the film, which has been banned for 'Children under Twelve and Natives'. While arguing over the exclusion of 'Natives' from the film, David discovers that Michael is 'Dora's Native', and calls on his fellow coloured friends to attack him. In a scene similar to the one in 'Mob Passion', a group ends up attacking a man simply because he has courted the affections of a woman from another apartheid-sanctioned group.

Michael is beaten to a pulp, and takes several days to recover under the care of his sister, Salome, and his lover, Dora. It is during the course of Michael's recovery that Salome discovers that Dora is Davie's sister. The story climaxes with the revelation that David Randolph is the unknown father of Salome's child. Salome had been hiding the identity of the father of her child from her family, including Michael, in an effort to protect Davie's reputation, and that of the Randolph family.

Themba reveals that the Randolphs' obsession with racial difference and shades of skin colour is nothing more than self-hatred.

He proves this by referencing Louisa's skin colour, Davie's ludicrous classification as black by government administrators, and the presence of Salome's child, who bears the blood of the two opposing families.

This is a recurring theme in Themba's writing, much as it was to become part of his own life story. His experience of romance with Jean Hart, a white woman, in a racially stratified society (as fictionalised in 'Crepuscule') is yet another example of the ways in which art and reality intertwined in Themba's world: there can be few more stark examples of 'star-crossed lovers' than a cross-racial couple in apartheid South Africa at the time of its Immorality Act.

Localising Shakespearean Imagery

In his creative output from his early *Drum* days, Can Themba used the basic tenets of Shakespeare's tragedies to explore African lives, borrowing Shakespeare's literary tropes to craft authentically African stories with characters that local readers would recognise.

But he did more than that: Themba 'conquered Shakespeare', according to legendary South African poet and former Sophiatown resident Don Mattera.[23] He was not referring to a conquest in the adversarial sense, but rather to Themba's capabilities in deconstructing Shakespeare's imagery and making it credible for local audiences.

Whereas in his early works Themba might not always have been conscious of the Shakespearean resonances, in his later works he is more deliberate in invoking Shakespeare. He adopts Shakespearean motifs to explore the present conditions of his society. In the stories published from the late 1950s onwards, we see a Can Themba who has assumed his own authorial voice, but is comfortable invoking Shakespeare's dramas in his analysis of African situations.

In *South Africa, Shakespeare, and Post-Colonial Culture,* Natasha Distiller observes that 'Themba draws Shakespeare into South Africa, makes the dramas speak of Sophiatown and other South African spaces, in contrast to [Anthony] Sampson's descriptions which utilise a Shakespearean sense of the absurd to amuse a delighted spectator'.[24]

Themba's piece 'Through Shakespeare's Africa' was first published in *The New African* in September 1963, after he was already in exile in Swaziland. In it he purposely employs the framework of Shakespearean drama to provide an analysis of the political situation in the Transkei, a Xhosa homeland located in the eastern part of South Africa. Here he narrates an unfolding political drama in this traditional African community, and likens it to one of Shakespeare's most famous tragedies, *Julius Caesar*. He introduces his analogy with the following observation: 'This Shakespeare would have understood without the interpolations of the scholars, and in this wise way the world of Shakespeare reaches out a fraternal hand to the throbbing heart of Africa ... Thus it comes with little surprise that the starting point in the Shakespearean odyssey for many an African who has staggered through literacy is *Julius Caesar*.'[25]

Themba goes on to narrate the story of the rise of Chief Kaiser Msi, who had ascended to the throne amid stiff competition from other chiefs who rivalled him in suitability for this prestigious portfolio. Chief Msi is obviously modelled on Chief Kaiser Matanzima, a Thembu traditional leader and graduate of the University of Fort Hare who became the chairman of the Transkei Traditional Authority in 1961, and was elected prime minister of the Transkei when it gained nominal independence under the apartheid 'homeland' scheme in 1976. The visionary Themba could foresee the potential for political drama in the Transkei when he wrote this piece as far back as 1963. His predictions were only too accurate in tracing the political drama that later ensued, culminating with the retirement, under a dark cloud of corruption, of Chief Matanzima in 1986.

With *Julius Caesar* the most obvious of the texts on which the story is modelled, adversaries who were formerly allies converge to plot an uprising against their new leader. To give their revolt substance, they have to solicit the support of a prominent chief to lead their campaign, and in the case of Themba's Transkei narrative, such a figure is Dilizintaba Sakwe, the equivalent of Shakespeare's Brutus. Given the closeness of Chief Sakwe to Chief Msi, the strategy is to claim to be putting public interest ahead of his relationship with the current chief. In this sense, Chief Sakwe convinces all and sundry that he is not Msi's adversary; rather, his revolution is an act of patriotism and innate allegiance to his beloved Transkei. This is a plot similar to that of *Julius Caesar*, where Brutus is lured into a conspiracy by Cassius, who claims that Caesar's assassination will be in the interests of Rome.

The drama culminating with the assassination of Julius Caesar is captured succinctly in Themba's narrative. In *Julius Caesar*, the protagonist's wife, Calpurnia, sees a vision of her husband's death in her dreams, something that Caesar initially dismisses offhand. After impassioned pleas from his worried wife, he agrees not to leave his house that day. When he confides this to Brutus, unaware that his friend is one of the conspirators, Caesar's reasoning seems ridiculous. Brutus deliberately misinterprets the dream, and entices Caesar to venture out. Convinced by Brutus's arguments, Caesar decides to leave the house, ignoring Calpurnia and the soothsayer who warned him to 'Beware the Ides of March', and he pays the price as he is stabbed to death by a group of Roman senators, which included his friend Brutus.

In a direct imitation of this plot, albeit in an African context, Themba writes: 'On the night before Ntsikana's Day Kaiser's wife, Nombulelo, dreamed of savage happenings. Worse still, the witch doctor, Makana the left-handed, warned Kaiser: "Beware the Day of Ntsikana!" But Kaiser brushed these ominous prognostications aside and went to the Ntsikana celebrations.'[26]

The above interpretation of Shakespeare's tragedy involves apportioning African names to the characters and events, including Ntsikana's Day (named after the famous Xhosa prophet Ntsikana), an obvious substitute in this case for the 'Ides of March'. Themba's choice of 'Ntsikana's Day' localises the story and gives it a historic resonance with the people he writes about.

As in Shakespeare's drama, the protagonist in Themba's story stubbornly walks straight to his own death. After the fatal wound is inflicted upon him by one of his most trusted lieutenants, as in the case of Brutus and Caesar, the last words of the paramount chief are: 'Tixo, nawe, mntwanenkosi!' The latter is a Xhosa phrase that translates loosely as 'You too, my brother!', clearly evoking Caesar's last words, 'Et tu, Brute?', after being stabbed by Brutus.

In 'Through Shakespeare's Africa', Themba goes on to allude to other Shakespearean texts, including *King Henry V* and *Othello*, which he transposes into the South African situation, taking ownership of Shakespeare for Africa. He states, 'But it is more than odd how many Shakespearean situations find echo in African life', to illustrate that the human story and Shakespeare's treatment of it is universal, and that Africa is part of the global village.[27]

Themba's classic short story 'The Suit', which was first published in 1963, also bears traces of Shakespearean influence. It is not dissimilar to Shakespeare's *Othello* for its thematic focus, plot and intense psychological engagement.

In 'The Suit', Maphikela informs Philemon about his wife's adulterous relationship with an unidentified young man. In Shakespeare's *Othello*, this role is played by Iago, who informs Othello about his wife's supposed adultery with Cassio – in Iago's case, however, he is lying out of malice, whereas Maphikela's report is the truth.

Both narratives engage the audience, creating feelings of anticipation, suspense and anxiety right until the end. The psychological elements prevalent in both *Othello* and 'The Suit' are spectacularly executed to keep the readers intimately involved. In *Othello*, we see the protagonist transitioning from loving and trusting his wife wholeheartedly, to a point where he begins to question her faithfulness. He ruminates on how his wife, Desdemona, whom he knows loves him dearly, could cheat on him with Cassio, his dearest and most trusted friend. In Themba's story, we see a similar transition: Philemon is loving and trusting until the devastating moment when he catches his wife, Matilda, cheating on him with another man, after which he asks: 'What makes a woman like this experiment with adultery?'[28]

We also learn that while punishing his wife, forcing her to carry around the suit left behind by her lover and dish food for it, he too suffered: 'Of course, she knew nothing of the strain he himself suffered from his mode of castigation.'[29]

Perhaps the most striking resemblance between the two stories is the use of a piece of cloth as a tool to develop the plot of the story. Shakespeare's *Othello* revolves around a piece of cloth – the handkerchief that is supposedly evidence of Desdemona's infidelity – while Themba's 'The Suit' revolves around a piece of cloth, the suit, which is also the title of the story. In *Othello*, Iago deliberately places the handkerchief in Cassio's house in order to suggest that it was mistakenly left by Desdemona after a secret tryst. Iago plots his conspiracy thus:

> I will in Cassio's lodging lose this napkin
> And let him find it. Trifles light as air
> Are to the jealous confirmations strong
> As proofs of holy writ. This may do something.[30]

After he discovers the handkerchief, Cassio requests Bianca, with whom he had an affair, to duplicate its attractive patterns for him. Bianca returns the handkerchief to Cassio in a fury, and Othello overhears that it was discovered in his friend's bedroom. To Othello this is clear evidence that his wife was cheating on him with Cassio, and, after a marathon of accusations, he kills Desdemona. It is only after killing his wife and hearing corroborating evidence both from Cassio and Emilia, Iago's wife, that Othello learns that Desdemona had no extramarital affair. Emilia reveals that she had stolen the handkerchief and given it to her husband, Iago, unaware of his evil intentions. In parallel scenes in Themba's narrative, Philemon uses the abandoned suit to castigate his wife. Both stories culminate in the dramatic deaths of the leading characters. Matilda dies in an apparent suicide, and Othello dies by his own hand.

The Shakespearean intertextuality that we see in 'The Suit' is a common element in Themba's stories. Even when the instances are not as direct as in the case of *Othello* and 'The Suit', such resonances leave traces in stories such as 'The Urchin' and 'The Dube Train'.

In a number of instances, Themba invokes specific phrases from Shakespeare to illustrate a point or describe a scene. In his tribute to his friend and colleague at *Drum*, Henry Nxumalo, who was brutally murdered on 31 December 1957, Themba quotes Shakespeare, repeating words from *Hamlet* in the scene where the ghost of Hamlet's father visits Hamlet to inform him of his father's murder at the hands of his brother, Hamlet's uncle. Here Themba echoes the words: 'It was "Murder most foul, as in the best it is, But this most foul, strange and unnatural."'[31] Here Themba makes use of inverted commas to underline that he is citing from Shakespeare's text.

Themba was neither the first nor the only South African writer to have experimented with the Bard's work in this manner. Writers like Sol Plaatje and R. R. R. Dhlomo were ahead of him, and subsequent generations have continued with this kind of experimentation and reinterpretation.

The late playwright Welcome Msomi, who had interactions with Themba during his exile days in Swaziland, was known for his adaptation of Shakespeare's *Macbeth* as *uMabatha*. In an extensive interview with Scott L. Newstok, Msomi spoke about the influence of Shakespeare, the genesis of the play and its impact on his life.[32] Msomi, like Themba and Plaatje before him, was able to localise Shakespeare so that the Bard speaks through African voices. In *uMabatha*, which is written in Zulu and reflects Zulu cultural dynamics, Msomi draws parallels between the era of Macbeth – power struggles in medieval Scotland – and incidents that occurred in nineteenth-century Zulu history. While there is a dance of witches in Shakespeare's *Macbeth*, Msomi's play opens with the music and dances of the diviners.

The universality of Shakespeare has been well documented, especially in academia. Almost every issue of the *Shakespeare in Southern Africa* journal carries an article that acknowledges this – as if the very existence of this journal is not indeed testimony to the Bard's influence. Distinguished Nigerian poet, novelist and essayist Ben Okri is another voice who has weighed in on the adaptability of Shakespeare to different cultural contexts. In his essay 'Leaping Out of Shakespeare's Terror', published in his collection of essays *A Way of Being Free*, he goes so far as to draw parallels between Shakespeare and Frantz Fanon: 'Frantz Fanon might have been thinking of the long nightmare at the end of Othello's sleep when he wrote in the closing sentences of *Black Masks, White Skins*: "O my body, make of me a man who questions."'[33]

In Themba's most successful literary works, especially the short stories, we see him retaining Shakespeare's influence by deliberately evoking and alluding to his works and style, but assuming his own unique voice. In other words, he borrows Shakespeare's dramatic scenarios, but gives his narratives a uniquely South African flavour replete with the idioms, imagery, rhythms and familiar settings of Africa. That this was done quite deliberately, and with both self-mockery and bombastic flair, is revealed in the words from 'Crepuscule': 'There are certain names that do not go with Mister, I don't have a clue why. But, for sure, you cannot imagine a Mr Charlie Chaplin or a Mr William Shakespeare or a Mr Jesus Christ. My name – Can Themba – operates in that sort of class.'[34]

In the same way that John Keats, though a great writer in his own right, is regarded as the most Shakespearean writer in the world, Can Themba is the most Shakespearean South African writer of his generation. The influence of Shakespeare lurks somewhere in the background of the majority of his works. He might have resented being called Mister; but there is no doubt that he deserved the title of 'Mr Shakespeare'.

15

The Suit for All Seasons

He also didn't neglect the dramas of personal life and of love life, the erotic side of life. And of course, 'The Suit' is the most wonderful example of that ... What punishment that the woman is left with a suit that a lover left quickly when the husband came home, but he did this – wickedly, but there was something very serious behind it.

Nadine Gordimer — Interview (2013)

If we had to single out a sole literary output as the most impactful in constructing the image of an artist, for Can Themba that story would undoubtedly be 'The Suit'. Notwithstanding the significance of all his other works, 'The Suit' stands out as the pinnacle of his literary oeuvre.

Intertextuality is an integral part of the writings and indeed the discourse of Themba. We have already seen, in the previous chapter, the extent to which he drew from and reinterpreted the works of others as a creative artist, intellectual, journalist and teacher. However, the converse is also true; his own writings have inspired adaptation and adoption in contemporary narratives and across genres, creating what might be called intergenerational dialogue across the decades. So far, 'The Suit' has been the most popular choice for experimentation, and has generated the most dynamic dialogue.

Themba's 'The Suit' has proved to be one of the most adaptable short stories ever written. This not only refers to cross-genre adaptation – it has been adapted for film, theatre and graphic comics – but includes intra-genre experimentation as well. This can be seen in the number of recent short stories that are in dialogue with 'The Suit', and continue to 'write back' to Can Themba. I am part of this discourse, and my own work will form part of my analysis in this chapter.

'The Suit' tells the story of a man, Philemon, who, acting on a tip-off from a neighbour, catches his wife (Matilda) in their marital bed with another man. The adulterer jumps out the window and escapes half-naked, leaving his suit behind. Instead of a predictably violent reaction, Philemon resorts to a psychological trick, using the presence of the suit in their home to punish Matilda. He forces his wife to treat the suit like a visitor, serving it food and carrying it with her when they walk in the streets. Matilda tries to devise measures to cope with her disgrace, joining a Cultural Club for married women as an antidote to the humiliation meted out by her husband. All seems to be getting better for Matilda, but her husband is already a few steps ahead; he humiliates her even further in front of her fellow Cultural Club members. The story ends with the death of Matilda in an apparent suicide and Philemon crying over her lifeless body.

In its first appearance in print, 'The Suit' headlined the inaugural issue of Nat Nakasa's *The Classic* magazine in 1963. It appeared alongside another contribution by Themba, a poem curiously entitled 'Dear God'. Other contributors to this issue included Lewis Nkosi, Richard Rive, Ezekiel Mphahlele and Casey Motsisi, all of whom were already among the leading literary voices on the continent. The likes of Nadine Gordimer, Nimrod Mkele and Philip Stein were on the board of trustees and editorial advisers. The magazine had been in the making for a long time, and by the time the first issue came out, Themba was already in exile in Swaziland. Nakasa wrote as part of his first editorial:

> It will be the job of *The Classic* to seek African writing of merit ... Although an effort will be made to use mostly South African writing, *The Classic* will welcome and solicit contributions from writers in Africa and the rest of the world. Particularly welcome will be the work of those writers with causes to fight for, committed men and women who look at human situations and see tragedy and love, bigotry and common sense, for what they are.[1]

The Classic had been given its name by Themba. In true '*Drum* Boys' style, he and Nakasa had decided that a visit to a nearby shebeen was in order to help them think clearly as they sought an appropriate name for the new journal. While they were cracking their skulls trying to figure out the best possible name, Themba asked the name of the dry-cleaning business behind which the shebeen was located. It was The Classic – and so the magazine got its name.

'The Suit' was to be republished multiple times after its first appearance in *The Classic*, and continues to resonate with different generations of readers. It demonstrates Harold Bloom's assertion about what he terms the 'anxiety of influence': 'The dead may or may not return, but their voice comes alive, paradoxically never by mere imitation, but in the agonistic misprision performed upon powerful frontrunners by only the most gifted of their successors.'[2] To this end, 'The Suit' has kept Themba's voice 'alive' for almost sixty years, ensuring that his name keeps reverberating through our cultural consciousness. It is among the many ironies of Themba's life that the story has had an independent existence for longer than its author – who died at 43.

Its influence has extended to the film and theatrical industries, with the story first adapted into a stage play by Mothobi Mutloatse and Barney Simon in 1993. After a successful run at local and international theatres, it was adapted as a musical theatre production by British playwright and director Peter Brook. This set its international trajectory on course, and it has now been performed in over 25 countries worldwide, including France, the United Kingdom and the United States. The play continues to make its mark locally, having been performed over the past decade at notable venues such as the Market Theatre and the National Arts Festival in Makhanda (formerly Grahamstown), as well as the Performing Arts Centre of the Free State in Bloemfontein. It finished another successful run at the Market Theatre in June 2017.

I myself penned a story entitled 'The Suit Continued', which was published in the *Southern African Short Story Review* in 2002.[3] The story experiments with Themba's 'The Suit', and is narrated from the perspective of the man who jumped out the window. 'The Suit Continued', in turn, instigated a series of further textual intersections with Themba's 'The Suit'. Mbulelo Mzamane saw it in the context of intertextuality: 'Thus while we can rightly speak of new directions in South African literature and society, there are inevitably echoes from the past that are evident in such work as Siphiwo Mahala's "The Suit Continued", based on Can Themba's "The Suit". Such inter-textual discourse goes on all the time among the new-order authors, in their endeavour to connect with the past.'[4]

Mzamane himself had embarked on a similar experimental endeavour as far back as 1981, with his short story 'The Dube Train Revisited', published in his collection *My Cousin Comes to Jo'burg*.[5] The story is obviously inspired by Themba's 'The Dube Train', which was first published in *Modern African Stories*, edited by Mphahlele, in 1964.[6] The story shares a similar setting and plot with Themba's original story, but the narrative style, the characters and the actions differ.

Mzamane was my principal at university, and our relationship strengthened over the years, with him playing the role of a mentor and Themba's writings forming an integral part of our common interests. Mzamane had been Themba's student in Swaziland and was instrumental in getting his collected works, *The Will to Die*, published posthumously in 1972. In this instance, Bloom's 'anxiety of influence' is clear in the connection between writers of three different generations.

My case of intertextuality with Themba's 'The Suit' developed organically. After reading 'The Suit' closely, I realised there was an aspect that was not explored in the narrative. 'The Suit' is based on a love triangle, yet it revolves around only two characters – the adulterous wife and her husband. The last we hear of Matilda's partner in adultery is that 'a man clad only in vest and underpants was running down the street'.[7] I was left wondering what happened to the man who had jumped out the window and fled the scene. To put it another way, what sets off the conflict in 'The Suit' is the discovery of an adulterous relationship; yet, the crucial presence of the fellow adulterer in the triangle remained unexamined. I began to ask: if the woman was cheating, what became of the man with whom she was cheating? This became the window through which I entered the story in an attempt to explore the unfolding events from the unnamed adulterer's point of view.

My entry point into Themba's narrative was more one of creative exploration than critical analysis, as it was preoccupied with imagining the fate of the character to whom adultery seems acceptable, while the woman had to bear the brunt of her husband's fury and retribution. The story begged all sorts of questions: Why was the man wearing a suit in a township? How did people react to the spectacle of a grown man running in the streets in only his underwear? And where did he run to? I asked myself these questions to enhance my imagination in the process of creative exploration, but, by virtue of attempting to close narrative gaps in Themba's original text, they inadvertently resulted in what might be described as 'creative criticism'. With every answer, more questions emerged; and thus began the journey towards the 'sequel' or continuation of 'The Suit', aptly titled 'The Suit Continued'.

Themba had provided the template in the form of Sophiatown of the 1950s as the setting, adultery as the source of conflict, as well as Philemon, Matilda and the suit itself as the central characters. My job was to enter into the realm that had already been created, and take the story in new directions while mindful of the historical context and social fabric of the original piece. Given the perspective from which my story is written – that of the unnamed adulterer, who tries to justify his nefarious deed – I had to create him as an unreliable and discordant narrator.

The decision to reimagine an existing text involves recognising the original as a formidable literary output in its own right, whether this is explicitly acknowledged or not. Apart from developing a storyline aligned with the already established plot, a major challenge with this process is that writing a period piece set in a different era poses dangers of anachronism. Avoiding this demands consistency in character portrayal, rational plot development, historical accuracy and a believable setting in order to maintain authenticity and stay true to the original prototype.

One of the fundamental aspects of my intervention was the use of the suit as a significant object in the furtherance of the story. In developing the narrative in 'The Suit Continued', I gave Matilda's partner in adultery (whom I named Terence) a teaching job, which accounted for his wearing a suit and being in the township during the day. Furthermore, as the suit was central to the original narrative, and stood as a symbol of masculinity representing the third party in the marriage, the 'character' of the suit deserved further exploration.

To amplify its symbolism, I bestowed the suit with new features that literally and figuratively developed its character. In its pockets, the suit has the man's wallet, house keys and his pass – without which Terence was legislatively reduced to a state of non-being as a black man under apartheid laws.

In addition, the suit also had a sentimental value, as it happened to be Terence's wedding suit – and this meant the creation of a fourth character, his wife Grace.

All these factors are heightened by the character of Grace, who, despite the dominant patriarchal culture, comes across as a strong and highly perceptive woman. While she performs the tasks traditionally assigned to women by patriarchal society, she uses these to stamp her authority and castigate masculinity. In this case, she irons her husband's clothes as per the dictates of the patriarchal society, but then she uses this as her power to ensure that he does not wear any other clothing until the suit is returned.

South African society is extremely patriarchal, and this was even more so in the 1950s, the period in which the story is set. Scholars such as Dorothy Driver have written extensively about the predominant patriarchal culture and misogyny among the *Drum* generation of writers, symbiotically linked to the societal culture of the time. In her essay 'The Fabulous Fifties: Short Fiction in English', Driver makes the following observation: 'Whereas *Drum* – its white editors and black journalists, but also the very context it sprang from and represented – arguably failed women writers, it helped concretise a historical moment through and against which black South African writers and readers would define and redefine themselves.'[8]

Whereas Driver's focus in this essay, and generally in her scholarship on the *Drum* generation of writers, is on the lack of gender representivity and, to some extent, the suppression of women's voices, she takes the broader societal complexities within her purview. In reimagining these historic moments, a writer must, on the one hand, create the most authentic reflection of the time and, on the other hand, challenge its conventions. Hence, in the case of 'The Suit Continued', Grace, while typical of a woman of the times, castigates her errant husband, leading to his thrashing around in an attempt to disentangle himself from his own web of lies. He is forced to borrow clothing from his much-shorter brother, with the result that he is subjected to a different kind of public humiliation.

Chronologically, Terence's tribulations happen alongside those of his fellow adulterer – Matilda, in Themba's story. This culminates in him abandoning his pride, and confessing to his wife that the suit has been 'confiscated'. Although he does not tell her the whole truth, which is consistent with his character, this gives Grace the opportunity to go with him to fetch the suit. It is at this point that the story reaches its climax, as Grace and Terence find Philemon helplessly crying over the lifeless body of Matilda. The story ends with the two men weeping alongside each other, both having lost the same lover.

Since I first published 'The Suit Continued', there have been a number of both critical and creative reactions, with scholars comparing my version with Themba's original, while creatives reimagined the plot. In 2006, Zukiswa Wanner wrote 'The Dress That Fed the Suit' as a creative response to my take on the subject, presenting the perspective of the woman – Matilda – whose voice is muted in both Themba's original story and 'The Suit Continued'. This necessary intervention completes the accounts of the three main characters involved in the love triangle.

'The Dress' is written as a suicide note from Matilda, the central female figure in both 'The Suit' and 'The Suit Continued'. This story keeps to the original motif as conceived by Themba, but, instead of the suit, Wanner uses a dress as the symbol representing the feminine figure. The following passage illustrates the perspective from a woman's position: 'Maybe a woman is not supposed to love only one man, but needs two to get all the qualities she needs in her perfect man. Because I loved you. I still do even as I pen these dying words. But in some odd way, I loved and still love Terry, too.'[9]

Here Matilda justifies her adulterous relationship with Terence, much as the latter did in 'The Suit Continued'. However, unlike Terence, Matilda is not seeking sympathy from the reader, but laying bare the truth – her own side of the story. The reader is aware that Matilda is going to die, as in Themba's original narrative she dies in an apparent suicide. However, towards the end of Wanner's story, she drops a bombshell: she is pregnant and is not sure of the paternity of the child. This revelation sets the whole narrative into a tailspin, and overrides the plot elements providing justifications for adultery.

In 2011, I wrote 'The Lost Suit', which was then published in *African Delights*. 'The Lost Suit' follows the theme of 'The Suit', but establishes a different plot and introduces the new shrewd and witty character of Stompie, a brother to Terence. The two brothers have similar characteristics, but while Terence is an irresponsible teacher, Stompie is a professional thief. The protagonist in this particular story is the embodiment of what Bloke Modisane calls an 'unheroic' hero: 'The hero is unheroic and is never on the side of law and order. This hero is measured by how much he can get away with: a hero is someone who commits a crime and is never discovered.'[10] Once again, the suit takes centre stage. Unlike Themba's original piece, what drives the plot in this case is the absence of the suit. In 'The Lost Suit', Stompie picks up a lover from a shebeen and goes to her place, after which he wakes up naked, with no lover in sight.

Fearing the fury of his wife, Doris, he embarks on a quest to find the suit, or at least a replacement.[11]

These four stories – 'The Suit', 'The Suit Continued', 'The Dress That Fed the Suit' and 'The Lost Suit' – are featured for the first time alongside each other in my short story collection *Red Apple Dreams & Other Stories.*[12] Conspicuous by their absence are Makhosazana Xaba's two rejoinders, 'Behind The Suit' and 'The Suit Continued: The Other Side', published in her collection *Running and Other Stories.* Although her book was published in 2013, it seems the two stories were written much earlier, even before Wanner wrote her story. In the acknowledgements to *Running*, Xaba writes:

> At the launch of *Words Gone Two Soon: A Tribute to Phaswane Mpe and K. Sello Duiker* in Grahamstown in 2005, I was fascinated by the pieces of writing in the book. Most intriguing was Siphiwo Mahala's story 'The Suit Continued'. As soon as I finished reading it, my mind began to race. It raced so fast that 'The Suit Continued: The Other Side' was written and complete in my head before the festival ended. Naturally, the first thing I did when I arrived back home was to empty my head. About two months later, 'Behind the Suit' began brewing in my head and again, I responded.[13]

'Behind The Suit' is the first story in Xaba's collection, and it is written in the form of a letter from a new character, Mondliwesizwe Mbatha, to his daughter. In this epistolary account, Mondliwesizwe reveals that he had a homosexual relationship with Philemon, the protagonist in the original by Themba. A logical explanation has to be given for the birth of the daughter to whom he is writing the letter. He explains that she was conceived in a rare moment of extraordinary sexual encounter: 'We each experienced our firsts: me with a woman and she with a black man. You, my darling angel, were to be the precious product of those firsts.'[14]

Similarly, 'The Suit Continued: The Other Side' is an account of Matilda's plight, in which she reveals that she had an affair with Gladys, a teacher who expanded her world, introducing her to corners and slopes of Sophiatown she did not know existed. With this revelation comes another startling detail about her marriage to Philemon: 'What I had never told even my closest friends was that Philemon had never taken me from the front. We had discussed this.

I really thought myself lucky, a man who was in no rush to prove his manhood by making me pregnant! We agreed it was the only form of contraception that guaranteed no pregnancy.'[15]

It is worth noting that while Xaba explores the idea originally conceived by Themba, hers is not necessarily a continuation of his plot, nor is it an attempt to provide a pastiche of the original. Instead, it is a recasting, carried out through a selection of elements from the preceding stories for her own purposes. In many ways, she subverts more conventional patterns of intertextual dialogue, and overturns established patriarchal and heterosexual templates. She ventures into previously unexplored terrain by bringing queer perspectives to this continuing intergenerational dialogue.

In Xaba's narratives, the setting extends from Sophiatown to Swaziland and England, something not found in the previous pieces, all of which are confined to Sophiatown. The character of Matilda, who in Themba's original piece is affectionately called Tilly, is deliberately referred to as Matty in Xaba's 'The Suit Continued: The Other Side'. However, in what appears to be an intertextual faux pas, Xaba refers to Can Themba's house as the House of Spirits, as opposed to the House of Truth, the name Themba gave his abode.[16]

Can Themba probably could not have dreamed that more than half a century after his passing, his classic story would still be inspiring responses and reworkings. Scholars might find it worth tracking to see if this work maintains the crossover appeal that has inspired such rich reinvention across generations.

Reading and Misreading 'The Suit'

While Themba's 'The Suit' may be revered, it is, of course, open to critical scrutiny. Having presented a rough summary of the story, it is worth stating the obvious: that 'The Suit' is a literary text, and any reading should ideally look beyond the 'facts' as presented by the plot. In his essay 'The Fiction Maker: The Short Story in Literary Education', Michael Chapman echoes my sentiments when he says the short story 'creates images which do not need to be elaborated and explained but which must be made to expand in the reader's mind'.[17]

A short story, by definition, is a piece of prose fiction that is short enough to be read in one sitting. In my article 'The Changing Topography of Short Story Writing in South Africa', I allude to some of the elements that make the short story a *short* story: 'To master the brevity of the short story, the author has to account for each and every word used, and every action the characters are involved in must move the plot forward. The plot is carried forward by a single dominant theme with limited characters who ought to be utilised optimally.'[18] The standing of 'The Suit' as a literary text, more specifically a short story, has often been overlooked by critics. Prosaic interpretations of 'The Suit' do great injustice to Themba's impeccable sense of irony, vivid imagery, solid structural organisation and captivating storyline.

Many critics have read 'The Suit' as a story of romantic drama, which at face value it is; but there is much more to it than the storyline of infidelity and the resulting cruelty unleashed as a form of castigation. It is how the story is presented rather than what the story presents that sustains its durability as a work of art.

The interest shown by many scholars in 'The Suit' stories attests to the impact of the stories both individually and collectively. The different creative responses to 'The Suit', including two stories by myself, another two by Xaba, and Wanner's intervention, have prompted contemporary critics to evaluate the suite of interrelated texts.

Several scholars, including Cheryl Stobie, Raphael d'Abdon and Julia Sertel, have grappled with the intersections of the various 'The Suit' stories.[19] The reason for the scholarly interest in this intertextual dialogue is captured in D'Abdon's essay, in which he notes that 'The Suit' 'stimulates literary conversations by leaving spaces for other writers to come in, and seeks to foreground continuities and echoes in the intra-African dialogues among three authors, whose responses to Themba (and to each other) are examined below'.[20]

In most of the critical texts that grapple with these intersecting stories, the most common weakness is the neglect of the central character in the original story by Themba – the suit. The suit sets Themba's story into motion and is the golden thread that runs through this intertextual dialogue. Chapman reminds us that 'the title is itself an important indicator of significance'.[21] Failure to recognise the suit itself as an integral element on which the plot hinges, and as a symbol of masculinity, weakens the arguments made by D'Abdon and Stobie, as the suit itself hardly features in their critique. Sertel, however, deduces meaning from the clothing item. She says, 'The suit that is left behind is not only the material evidence for Matilda's adultery, but also symbolic of the constant presence of its owner hovering over the marriage.'[22]

Given the gendered nature of the stories, there is an understandable scholarly impulse to interrogate and explore gender binaries in these analyses. What Stobie misses in the symbolism of the suit, she makes up for in her interrogation of patriarchy and gender representivity. She makes a cogent argument about the patriarchal tendencies prevalent in 'The Suit Continued' in particular, and outlines the subversive efforts made by Xaba in dismantling the established patriarchal order in her stories. Stobie also avoids the trap of confusing character representation with the author's own views. Talking about Themba's 'The Suit', Stobie says: 'While the structural violence of misogyny is detailed in the short story, I would argue that is not authorially endorsed, but criticised, as Themba provides us with a clear view of Matilda's abject humiliation and her horror at Philemon's "evil", "sheer savagery", "brute cruelty" and demonical rage.'[23]

In making this observation, Stobie acknowledges Themba's construction of the character of his protagonist, presenting him at first as a remarkably chivalrous husband who would wake up and make tea for his wife, something unusual in a patriarchal society. However, there is a subtle hint of the storm to come – he is reading a book on abnormal psychology. This is a crucial hint, given that 'The Suit' is a deeply psychological story. It speaks to Chapman's assertion that '[w]hat in a novel is a record of linked events becomes, in the story, a picture'.[24] The picture presented here should prompt us to look beyond the external and dramatic events of the story, and immerse ourselves in the minds of the characters.

The transition in Philemon's character after finding his wife in bed with another man is unexpected, while the implied suicide of Matilda invites us to empathise with her humiliation – the point at which Wanner picks up the narrative and runs with it, giving voice to Matilda's silence.

Because, in terms of chronology, I was the first among contemporary writers to experiment with Themba's 'The Suit', my story 'The Suit Continued' is often a starting point for scholars seeking to do a collective study of the various stories. 'The Suit Continued' is a first-person narrative told from the point of view of Terence, an unreliable first-person narrator.

One hazard of employing the agency of an unreliable narrator to advance the story is the potential for misreading or conflating the articulations of the character with the views of the author. This can be seen in D'Abdon's essay, where he focuses on the same patriarchal scenario explored by Stobie, but reduces it to a duel fought between opposing binaries of 'male voices' versus 'female voices', wherein he concludes that 'Can Themba's and Siphiwo Mahala's stories are superseded by Xaba's and Wanner's rewritings'.[25] A writer's opinion hardly matters in how readers receive their text, but certainly none of the authors had any intention of competing with the others in writing these stories – much less trying to supersede an iconic text like 'The Suit', which established its own reputation decades before the others were written. It is a pity that a scholarly paper sets such rigid and antagonistic binaries, which suggest insufficient attention to the respective authors' handling of the plot, character development, symbolism and other aesthetic elements.

Sertel presents a different interpretation. Scrutinising the narrative approach in which the protagonist is the first-person narrator, she observes:

> As he [Terence] interprets the incidents in accordance with a specific personal goal, he must be regarded as an unreliable narrator. His statement that 'this is not a confession, but a testimony' (Mahala 2011: 15) implies that he is convinced of his innocence. In his understanding Terence even experiences a double victimization by Can Themba on a meta level, who portrays him as the victim of his 'propaganda piece' (15), as well as by women in general and Matilda in particular, who 'take advantage of [us] men'.[26]

A fundamental element leading to misreadings of Can Themba's 'The Suit' is the tendency to try to see it for what it is not. The short story, Chapman reminds us once more, 'if it is to be done justice, needs to be approached and appreciated on its own terms'.[27] While it might be expedient to bend the text to fit our conceptions, these are not necessarily those of the author. As Mzamane put it, 'There's no point in taking the clay pot to task because it lacks some of the qualities a top hat possesses: sophistication, style and so on. The creator of the clay pot had no intentions of reproducing a top hat. Let's be judged by what we set out to achieve.'

PART V

A Writer's Immortality

16

Re-Membering the Fragments

I see him [Can Themba] as a living ancestor. That's why I don't memorialise him as if he didn't have a background. I find it difficult to see him as if he's gone.

Mothobi Mutloatse — Interview (2013)

The above epigraph speaks of the transcendent ability of art to survive beyond the lifetime of its creator. More than fifty years after his passing, Can Themba's works are not only alive and well; they have the potential and vigour to remain part of the public discourse for the foreseeable future.

At the time of his passing in 1967, Themba had been banned for about a year by the South African government. This effectively meant that he was an illegal writer. In this way, the government hit him where it hurt the most – making it impossible for him to practise his innate vocation. Although Themba's articles and short stories had been featured in newspapers, magazines and journals all over the world, he had not yet completed a book. Not only was it his intention to write a book while in Swaziland, according to his wife, he also had intricate discussions with Casey Motsisi about collaborating in writing a short story collection.

But banning meant he could neither be published nor quoted in South Africa, which probably discouraged him from writing, as the chances of being published were greatly diminished. This also erased any hope of earning royalties, as had been his dream since his first interview with Henry Nxumalo in 1952, in which he shared that he wanted to be a famous author one day. Until his work could be legally circulated – which, as described below, did not occur until decades after his death – he could not publish a book or indeed any other writing.

Themba was not the only one silenced by apartheid legislation. According to Mbulelo Mzamane in his introduction to *Hungry Flames and Other Black South African Short Stories*, Themba was one of 46 writers and social activists banned under the Suppression of Communism Amendment Act of 1965: 'Between 1960 and 1966, the government made a desperate bid to wipe out the literary achievements of the preceding decades. A Government Gazette of 1966 named 46 exiles as "Statutory Communists" – among them Abrahams, Mphahlele, Modisane, Themba, Maimane and La Guma, all of whom could neither be read nor quoted in South Africa.'[1]

The government's attempts to muffle Themba's voice and those of his contemporaries were aimed not only at preventing the spread of their influence to their immediate audiences; the intention was to wipe them from the face of history. While the apartheid state attained some measure of success in terms of silencing and frustrating Themba during his lifetime, they could not suppress his legacy: since his death, he has continued to rise like a phoenix.

A novice to the South African literary and journalism landscapes might understandably wonder why a man who died far from home, without ever publishing a book, is part of the national memory more than fifty years after his death.

The question of the extent of Themba's artistic contribution further prompts investigation of the understanding of memory and the notions of 're-membering' and 'reconstruction'. In his book *Re-Membering the Black Atlantic: On the Poetics and Politics of Literary Memory*, Lars Eckstein describes the importance of literature in telling a people's history – not just its role in preserving knowledge, but its capacity to do so. In his introduction, he makes a bold statement: 'Literature must also be reckoned as a special form of cultural memory in itself.'[2]

This also presents history as more than a series of dates and facts, but as a crucible in which we endeavour to measure human progress. In his book *Zones of Re-membering: Time, Memory and (un)-Consciousness*, Don Gifford argues, 'Our individual and collective memory is stored in the arts.'[3] The arts, particularly literature, are one of the most efficient vehicles for preserving memory and transmitting it from generation to generation. From this, we are able to construct the notion of 're-membering', reconnecting what has been dis-membered, as opposed to merely remembering as a form of retrieving information from the crevices of memory. This notion of re-membering speaks to the process of putting together fragments of memory to make a composite whole, reassembling dispersed particles of a singular object. In this case, our object is Can Themba.

Literary art and journalism are the media that Themba chose as his form of self-expression. It is the resilience of these two mediums that has ensured that he remains a significant part of our collective and national memory. He did not only write about his country and the events of the day; in many ways Themba chronicled his own life story through the poems, short stories and articles he published. His personal story can be sifted out not only from his own writings, but also from writings by others about him and his era.

Here it must be noted that memory is not always consistent and reliable. Not only are there lapses in memory; as a story is told, it also has the potential to travel, assume different interpretations, shapes and forms, and diverge into something completely different from its original version. The epistemology of re-membering is premised on the view that memory is susceptible to loss or diversion. It concedes that vital elements of a story can be dis-membered. We have already seen in earlier chapters how Themba's identity was reinterpreted or recast according to who was documenting his life, the particular moment or context in history, and the availability of the full facts. And as discussed below, even a fact as concrete as the year of Themba's death was muddled by various sources.

Themba's early demise did not only end his life, it also rendered fragments of his story dispersed, missing or distorted. The evolution of Can Themba's name as a writer and artist took the form of a gradual reconstruction, a re-membering of fragments of history – a reassembling of a dis-membered tale into a composite whole.

The first significant moment of reconstruction after his passing came at the occasion of his funeral, held at St Joseph's Catholic Mission School in Umzimpofu, outside Manzini in the Kingdom of eSwatini. A man who professed to be an atheist, an existentialist, and who was dubbed a romantic nihilist – Can Themba, the boisterous, beloved boozer – was buried like a bishop, becoming the first 'civilian' to be interred in the St Joseph's cemetery.

Retrospectively this baffled even his widow, Anne Themba, who confessed that she never gave much thought to the significance of the burial, along with full Catholic rites. Father Angelo Ciccone of St Joseph's Mission offered to preside, and the family readily agreed. The man of the cloth, an Italian émigré, had struck up a strong friendship with Themba during his last days in Swaziland.

Themba had made plans for his burial, indicating to his wife that she should never mourn him, and that only one speaker should be allowed to eulogise him at the funeral. The writer and scholar G. D. Trevelyan, who attended the funeral even though he did not know much about Themba or his writing, reported the event in his article published in the South African literary journal *Contrast*.[4] Trevelyan described the single eulogist as someone who knew Themba from his days as a high-school student – Trevelyan himself did not know the speaker's name.

According to Trevelyan, the chosen speaker had known Themba since primary school days, and later shared a room with him at boarding school, where Themba sacrificed his own bed for the speaker: 'Can had entered his life as a friend of his brother in primary school, but it was in his first high school year that he really became acquainted with Can. The school they attended was a boarding school and there weren't enough beds. So, as a junior he was allocated a blanket and the floor, until Can allowed him part of his bed. This he had for the rest of the year.'[5]

Given the fact that the speaker knew Themba from a young age, and that he lived in Swaziland at the time of Themba's death, establishing his identity poses an excellent quest for the literary detective.

Mzamane also claimed to have attended his former teacher's funeral. He had received his high-school education in Swaziland, and had benefited from Themba's tutelage during those days. At the time of Themba's death, Mzamane was exiled in the Kingdom of Lesotho, where he was a student at Roma University. Mzamane's recollections of the funeral indicated that the speaker might have been Rosette Ndziba, one of the founders of the Pan Africanist Congress (PAC) in South Africa.

A fellow teacher at the nearby Salesian school in Manzini, Ndziba had intimate knowledge of Themba. Not only had they shared a room in high school, they had both studied at the University of Fort Hare, and both had ended up as teachers exiled in Swaziland. According to Mzamane, speaking at his friend's funeral provided

Ndziba with an opportunity to deride his detractors. Pitika Ntuli, who says Themba and Ndziba used to engage in intellectual debate for hours on end, also confirmed the friendship between Ndziba and Themba: 'He actually liked Rosette Ndziba, who was one of the PAC leading intellectuals who was in Swaziland. When that guy would actually join, you could see kind of sparks of intellect; there will be a bottle here of brandy sitting there untouched because the minds were so actually engaged.'[6]

In our interview, Mzamane told me that Ndziba came from a religious family, his father having been a priest in the Methodist church. By virtue of his religious background, Ndziba was an obvious choice of speaker at occasions such as funerals. Apparently Ndziba's eulogy started innocuously enough, reflecting on the positive traits of the departed friend. He then moved on to the devastation caused by his death, questioning the reasoning and fairness of a god who would take such a good man instead of eliminating the white mercenaries from the South African apartheid government who were killing innocent people.

Ndziba's eulogy had evocations of Themba's widely cited speech at the funeral of Oubaas (used by Lewis Nkosi as an epigraph in his tribute to Themba), where Themba had reportedly said: 'The son of a bitch had no business to die!'[7] Oubaas was a promising scribe and teacher from Sophiatown who had died in a car accident while on a drinking spree with Themba and *Drum* photographer Bob Gosani. Anthony Sampson had this to say: 'Oubaas was killed, Can's face was smashed and Bob lost his lung. It was a fearful reckoning. Can afterwards liked to chant a toast in shebeens to Oubaas with the words "the son of a bitch had no right to lead such a dangerous life".'[8]

Meanwhile, Ndziba's eulogy took yet another turn, addressing matters at hand, which included squaring up with those who had not been too friendly to him and his departed friend. Ndziba presented different options to the Creator, saying if it was not his intention to eliminate the Boers, he could at least have taken some of Themba's detractors, including one W. D. Madikizela and Mokgokong, a colleague of Ndziba's at the Salesian school who had clearly incurred his wrath. (The story goes that Madikizela's crime had been to deny Themba entry into his house in the middle of a rainy night after Themba, a married man whose family was in Mbabane, had arrived in the company of a woman with whom he clearly had an adulterous relationship. This experience had left a sour taste not only in Themba's mouth; his good friend Ndziba had taken umbrage on his behalf.)

One of the greatest ironies about Themba's life is that his burial symbolically marked the beginning of a new life for him. It stands as a metaphor for the reincarnation of the scribe in accordance with the Christian doctrine of resurrection: from his grave, Themba was 'born again', to use the favoured term of charismatic Christianity. Indeed, Themba's name took on a completely new life after his burial; it can be argued that with time he became a more prominent and widely recognised figure in death than he was while he was still alive.

A number of significant initiatives took place following Themba's burial. To begin with, some of the earliest elements of Themba's biography were published a few months after his burial, in the form of Trevelyan's piece in the journal *Contrast.*[9] This piece settles the contentious issue of the year of Themba's death, which until recently fluctuated between 1967 and 1969, depending on which source is referred to. One confusing element regarding Themba's biographical details is that even seemingly authoritative texts like *The World of Can Themba* have published incorrect details; the latter states that the author died in 1968, something disproved by Trevelyan's article, which describes the funeral as taking place in September 1967. To further muddy the waters, an article by Sthembiso Hlongwane of *Drum* magazine, written after a visit to Swaziland in 2013, and which included an extensive interview with Father Ciccone, suggests that Themba died in 1969. This, again, is contradicted by more reliable records that register Themba's passing in 1967.

A year after his passing, *The Classic* literary journal, which he had helped to found, published a tribute edition to Themba in 1968. Since Themba remained a banned person even in death, the tribute edition could not contain any of his works. Instead, it featured eulogies by some of his former colleagues and fellow writers, including Harry Mashabela, Juby Mayet, Casey Motsisi and Stanley Motjuwadi.

Mzamane revealed that it was at the funeral that the idea of publishing Themba's works in a book was first mooted. He had travelled to Swaziland with two academics, professors Roy Holland and Donald Stuart, the latter having taught Themba at the University of Fort Hare. Mzamane informed them about the stacks and stacks of books he had seen on the occasions that he visited Themba in his flat in Manzini. He introduced them to Themba's widow, Anne, which resulted in Themba's stories being collected and compiled into a manuscript. Mzamane meanwhile started teaching Themba's stories to his students even before they were published in book form.

Mzamane tells the story as follows:

> Somebody described Can Themba at one point as maybe the greatest living author who was never published as well. So that kind of thing stuck, and I knew Aunt Anne, his wife, as well, so we decided to go to the funeral but also to find out whether or not we could not pick up some of the pieces and probably anthologise some of the work that had come before. That is how *The Will to Die* actually was conceived and executed.[10]

This process culminated in the publication of Themba's debut collection, *The Will to Die*, five years after his passing, by Heinemann Educational Books in London in 1972. The book was distributed across the world, but could not circulate legally inside South Africa. It nevertheless launched Themba's work into the African literary canon, as the book was published as part of the prestigious African Writers Series, founded by Chinua Achebe in 1962. Themba's stature as a literary figure grew as he was celebrated in parts of the continent where *Drum* magazine was distributed and beyond. In an unrecorded conversation in 2017, the distinguished writer Ngũgĩ wa Thiong'o alluded to the positive influence that Themba and the rest of his colleagues from the *Drum* Decade had on his own literary appreciation.

Meanwhile, in 1982, 15 years after Themba's passing, J. W. Price of David Philip Publishers wrote to the Directorate of Publications in Cape Town to request permission to publish and distribute *The Will to Die* inside South Africa. The application went through stringent government processes with very elaborate deliberations. An equally elaborate assessment was written in Afrikaans, which, in translation, partly reads:

> This work is a collection of some of his short stories as well as certain shorter articles he wrote for the various newspapers. The stories and reports are mainly about conditions in the black neighbourhoods of

> Johannesburg and it is clear that he knew the tsotsi elements and shebeens very well. Of course, Can Themba himself was a person who drank a lot. (See the preface p. ix.) The stories and reports are all of a very good standard. There is really nothing in this book that makes it undesirable.[11]

With this positive recommendation, the government's application acknowledged that 'this publication was previously found to be undesirable by a committee of Publications under the Publications Act, 1974–1977'. It then made the recommendation: 'This publication is not undesirable. The decision was unanimous.'[12] With that, David Philip obtained the rights to republish *The Will to Die*, thus restoring Can Themba's voice, and reconnecting him with readers in his land of birth for the first time in nearly 15 years.

The availability and legal distribution of Themba's works inside South Africa instigated considerable interest in his works. Reprints of *The Will to Die* were followed in 1985 by a more substantial collection of his works, edited by Essop Patel and titled *The World of Can Themba*.[13] The latest and arguably the most comprehensive collection of Themba's works so far was published in 2006, under the title *Requiem for Sophiatown*.[14]

The availability of Themba's collected works in the public domain elevated his status as a major contributor to South Africa's literary architecture. The interest in his literary output has attracted literary criticism that focuses not only on the author's individual contribution, but on the generation of writers to which he belonged, as well as the patterns in our literary growth. In re-membering the fragments of his life and works, a colossus has been reconstructed.

Transcendent Narratives

In considering how the life and works of Can Themba have had to be literally reconstituted, it is worth looking at the fluctuations of the scholarship and critique surrounding his work, especially by his peers.

His works earned him respect among his contemporaries from the moment he first published in *SANC* and *The Fort Harian* as a student at the University of Fort Hare, to his pieces appearing in *Zonk* magazine, to his breakthrough at *Drum* magazine, and then at the *Golden City Post*, *Africa!*, *Africa South* and the other publications in which his works appeared. But beyond the impact of his published works, Themba's contemporaries revered him for his intellectual brilliance.

The disjuncture between Themba's enormous potential as a creative intellectual and his actual output is often remarked upon by his critics. David Rabkin's assertion cited in the Introduction that 'much more has been written about Themba than he has written himself' is both poignant and accurate.[15]

It is probably on the basis of knowing his capabilities that Lewis Nkosi, despite acknowledging Themba's superior intellectual capacity, was dissatisfied with his actual output. In his piece 'Fiction by Black South Africans', Nkosi states that among the black South African writers of the time, Themba stood out for his intellect and language proficiency, but his final literary contribution was minuscule: 'Themba has perhaps the liveliest mind and the best command of the English language; but apart from his recent story published in *Modern African Prose* he has been annoyingly shiftless, throwing off cheap potboilers when magazines demanded them.'[16]

It has already been noted that Nkosi's tribute to Themba claims that Can's achievements are disappointing (compared to Nat Nakasa's) because 'his learning and reading were more substantial and his talent proven'.[17] What is conspicuous by its omission from his first piece ('Fiction by Black South Africans') was an acknowledgement of Themba's writing talent, which he clearly referenced in his homage to the departed scribe.

It should be noted, however, that Nkosi's essay on 'Fiction by Black South Africans' was written in 1965, before Themba's works could be collected and published in book form. While they were colleagues at *Drum* and at *Golden City Post* before Nkosi went into exile in 1961, it is unlikely that the latter managed to follow and read closely all Themba's works in other publications in order to make a conclusive assessment of his literary oeuvre. While Nkosi made a valid point about the meagre nature of Themba's literary contribution, he failed at first to acknowledge the aesthetic value of the little that Themba had published. It could be argued that this is a simple matter of quantity versus quality.

There was also a failure to take into consideration the kind of material published on platforms like *Drum* magazine, the main outlet in which Themba published in the 1950s. *Drum*'s focus was on popular culture, and the majority of the stories they published were indeed of that nature. There is a significant difference both in terms of content and literary aesthetics, for instance, between the stories that Themba published in *Drum* magazine and the ones he published in *The Classic*, a literary journal, as has been pointed out by scholars such as Rob Gaylard.[18] Some of Themba's most revered short stories, including 'The Suit', 'The Urchin' and 'The Dube Train', were published in *The Classic*. The same applies to his colleagues; even though they had their breakthroughs in *Drum*, they did not publish their best stories there. Stories like Bloke Modisane's 'The Dignity of Begging', first published in *Drum*, was later modified; the version that is now circulated is the refined one tailor-made for literary journals.

Moreover, in our 2013 interview, Keorapetse Kgositsile emphasised the importance of considering the context within which Themba wrote. He argued Themba never really had time to sit and focus on writing, a luxury that many might take for granted: 'When you consider that everything you've read by Can Themba was written on the run, so to speak, [or] to beat the deadline, the guy was a genius. I mean, I don't know how really to put it, that where some people have blocks of time devoted to writing, without interference, Can didn't have that.'[19]

Themba's constant 'running' included juggling journalism and teaching work, avoiding the police, skipping the country and trying to publish despite a banning order. This included writing under pseudonyms: Parks Mangena revealed that at times Themba asked to publish stories under his name.

Then there is the mystery of the missing material and the fabled tartan attaché case. With regard to the quantity of Themba's published works, and to account for the material that he supposedly was working on before his untimely death in Swaziland, his widow Anne wrote 'The Wife Remembers' in a special publication prepared for the maiden performance of *The Suit*: 'Can kept scripts in a tartan attaché case which went missing. I had to make do with the odd scripts in my possession, with the remainder collected from *Drum* offices. I am grateful for the joint efforts of Jim Bailey, former *Drum* owner, Professor Donald Stuart and Roy Holland, who pieced together what became *The Will to Die*.'[20]

The Will to Die was published only in 1972, seven years after Nkosi published his first critical essay on Themba. Following the publication of this collection, there is a noticeable transition in Nkosi's opinions about Themba's work, almost certainly as a result of Can's work now being available in book form. In his essay 'The Late Can Themba: An Appreciation', first published in *The Transplanted Heart* in 1975,[21] Nkosi acknowledged Themba's writing talent; it is tempting to speculate that this could have been the result of exposure to a wider range of his former colleague's writing. Nkosi's swift acknowledgement of Themba's creative genius was nevertheless indicative of the growing stature of Themba as a creative intellectual.

Aggrey Klaaste makes an interesting point about Nkosi's fluctuating views about the writings of his South African peers: 'His writing went through various stages. When he started working as an academic in London, he suddenly discovered that black writing in South Africa had no depth, no breadth.'[22] Nkosi was studying literature at Sussex University in the United Kingdom at the time of writing most of his disparaging essays. This pattern was not unique to Nkosi. When Muxe Nkondo wrote his review of Themba's *The Will to Die*, he was pursuing a degree in Modern English Studies at Leeds University.[23] In his advanced age, he also blames his English education for the rigidity of its structural impositions when applied to scholarship on writing.

In his introduction to his book *Hungry Flames and Other Black South African Short Stories*, Mzamane observes: 'Can Themba writes about the underworld life of Sophiatown in a highly evocative manner and with unrivalled authenticity.'[24] This is the sentiment that would later be shared by numerous other critics, including Rabkin in his doctoral thesis, '*Drum* Magazine (1951–1961): And the Works of Black South African Writers Associated with It', when he says: 'What he notes, in his reportage as in his fiction, is the way in which the black people, among whom he lives, cope with the complex and far-flung web of restrictions and definitions imposed upon them. To this task Themba brought a fine ear and eye for the absurd and the idiosyncratic.'[25]

The increased attention that could be paid to Themba's works once *The Will to Die* had been published (and later, unbanned in South Africa) unleashed a whole new era in the appreciation of his works. The citations from Rabkin and Mzamane both show their recognition of Themba's unique contribution to the literary landscape, rather than continuing to lump him together with a coterie of writers as if they were homogeneous.

So far, there are only three published collections of Themba's works (*The Will to Die*, *The World of Can Themba* and *Requiem for Sophiatown*), and many of these publications are duplicative in nature, as the same stories crop up in all three collections, with 'The Suit' being the most reproduced of his pieces. But his stories, articles and poems have been published (and to some extent, scattered) in various journals, magazines and anthologies across the world. A few works are available in archival collections, which include stories that he may have written under known or unknown pen names. For example, 'The Wanton Waif', a story published under the name Morongwa Sereto – a combination of his eldest daughter's first name and her mother's maiden name – is an example of his work that may go unnoticed and unrecognised as part of his literary output.[26]

It is largely due to his ability to straddle the social and intellectual strata that Themba's influence transcends and connects different generations. There is no other South African writer whose short stories have been reimagined through works of creative expression as much as Themba's stories have. From 'The Dube Train Revisited' by Mzamane, based on Themba's 'The Dube Train', to my 'The Suit Continued', Zukiswa Wanner's 'The Dress that Fed the Suit', Makhosazana Xaba's 'Behind The Suit' and 'The Suit Continued: The Other Side', we witness the growing influence of a writer long after his demise.

Although he may not have been aware of the extent of the intergenerational dialogue that Themba would later inspire, Michael Chapman makes a poignant statement about Themba's influence in sustaining intergenerational dialogue: 'By placing Themba, as a writer of the fifties, in infinite dialogue with our own times, we realise something of the nature of his stories as the conditions of a practice. Can Themba's style takes its strength from its epochal delineations; his human and literary pursuit, in its search for identity and purpose in a restrictive socio-political system, constitutes a continuing challenge.'[27]

What is remarkable about this particular statement are not only Chapman's apt observations about the epochal nature of Themba's works, but Themba's own transcendence from the text to his human pursuit. This augurs well for the theoretical approach that undergirds this book, which extends from the text to the biographical detail of the author. In such a scenario, we are able to trace and assemble Themba's nuggets of influence not only in literary circles, but throughout the various provinces of life. Chapman emphasises Themba's epochal resonance as a vital tool in consolidating memory: 'In his attempts to write stories out of the detritus of Sophiatown, his voice resonates, paradoxically, because it is so true to its own milieu. And given our need, variously, for memory, idealisation and dialectical enquiry, we may continue to enter into processes of both identification and exchange with Themba's stories.'[28]

It is perhaps Mzamane who took the most trouble to trace the epistemology of Themba's sustained intergenerational dialogue with contemporary writers beyond the year 2000. In *Words Gone Two Soon*, an anthology that pays homage to two writers who passed away at a relatively young age, Phaswane Mpe (10 September 1970 – 12 December 2004) and K. Sello Duiker (13 April 1974 – 19 January 2005), Mzamane brought together a kaleidoscope of cross-generational South African writers.

In his introduction, Mzamane lauded the significance of the anthology in spearheading intergenerational discourse in South African literature, drawing ontological connections between the works of seasoned writers such as Mazisi Kunene, Keorapetse Kgositsile and Zakes Mda; and the younger generation of Tiisetso Makube, Zachariah Rapola, McQueen Motuba and others. Mzamane further emphasises the importance of the collection in bridging the generation gap.[29]

This injunction comes across as an antidote to the earlier diagnosis Mzamane made in his introduction to *Hungry Flames*, where he bemoaned the apartheid government's deplorable efforts in trying to cut one generation from the next through banishment. Despite all the adversarial forces lined up to disrupt the longevity of Themba's influence, his works seem to have acquired an aura of immortality. The manner in which Themba's writing keeps resurfacing suggests the fulfilment of Nkondo's wistful words: 'We must find a way of televising Can Themba in such a way that he becomes a celebrity, like a football player. He becomes available as part of popular culture without losing his seriousness.'[30]

Postscript: The Three Burials of Can Themba

Can won't die. He won't die. Actually, his writing is breathing life into him all over again.

Mothobi Mutloatse — Interview (2013)

Can Themba has been buried three times since 1967; yet he refuses to die. Each burial gives him a new lease on life, and each new life opens a fresh chapter in scholarship on and appreciation of his work.

The availability of Themba's collected works in book form has enabled thorough engagement with his oeuvre, and restored his place in the annals of South African cultural heritage. His works have not only outlived him, but they continue to hold meaningful value as the decades pass.

The intergenerational dialogue that Themba spearheaded through his works is a clear affirmation of Mothobi Mutloatse's assertion that Can Themba will never die. His writings keep him alive by engaging in a continuous dialogue with different generations, not only of readers, but also of writers and other practitioners in the arts sector who reimagine his works through graphics, stage plays and films.

Over the years, he has received numerous accolades that affirm his remarkable contribution to both the literary and journalistic landscapes. Obviously, it has only been possible to award these posthumously, but they give at least retrospective recognition, thus restoring part of the public memory.

One of the first such accolades Themba received was recognition by the Congress of South African Writers (COSAW) in 1989. COSAW was a national association of writers established in 1987, during the dying days of apartheid. This organisation aligned itself with the liberation struggle, particularly with the ANC as the biggest and oldest liberation movement in South Africa. The ANC and other major political parties were banned at the time, and it was mainly civil movements and cultural structures that kept the revolutionary fires burning at home, often spreading the philosophy and ethos of Black Consciousness.

The Black Consciousness Movement, whose major proponent was Steve Biko, flourished from the early 1970s through to the 1980s. This was the period when all anti-apartheid political organisations were banned, many political activists were detained, imprisoned and murdered, and more still were exiled. The banning of political activity, coupled with the banning of 46 writers under the Suppression of Communism Amendment Act, led to many writers and political activists streaming out of the country, particularly in the 1960s.

In his chapter 'The Impact of Black Consciousness on Culture', Mbulelo Mzamane points out that two of Themba's protégés, Casey Motsisi and Stanley Motjuwadi, served as links that ensured continuity between generations: 'Casey Motsisi and Stanley Motjuwadi, both of whom had emerged towards the end of the Sophiatown renaissance, also bridged the gap between the evolving writers and their exiled predecessors. Both were journalists who provided some degree of continuity with the past … The literary revival of the Black Consciousness era was to a degree made possible through the inspiration and example of these writers.'[1]

In the first instance, what this excerpt from Mzamane illustrates is that even though Themba had long departed by the time of the emergence of the Black Consciousness Movement, he played a catalytic role in its development through his colleagues and mentees, who remained the vital link that connected different generations, particularly the *Drum* generation with the Black Consciousness Movement. The other connection that Mzamane makes here, between a political movement and culture, assumes that it is widely understood that literary activity, particularly in South Africa, was linked to political struggle against apartheid. In his chapter, Mzamane shows how platforms for poetry, theatre and music were used to exhort people into action and, perhaps still more importantly, to take pride in who they were and what they achieved.

The recognition by COSAW of Themba's contribution to public memory was a vital step in the project to restore his reputation. It happened just a month before the then president, P. W. Botha, handed over power to the younger F. W. de Klerk, due to economic pressures as a result of international sanctions against South Africa.

Botha had announced his retirement in April 1989, and De Klerk would announce the unbanning of political parties within the first four months of his rule, thus ending almost three decades of banishment of almost all political activity in South Africa. This is the context within which Themba was recognised by the writers' movement, which made him a pioneering figure in the transitional period from apartheid to democracy. By that time, it was already clear that the political tide was turning, and writers' movements understood the importance of restoring public memory by recognising predecessors such as Themba. Academic and activist Andries Oliphant explained in an article in *New Nation* in August 1989 that naming a library after Themba was 'a tribute to the spirit of the fifties': 'The decision to name the library after Can Themba was motivated by the fact that his work epitomised the spirit of resistance, innovation and wit of his generation. By remembering him, the tradition of resistance dating back to the fifties finds a continuation in present cultural struggles ... The launch of the Can Themba library and the events which accompany it underlined the extraordinary advances and gains made by cultural workers under extremely difficult circumstances.'[2]

The specific mention of Themba's 'resistance' as one of the key elements for which he was recognised is a clear indication of the political inclination of COSAW. The newspaper in which Oliphant published the article, *New Nation,* was a progressive paper that aligned itself with the discourse of liberation. Zwelakhe Sisulu, son of famous liberation struggle stalwarts, Walter and Albertina Sisulu, was one of its senior contributors and later the editor. The motivation given by Oliphant above is similar to that given when then president Thabo Mbeki posthumously bestowed the Order of Ikhamanga on Themba in 2006. The citation recognised him for his 'excellent achievement in literature, contributing to the field of journalism and striving for a just and democratic society in South Africa'.[3] The Order of Ikhamanga remains the highest accolade Themba has received from the government of South Africa to date.

In 2013, on the fiftieth anniversary of the publication of 'The Suit', the Department of Arts and Culture hosted the Can Themba Memorial Lecture to coincide with what would have been his 89th birthday. The occasion was supported by *Drum* magazine, the Centre for the Book (a component of the National Library of South Africa) and the State Theatre. The guest speakers included Nobel laureate and Themba's contemporary, Nadine Gordimer, writer and academic Mbulelo Mzamane, and Joe Thloloe. Gordimer presented a paper, 'Can Themba',[4] while Thloloe and Mzamane engaged in a panel discussion giving insights on the life and times of Themba in a way that had not been publicly done since his funeral in 1967.

In his message for the occasion, the Minister of Arts and Culture, Paul Mashatile, who was unable to attend the event, said Themba was 'a writer of exceptional talent'. Mashatile was represented at the event by his special adviser, Keorapetse Kgositsile, who had known Themba personally. Kgositsile read the minister's speech, which included the following excerpt: 'The icon that we are celebrating this evening is remembered as an eloquent debater, immensely talented writer and a daring journalist ... He distinguished himself from most of his peers with his incisive intellect and a prose style deeply steeped in the nuances and rhythms of life in the township.'

Over the years, in a number of productions that focused on either Sophiatown or the *Drum* era, including books, theatre and films, Themba is always featured as one of the characters, or sometimes certain characters are based on his life. These include the play *Sophiatown* by Malcolm Purkey, *Baby Come Duze*, a play by Mothobi Mutloatse, *Who Killed Mr Drum?* by Sylvester Stein, and *Drum*, a film by Zola Maseko starring Hollywood actor Taye Diggs.

The year 2016 saw increased representation of Themba in theatre. The Market Theatre hosted the adaptation of Themba's short story 'Crepuscule', which was later performed at the 2016 Grahamstown National Arts Festival. The same festival also saw the premiere of *The House of Truth*, the first bioplay based on the life of Themba on 30 June 2016. In September 2018, I convened the first Can Themba Symposium at the Market Theatre in Johannesburg, offering 'a unique opportunity for participants to interrogate Themba's writings, life and legacy'.[5]

In 2010, Can Themba's family quietly disinterred his mortal remains from the St Joseph's cemetery where he had been buried in 1967. This reburial was organised by the family without any fanfare or state involvement. His remains were reburied at the Westpark Cemetery in Johannesburg. His reburial was quite distinct from that of Nat Nakasa's, for instance, whose mortal remains were repatriated from the United States with much fanfare in August 2014. Nathi Mthethwa, the Minister of Arts and Culture, described the objective of returning Nakasa's remains as restoring his dignity and his nationhood. The same can be said about Can Themba's reburial – he would no longer lie in foreign soil. The fiftieth anniversary of his passing solicited a number of tributes across the arts, culture and media fraternities. After her passing in 2014, his wife was buried alongside her husband.

The third burial coincided with the fiftieth anniversary of his death. On Saturday, 30 September 2017, the Department of Arts and Culture, working in close collaboration with his surviving family, hosted the unveiling of his tombstone. This ceremony was the culmination of a number of activities that focused on paying tribute to Themba during the month of September, which is also commemorated as heritage month in South Africa, with 24 September being national Heritage Day. This unveiling marked the third burial of Can Themba. His remains, along with those of his wife, were exhumed and reburied in a different section of the cemetery – Heroes Acre – where he lies next to other South African cultural icons.

These events affirm the view that Can Themba's life is an apparently infinite journey. He keeps reinventing himself, opening new chapters and inspiring new ways of perceiving. This biographical text is part of that journey of rediscovery. While it does not complete his life story – the Can Themba phenomenon refuses that kind of rigidness – my hope is that it marks a significant contribution to our understanding of who Can Themba was, and is.

Notes

Introduction

1 Can Themba, 'The Suit', *The Classic* 1, no. 1 (1963): 6–16. The story of the genesis of *The Classic* is told in Chapter 15.

2 Aggrey Klaaste, 'Can Themba's Work Lives On', *Sowetan*, 26 August 1985, 10.

3 David Rabkin, '*Drum* Magazine (1951–1961): And the Works of Black South African Writers Associated with It' (PhD diss., University of Leeds, 1975).

4 Ursula A. Barnett, *A Vision of Order: A Study of Black South African Literature in English (1914–1980)* (Cape Town: Maskew Miller Longman, 1983), 185.

5 Doc Bikitsha, 'Let the Township Idiom Ring through Their Writings', *Rand Daily Mail*, 27 January 1983, 3.

6 Mcebisi Ndletyana, *African Intellectuals in 19th and Early 20th Century South Africa* (Cape Town: HSRC Press, 2008), 1.

7 Trevor Huddleston, *Naught for Your Comfort* (London: Collins Fontana, 1956), 97.

8 In Michael Chapman, ed., *The Drum Decade: Stories from the 1950s* (Pietermaritzburg: University of Natal Press, 2001 [1989]), 18.

9 Interview, Muxe Nkondo, 2015.

10 *Come Back, Africa,* produced and directed by Lionel Rogosin, Lionel Rogosin Films, 1959.

11 Can Themba, *Requiem for Sophiatown* (Johannesburg: Penguin, 2006), 57.

12 Paul Gready, 'Sophiatown Writers of the Fifties: The Unreal Reality of Their World', *Journal of Southern African Studies* 16, no. 1 (1990): 155.

13 Harry Mashabela, 'Can Remembered', *The Classic* 2, no. 4 (1968): 12.

14 Lindy Stiebel and Michael Chapman, eds., *Writing Home: Lewis Nkosi on South African Writing* (Pietermaritzburg: UKZN Press, 2016), 209.

15 Stiebel and Chapman, eds., *Writing Home*, 163, 205.

16 Lucky Mathebe, 'Ideology and the Crisis of Affiliation and Association in the Professional Life and Career of the Drum School Writer, Can Themba (1924–1968)', *South African Review of Sociology* 47, no. 2 (2016): 78–94, https://doi.org/10.1080/21528586.2016.1147981.

Chapter 1 A Knock on the Door

1 Interview, Pitika Ntuli, 2013.
2 Interview, Mangosuthu Buthelezi, 2015.
3 Essop Patel, ed., *The World of Can Themba: Selected Writings of the Late Can Themba* (Johannesburg: Ravan Press, 1985), 6.
4 Patel, ed., *The World of Can Themba*, 6.
5 Casey Motsisi, 'Can Remembered', *The Classic* 2, no. 4 (1968): 7.
6 Interview, Muxe Nkondo, 2015.
7 Sylvester Stein, *Who Killed Mr Drum?* (London: Corvo Books, 2003 [1999]), 118.
8 Anthony Sampson, *Drum: A Venture into the New Africa* (London: Collins, 1956), 147.
9 Sampson, *Drum*, 150.
10 Jürgen Schadeberg, *The Fifties People of South Africa* (Johannesburg: Bailey's African Photo Archives, 1987), 87.
11 Sampson, *Drum*, 151.
12 Interview, Pitika Ntuli, 2013.
13 Interview, Anne Themba, 2013.
14 Interview, Pitika Ntuli, 2013.
15 Willard Motley, *Knock on Any Door* (New York: Appleton and Co., 1947).
16 Can Themba, *Requiem for Sophiatown* (Johannesburg: Penguin, 2006); Schadeberg, *The Fifties People*, 70.
17 Stein, *Who Killed Mr Drum?*, 250.

Chapter 2 The Poet Laureate of Fort Hare

1 *Zonk*, December 1949, 50.
2 Can Themba, 'Thirst in the Hearts of Men', *SANC Journal* (Summer 1945): 37.
3 Can Themba, 'Dedication', *The Fort Harian*, 1947; Can Themba, 'Revelation', *The Fort Harian*, 1947.
4 University of Fort Hare Archives, Annual Calendar of the South African Native College, 1946.
5 University of Fort Hare Archives, Letter from Can Themba to Mendi Memorial Scholarship Fund, 24 October 1944.

6 University of Fort Hare Archives, Letter from the Registrar to Can Themba, 15 February 1945.
7 Tyrone August, *Dennis Brutus: The South African Years* (Cape Town: HSRC Press, 2020), 57.
8 August, *Dennis Brutus*, 62.
9 University of Fort Hare Archives, Syllabus, Bachelor of Arts, 1945.
10 August, *Dennis Brutus*, 61.
11 Daniel Massey, *Under Protest: The Rise of Student Resistance at the University of Fort Hare* (Pretoria: UNISA Press, 2010), 42.
12 Lewis Nkosi, *Home and Exile and Other Selections* (London: Longman, 1965), 3.
13 Massey, *Under Protest*, 42.
14 Interview, Mangosuthu Buthelezi, 2015.
15 Can Themba and Todd Matshikiza, 'Special Branch Tries to Keep the Lid on Political Change', *Drum*, April 1957.
16 Interview, Mangosuthu Buthelezi, 2015.
17 Interview, Mangosuthu Buthelezi, 2015.
18 Themba, 'Thirst in the Hearts of Men', 37.
19 Can Themba, 'The Ciskeian Maid', *The Fort Harian*, August 1951, 8.
20 August, *Dennis Brutus*, 57.

Chapter 3 The Teacher of Life and Letters

1 Stanley Motjuwadi, 'Can Remembered', *The Classic* 2, no. 4 (1968): 12.
2 Essop Patel, ed., *The World of Can Themba: Selected Writings of the Late Can Themba* (Johannesburg: Ravan Press, 1985), 5.
3 Nelson Mandela, *Long Walk to Freedom* (London: Little, Brown and Company, 1994), 47–48.
4 Patel, ed., *The World of Can Themba*, 4.
5 Casey Motsisi, 'Can Remembered', *The Classic* 2, no. 4 (1968): 7.
6 Patel, ed., *The World of Can Themba*, 206.
7 Patel, ed., *The World of Can Themba*, 208.
8 Mothobi Mutloatse, ed., *Casey & Co: Selected Writings of Casey Motsisi* (Johannesburg: Ravan Press, 1980), vii.
9 Mike Nicol, *A Good-Looking Corpse* (London: Secker & Warburg, 1991), 220.
10 Jürgen Schadeberg, *The Fifties People of South Africa* (Johannesburg: Bailey's African Photo Archives, 1987), 72.
11 Motsisi, 'Can Remembered', 8.
12 Interview, Sol Rachilo, 2015.
13 Interview, Muxe Nkondo, 2013.
14 Interview, Sol Rachilo, 2015.

15 University of Fort Hare Archives, Letter from Can Themba to the Burser, 19 March 1952.
16 University of Fort Hare Archives, Letter from Can Themba to Professor Dent, 25 June 1952.
17 University of Fort Hare Archives, Letter from Can Themba to Fort Hare, 3 February 1953.
18 University of Fort Hare Archives, Letter from Rhodes University to Can Themba, 5 February 1953.
19 University of Fort Hare Archives, Letter from the Registrar to Can Themba, 18 August 1953.
20 'Hendrik Verwoerd: 10 Quotes by Hendrik Verwoerd', *South African History Online*, 20 September 2016, https://www.sahistory.org.za/archive/hendrik-verwoerd-10-quotes-hendrik-verwoerd-politics-web-20-september-2016.
21 Chinua Achebe, *Hopes and Impediments: Selected Essays, 1965–1987* (London: Heinemann, 1988), 96.
22 Can Themba Memorial Lecture, Pretoria State Theatre, 21 June 2013, addressed jointly by Nadine Gordimer, Joe Thloloe and Mbulelo Mzamane.
23 Interview, Lucas Ledwaba, 2015.
24 Interview, Joe Thloloe, 2013.
25 Interview, Juby Mayet, 2015.
26 Interview, Lindiwe Mabuza, 2019.
27 Motsisi, 'Can Remembered', 8.

Chapter 4 From Marabastad to Sophiatown and Beyond

1 J. R. A. Bailey, ed., *The Beat of the Drum: The Story of a Magazine that Documented the Rise of Africa, Vol. 1* (Johannesburg: Ravan Press, 1982), 126.
2 Can Themba, *Requiem for Sophiatown* (Johannesburg: Penguin, 2006), 51.
3 Nelson Mandela, *Long Walk to Freedom* (London: Little, Brown and Company, 1994), 144–142.
4 Mike Nicol, *A Good-Looking Corpse* (London: Secker & Warburg, 1991), 179.
5 Can Themba, *The Will to Die* (Cape Town: David Philip, 1985 [1972]), 46–47.
6 Ezekiel Mphahlele, *Down Second Avenue* (London: Faber & Faber, 1959).
7 Sylvester Stein, *Who Killed Mr Drum?* (London: Corvo Books, 2003 [1999]), 86.
8 Interview, Anne Themba, 2013.

9 He did not complete this degree.
10 Nicol, *A Good-Looking Corpse*, 159.
11 Jürgen Schadeberg, *The Way I See It* (Johannesburg: Picador Africa, 2017), 216.
12 Bailey, ed., *The Beat of the Drum*, 16.
13 Harry Mashabela, 'Can Remembered', *The Classic* 2, no. 4 (1968): 10.
14 Mashabela, 'Can Remembered', 11.
15 It is almost certain that Themba first wrote 'finish and klaar', a quintessentially South African idiom. The cited sources however, were edited abroad, and the ensuing 'correction' may have been responsible for this formulation.

Chapter 5 The *Drum* Seduction

1 Michael Chapman, ed., *The Drum Decade: Stories from the 1950s* (Pietermaritzburg: University of Natal Press, 2001 [1989]), 187.
2 David Rabkin, '*Drum* Magazine (1951–1961): And the Works of Black South African Writers Associated with It' (PhD diss., University of Leeds, 1975), 51.
3 J. R. A. Bailey, ed., *The Beat of the Drum: The Story of a Magazine that Documented the Rise of Africa, Vol. 1* (Johannesburg: Ravan Press, 1982), 15.
4 Bailey, ed., *The Beat of the Drum*, 15.
5 Mike Nicol, *A Good-Looking Corpse* (London: Secker & Warburg, 1991), 159.
6 *Drum*, March 1953.
7 *Drum*, March 1953.
8 Interview, Jürgen Schadeberg, 2018.
9 Bailey, ed., *The Beat of the Drum*, 16.
10 Jürgen Schadeberg, *The Way I See It* (Johannesburg: Picador Africa, 2017), 240.
11 Sylvester Stein, *Who Killed Mr Drum?* (London: Corvo Books, 2003 [1999]), 39, 52.

Chapter 6 Occasions for Loving

1 Aggrey Klaaste, 'The "Tyranny of Time and Place": The Crisis of Black South African Writing of the 1960s', in *African Studies Forum*, ed. Romaine Hill, Marie Muller and Martin Trump (Pretoria: HRSC, 1991), 104.
2 Anthony Sampson, 'Editorial', *Drum*, August 1953.
3 Interview, Anne Themba, 2013.

4 Interview, Anne Themba, 2013.
5 Interview, Anne Themba, 2013.
6 Mike Nicol, *A Good-Looking Corpse* (London: Secker & Warburg, 1991), 179.
7 Interview, Lindiwe Mabuza, 2019.
8 Jürgen Schadeberg, *The Fifties People of South Africa* (Johannesburg: Bailey's African Photo Archives, 1987), 67.
9 Can Themba, 'Dolly and Her Men', *Drum*, January 1957, 37.
10 Schadeberg, *The Fifties People of South Africa*, 67.
11 Essop Patel, ed., *The World of Can Themba: Selected Writings of the Late Can Themba* (Johannesburg: Ravan Press, 1985), 183.
12 Patel, ed., *The World of Can Themba*, 186.
13 Patel, ed., *The World of Can Themba*, 204–205.
14 Can Themba, *Requiem for Sophiatown* (Johannesburg: Penguin, 2006), 51.
15 Juby Mayet, 'Can Remembered', *The Classic* 2, no. 4 (1968): 14.
16 Interview, Juby Mayet, 2015.
17 'Malay' was a term used under the apartheid racial classification system of the time to designate people of mixed-race/slave descent and Muslim practice.
18 Nicol, *A Good-Looking Corpse*, 181.
19 Nicol, *A Good-Looking Corpse*, 181.
20 Nicol, *A Good-Looking Corpse*, 181.
21 Sylvester Stein, *Who Killed Mr Drum?* (London: Corvo Books, 2003 [1999]), 133.
22 Interview, Juby Mayet, 2015.
23 Malcolm Hart, *A Life of Unintended Consequences* (London: H. H. Dervish), 5.
24 Hart, *A Life of Unintended Consequences*, 17.
25 Hart, *A Life of Unintended Consequences*, 38–39.
26 *Drum*, November 1955, 126.
27 Hart, *A Life of Unintended Consequences*, 41.
28 Hart, *A Life of Unintended Consequences*, 58.
29 Hart, *A Life of Unintended Consequences*, 57.
30 Nicol, *A Good-Looking Corpse*, 181.
31 Nicol, *A Good-Looking Corpse*, 181.
32 Hart, *A Life of Unintended Consequences*, 61.

Chapter 7 Drumming up a Storm

1 Jürgen Schadeberg, *The Way I See It* (Johannesburg: Picador Africa, 2017), 170.

2 Bloke Modisane, *Blame Me on History* (Johannesburg: Ad Donker, 1986 [1963]), 190.
3 Sylvester Stein, *Who Killed Mr Drum?* (London: Corvo Books, 2003 [1999]), 89.
4 Modisane, *Blame Me on History*, 199.
5 Can Themba, *The Will to Die* (Cape Town: David Philip, 1985 [1972]), 75.
6 Interview, Peter Magubane, 2014. To '*moer*' is to beat or thrash.
7 Themba, *The Will to Die*, 76.
8 Interview, Jürgen Schadeberg, 2018.
9 Lewis Nkosi, *Home and Exile and Other Selections* (London: Longman, 1965), 10.
10 Can Themba, 'Banned to the Bush', *Drum*, August 1956, 22.
11 Themba, 'Banned to the Bush', 22.
12 Can Themba and Todd Matshikisa, 'A Country Marching into Trouble', *Drum*, April 1957, 23.
13 Themba and Matshikisa, 'A Country Marching into Trouble', 23.
14 Themba and Matshikiza, 'A Country Marching into Trouble', 21.
15 Can Themba, 'World's Longest Walk to Work', *Drum*, March 1957, 28.
16 Themba and Matshikisa, 'A Country Marching into Trouble', 22.
17 Can Themba, 'Treason Arrests', *Drum*, January 1957, 17.
18 Interview, Peter Magubane, 2014.
19 Can Themba, 'Zeerust: The Women's Battle', *Drum*, May 1958, 22–27.
20 Themba, 'Zeerust'.
21 Themba, 'Zeerust'.
22 Themba, 'Zeerust'.
23 Themba, 'Zeerust'.
24 Essop Patel, ed., *The World of Can Themba: Selected Writings of the Late Can Themba* (Johannesburg: Ravan Press, 1985), 160.
25 David B. Coplan, *In Township Tonight: South Africa's Black City Music and Theatre* (Johannesburg: Ravan Press, 1985), 145.
26 Lindy Stiebel and Michael Chapman, eds., *Writing Home: Lewis Nkosi on South African Writing* (Pietermaritzburg: UKZN Press, 2016), 26.
27 Patel, ed., *The World of Can Themba*, 161.
28 Stein, *Who Killed Mr Drum?*, 133.

Chapter 8 Destruction and Demise

1 Sylvester Stein, *Who Killed Mr Drum?* (London: Corvo Books, 2003 [1999]), 250.
2 Lindy Stiebel and Michael Chapman, eds., *Writing Home: Lewis Nkosi on South African Writing* (Pietermaritzburg: UKZN Press, 2016), 23.

3 Stiebel and Chapman, eds., *Writing Home*, 205.
4 Stiebel and Chapman, eds., *Writing Home*, 207.
5 Stein, *Who Killed Mr Drum?*, 73.
6 Stiebel and Chapman, eds., *Writing Home*, 207.
7 Stiebel and Chapman, eds., *Writing Home*, 207.
8 Stein, *Who Killed Mr Drum?*, 74.
9 Mike Nicol, *A Good-Looking Corpse* (London: Secker & Warburg, 1991), 180.
10 Stiebel and Chapman, eds., *Writing Home*, 15–48.
11 Stiebel and Chapman, eds., *Writing Home*, 24.
12 Ryan Brown, *A Native of Nowhere: The Life of Nat Nakasa* (Johannesburg: Jacana Media, 2013).
13 Nicol, *A Good-Looking Corpse*, 352.
14 Nicol, *A Good-Looking Corpse*, 352.
15 Tom Hopkinson, *In the Fiery Continent* (London: Victor Gollancz, 1962), 96.
16 Hopkinson, *In the Fiery Continent*, 96.
17 Can Themba, *The Will to Die* (Cape Town: David Philip, 1985 [1972]), 22.
18 Nicol, *A Good-Looking Corpse*, 257.
19 Stein, *Who Killed Mr Drum?*, 96.
20 Stein, *Who Killed Mr Drum?*, 236.
21 Hopkinson, *In the Fiery Continent*, 63.
22 Hopkinson, *In the Fiery Continent*, 159.
23 Stein, *Who Killed Mr Drum?*, 159.
24 Yvonne Themba, 'Daughters Remember', in 'The Duze Workshop Ensemble Presents *The Suit*', Johannesburg, 1993, 4.
25 Mari Snyman, 'Can Themba: The Life of a Shebeen Intellectual' (Master's thesis, University of Joahnnesburg, 2003).
26 Jürgen Schadeberg, *The Way I See It* (Johannesburg: Picador Africa, 2017), 215.
27 The full transcript of the interview is included as an appendix to her thesis. See Snyman, 'Can Themba', 109–112.
28 Snyman, 'Can Themba', 109.
29 Interview, Jürgen Schadeberg, 2018.
30 Schadeberg, *The Way I See It*, 260.
31 Essop Patel, ed., *The World of Can Themba: Selected Writings of the Late Can Themba* (Johannesburg: Ravan Press, 1985), 164.
32 Can Themba, *Requiem for Sophiatown* (Johannesburg: Penguin, 2006), 161.
33 Themba, *Requiem for Sophiatown*, 155.

34 Brown, *A Native of Nowhere*, 49.
35 Interview, Juby Mayet, 2015.
36 Stiebel and Chapman, eds., *Writing Home*, 26.
37 Stiebel and Chapman, eds., *Writing Home*, 29.
38 Taban Lo Liyong, 'The Influence of *Drum* Magazine on Me since 1952', unpublished paper, 1999.
39 Harry Mashabela, 'Can Remembered', *The Classic* 2, no. 4 (1968): 11.
40 Themba, *Requiem for Sophiatown*, 56–57.
41 Stein, *Who Killed Mr Drum?*, 270.
42 Themba, *Requiem for Sophiatown*, 91.
43 Themba, *Requiem for Sophiatown*, 57.
44 Themba, *Requiem for Sophiatown*, 64.
45 Themba, *Requiem for Sophiatown*, 92.
46 Hopkinson, *In the Fiery Continent*, 90.
47 No further particulars are available as to who 'Butch' was, other than a *Drum* staffer.
48 Hopkinson, *In the Fiery Continent*, 90.
49 Samuel Klagsbrun, 'Self-Destructive Behavior: Slow Dying', in *The Will to Live vs. the Will to Die*, edited by Norman Linzer (New York: Human Sciences Press, 1984), 235.
50 Nicol, *A Good-Looking Corpse*, 181–182.
51 Interview, Keorapetse Kgositsile, 2013.
52 Stiebel and Chapman, eds., *Writing Home*, 34.
53 Themba, *Requiem for Sophiatown*, 53.

Chapter 9 The Road to Swaziland: A Kind of Suicide

1 Can Themba, 'The Man Who Took the Lonely Road to Ghana', *Drum*, June 1960, 59.
2 Can Themba, *Requiem for Sophiatown* (Johannesburg: Penguin, 2006), 54.
3 *Changing World; 7; South African Essay, Part 1: Fruit of Fear*, documentary, 1965, https://americanarchive.org/catalog/cpb-aacip_15-51vdnrj3.
4 Siphiwo Mahala, *The House of Truth* (Pretoria: Iconic Productions, 2017), 57.
5 Anne Themba, 'The Wife Remembers', in 'The Duze Workshop Ensemble Presents *The Suit*', Johannesburg, 1993, 2.
6 Interview, Lindiwe Mabuza, 2019.
7 Themba, *Requiem for Sophiatown*, 161.
8 Can Themba, 'This is Why I Am Not a Communist', *Golden City Post*, 15 May 1955.

9 Sylvester Stein, *Who Killed Mr Drum?* (London: Corvo Books, 2003 [1999]), 250.
10 Stein, *Who Killed Mr Drum?*, 203.
11 Interview, Anne Themba, 2013.
12 Interview, Don Mattera, 2013.
13 Wopko Jensma, *Sing for Our Execution* (Johannesburg: Ravan Press, 1973), 5.
14 Nadine Gordimer, 'Can Themba', Can Themba Memorial Lecture, Pretoria State Theatre, 21 June 2013.

Chapter 10 Black Englishman or Detribalised African? A Quest for Shared Identities

1 Daniel Massey, *Under Protest: The Rise of Student Resistance at the University of Fort Hare* (Pretoria: UNISA Press, 2010), 32.
2 Mark Gevisser, *Thabo Mbeki: The Dream Deferred* (Johannesburg: Jonathan Ball, 2007), 140.
3 Gevisser, *Thabo Mbeki*, 141.
4 This later manifested in the apartheid establishment of the Bantustan or 'homeland' system, which gave nominal independence to specific tribes in certain reserves.
5 Ntongela Masilela, 'The New African Movement: The Early Years', http://pzacad.pitzer.edu/NAM/general/Early%20Years-%20Movement.pdf.
6 Es'kia Mphahlele, *Es'kia* (Cape Town: Kwela Books, 2002), 87.
7 R. R. R. Dhlomo, *An African Tragedy* (Lovedale: Lovedale Institution Press, 1928).
8 Can Themba, *Requiem for Sophiatown* (Johannesburg: Penguin, 2006), 77.
9 Themba, *Requiem for Sophiatown*, 79.
10 In Mbulelo V. Mzamane, ed., *Words Gone Two Soon: A Tribute to Phaswane Mpe and K. Sello Duiker* (Pretoria: Umgangatho Media and Communications, 2005), 212.
11 John S. Mbiti, *African Religions and Philosophy* (Nairobi: East African Educational Publishers, 1969). Cattle were central in the spiritual connection of families and their ancestors. When elders die, a beast is often slaughtered in their honour, and when families want to communicate with their ancestors, sacrifices are performed, usually including the slaughtering of a beast. Cattle also produce milk, which is seen as physical and symbolic food for siblings, not only because they drink milk from the same cattle in a household, but also because they suckle

from the same breasts as infants. So milk (or the cattle) becomes the glue that holds the family together.

12 Can Themba, *The Will to Die* (Cape Town: David Philip, 1985 [1972]), 16.
13 Harry Mashabela, 'Can Remembered', *The Classic* 2, no. 4 (1968): 12.
14 Interview, Simon Maziya, 2017.
15 Interview, Muxe Nkondo, 2015.
16 Can Themba, 'The Ban on Congress', *Drum* East Africa, May 1958, 17.
17 Mike Nicol, *A Good-Looking Corpse* (London: Secker & Warburg, 1991), 179.
18 Can Themba, 'The Ciskeian Maid', *The Fort Harian*, August 1951, 8.
19 Lindy Stiebel and Michael Chapman, eds., *Writing Home: Lewis Nkosi on South African Writing* (Pietermaritzburg: UKZN Press, 2016), 24.
20 Bloke Modisane, *Blame Me on History* (Johannesburg: Ad Donker, 1986 [1963]), 94.
21 Lewis Nkosi, *Home and Exile and Other Selections* (London: Longman, 1965), 32.
22 Zakes Mda, *The Heart of Redness* (Oxford: Oxford University Press, 2000).
23 Michael Chapman, 'Can Themba, Storyteller and Journalist of the 1950s: The Text in Context', *English in Africa* 16, no. 2 (1989): 21.
24 Ryan Brown, *A Native of Nowhere: The Life of Nat Nakasa* (Johannesburg: Jacana Media, 2013).
25 Nicol, *A Good-Looking Corpse*, 292–293.
26 Nicol, *A Good-Looking Corpse*, 292.
27 Modisane, *Blame Me On History*, 96.
28 Modisane, *Blame Me on History*, 158.
29 Tom Hopkinson, *In the Fiery Continent* (London: Victor Gollancz, 1962), 111.
30 Nicol, *A Good-Looking Corpse*, 179.
31 Themba, *Requiem for Sophiatown*, 156–157.
32 Es'kia Mphahlele, 'The Tyranny of Place and Aesthetics', in *Race and Literature*, ed. Charles Malan (Durban: Owen Burgess, 1987), 49.
33 Essop Patel, ed., *The World of Nat Nakasa* (Johannesburg: Ravan Press, 1975), 203.
34 South Africa only attained freedom from the minority apartheid rule that enforced racial discrimination in 1994.
35 Themba, *The Will to Die*, 4.
36 Jürgen Schadeberg, *The Fifties People of South Africa* (Johannesburg: Bailey's African Photo Archives, 1987), 70.
37 *Come Back, Africa,* produced and directed by Lionel Rogosin, Lionel Rogosin Films, 1959.

Chapter 11 A Politico in a Poet

1 Nadine Gordimer, 'The Essential Gesture: Writers and Responsibility', The Tanner Lectures on Human Values, University of Michigan, 12 October 1984, https://tannerlectures.utah.edu/_resources/documents/a-to-z/g/gordimer85.pdf.
2 George Orwell, 'Why I Write', *Gangrel* 4 (Summer 1946), https://www.orwellfoundation.com/the-orwell-foundation/orwell/essays-and-other-works/why-i-write/.
3 Langston Hughes, *An African Treasury: Stories, Poems, Articles and Essays by Black Africans* (New York: Outlet, 1960), ix.
4 Hughes, *An African Treasury*, ix.
5 Michael Chapman, 'Can Themba, Storyteller and Journalist of the 1950s: The Text in Context', *English in Africa* 16, no. 2 (1989): 21.
6 Anthony Sampson, *Drum: A Venture into the New Africa* (London: Collins, 1956), 127.
7 Es'kia Mphahlele, 'Themba: Rebel Par Excellence', *Sowetan*, 1985, 8.
8 Ezekiel Mphahlele, *Down Second Avenue* (London: Faber & Faber, 1959), 178.
9 Bloke Modisane, *Blame Me on History* (Johannesburg: Ad Donker, 1986 [1963]), 139.
10 Presentation at the Grahamstown National Arts Festival, 2007.
11 Chapman, 'Can Themba, Storyteller and Journalist', 28.
12 Paul Gready, 'Sophiatown Writers of the Fifties: The Unreal Reality of Their World', *Journal of Southern African Studies* 16, no. 1 (March 1990): 152–153.
13 Mari Snyman, 'Can Themba: The Life of a Shebeen Intellectual' (Master's thesis, University of Johannesburg, 2003), 78.
14 Can Themba, *Requiem for Sophiatown* (Johannesburg: Penguin, 2006), 59.
15 Lindy Stiebel and Michael Chapman, eds., *Writing Home: Lewis Nkosi on South African Writing* (Pietermaritzburg: UKZN Press, 2016), 34.
16 Can Themba, 'Treason Arrests', *Drum*, January 1957, 19.
17 Snyman, 'Can Themba', 101.
18 Mike Nicol, *A Good-Looking Corpse* (London: Secker & Warburg, 1991), 181.
19 Sampson, *Drum*, 127.
20 Tom Hopkinson, *In the Fiery Continent* (London: Victor Gollancz, 1962), 110.

21 Sylvester Stein, *Who Killed Mr Drum?* (London: Corvo Books, 2003 [1999]).
22 Stiebel and Chapman, eds., *Writing Home*, 34.
23 Can Themba, *The Will to Die* (Cape Town: David Philip, 1985 [1972]), 3.
24 Themba, *The Will to Die*, 112.
25 Themba, *The Will to Die*, 113.
26 Michael Chapman, *The Drum Decade: Stories from the 1950s* (Pietermaritzburg: University of Natal Press, 2001 [1989]), 183.
27 Sam Mathe, 'Theatre: Can Themba: The Man from the House of Truth', *Jazz Life Magazine*, 5 February 2017.
28 Jürgen Schadeberg, *The Way I See It* (Johannesburg: Picador Africa, 2017), 168.
29 Stein, *Who Killed Mr Drum?*, 66.
30 Can Themba, 'This is Why I Am Not a Communist', *Golden City Post*, 15 May 1955, 15.
31 Can Themba, 'I Am Not a Fascist Either', *Golden City Post*, 22 May 1955, 16.
32 Themba, 'I Am Not a Fascist Either', 16.
33 Interview, Keorapetse Kgositsile, 2013.
34 Essop Patel, ed., *The World of Can Themba: Selected Writings of the Late Can Themba* (Johannesburg: Ravan Press, 1985), 167.
35 Hopkinson, *In the Fiery Continent*, 270.
36 *Changing World; 7; South African Essay, Part 1: Fruit of Fear,* documentary, 1965, https://americanarchive.org/catalog/cpb-aacip_15-51vdnrj3.
37 *Changing World; 7; South African Essay, Part 1.*

Chapter 12 The People's Intellectual

1 Toyin Falola, *Nationalism and African Intellectuals* (Rochester, NY: University of Rochester Press, 2001), 16.
2 Antonio Gramsci, *Prison Notebooks, Volume 1* (New York: Columbia University Press, 1992).
3 Sylvester Stein, *Who Killed Mr Drum?* (London: Corvo Books, 2003 [1999]), 86.
4 Stein, *Who Killed Mr Drum?*, 274.
5 Mcebisi Ndletyana, *African Intellectuals in 19th and early 20th Century South Africa* (Cape Town: HSRC Press, 2008), 5.
6 Ndletyana, *African Intellectuals*, 1.
7 Essop Patel, ed., *The World of Can Themba: Selected Writings of the Late Can Themba* (Johannesburg: Ravan Press, 1985), 1.

8 Nadine Gordimer, 'Can Themba', Can Themba Memorial Lecture, Pretoria State Theatre, 21 June 2013.
9 Jürgen Schadeberg, *The Way I See It* (Johannesburg: Picador Africa, 2017), 253.
10 Interview, Don Mattera, 2013; Gordimer, 'Can Themba'.
11 Aggrey Klaaste, 'More Comments about Can Themba', in 'The Duze Workshop Ensemble Presents *The Suit*', Johannesburg, 1993.
12 Gilles Deleuze and Michel Foucault, 'Intellectuals and Power', 1972, https://theanarchistlibrary.org/library/gilles-deleuze-michel-foucault-intellectuals-and-power.
13 Tom Hopkinson, *In the Fiery Continent* (London: Victor Gollancz, 1962), 94.
14 Mari Snyman, 'Can Themba: The Life of a Shebeen Intellectual' (Master's thesis, University of Johannesburg, 2003).
15 Lindy Stiebel and Michael Chapman, eds., *Writing Home: Lewis Nkosi on South African Writing* (Pietermaritzburg: UKZN Press, 2016), 26.
16 Mike Nicol, *A Good-Looking Corpse* (London: Secker & Warburg, 1991), 179.
17 Interview, Keorapetse Kgositsile, 2013.
18 Gordimer, 'Can Themba', as reported by Mpulo, 'Celebrating Can Themba', 90.
19 Patel, ed., *The World of Can Themba*, 164–165.
20 Anthony Sampson, *Drum: A Venture into the New Africa* (London: Collins, 1956), 68.

Chapter 13 No Ordinary Storyteller

1 Es'kia Mphahlele, 'Themba: Rebel Par Excellence', *Sowetan* 1985, 8.
2 Harry Mashabela, 'Can Remembered', *The Classic* 2, no. 4 (1968): 12.
3 G. M. Nkondo, 'Reviews: Posthumous Collection: *The Will to Die*', *The Journal of Commonwealth Literature* 8, no. 1 (1973): 112.
4 Can Themba, *The Will to Die* (Cape Town: David Philip, 1985 [1972]), 3.
5 Themba, *The Will to Die*, 6, 8.
6 Ezekiel Mphahlele, *Down Second Avenue* (London: Faber & Faber, 1959); Bloke Modisane, *Blame Me on History* (Johannesburg: Ad Donker, 1986 [1963]).
7 Bloke Modisane, 'Short Story Writing in Black South Africa', *AMSAC Newsletter*, March 1963, 3.
8 Ezekiel Mphahlele, *The Wanderers* (London: Macmillan, 1971).
9 Lindy Stiebel and Michael Chapman, eds., *Writing Home: Lewis Nkosi on South African Writing* (Pietermaritzburg: UKZN Press, 2016), 73.

10 Can Themba, 'The Man Who Took the Lonely Road to Ghana', *Drum*, June 1960, 69.
11 Can Themba, 'How Different is the North', *Drum*, July 1960, 65.
12 Peggy Rutherford, ed., *Darkness and Light: An Anthology of African Writing* (London: Faith Press, 1958).
13 Can Themba, 'Here It Is at Last', *Drum*, May 1959; also published in Can Themba, *Requiem for Sophiatown* (Johannesburg: Penguin Books, 2006).
14 Themba, *Requiem for Sophiatown*, 44.
15 Ngũgĩ wa Thiong'o, *Decolonising the Mind: The Politics of Language in African Literature* (Nairobi: East African Educational Publishers, 1981).
16 Chinua Achebe, *The Education of a British-Protected Child* (London: Penguin, 2009); Chinua Achebe, *Morning Yet on Creation Day* (London: Heinemann Educational Books, 1975).
17 Achebe, *Morning Yet on Creation Day*, 87.
18 Themba, *Requiem for Sophiatown*, 47.
19 Stiebel and Chapman, eds., *Writing Home*, 49–62.
20 Nadine Gordimer, 'Can Themba', Can Themba Memorial Lecture, Pretoria State Theatre, 21 June 2013.
21 Michael Chapman, 'Can Themba, Storyteller and Journalist of the 1950s: The Text in Context', *English in Africa* 16, no. 2 (1989): 27.
22 Interview, Muxe Nkondo, 2015.
23 T. S. Eliot, *The Sacred Wood: Essays on Poetry and Criticism* (New York: Alfred A. Knopf, 1921), 54.
24 Interview, Muxe Nkondo, 2015.
25 Michael Chapman, ed., *The Drum Decade: Stories from the 1950s* (Pietermaritzburg: University of Natal Press, 2001 [1989]), 209.
26 Nkondo, 'Reviews', 118.
27 Ezekiel Mphahlele, ed., *African Writing Today* (London: Penguin, 1967).
28 Ellis Ayitey Komey and Ezekiel Mphahlele, eds., *Modern African Stories* (London: Faber & Faber, 1964).
29 Essop Patel, 'More Comments about Can Themba', in 'The Duze Workshop Ensemble Presents *The Suit*', Johannesburg, 1993.
30 Patel, 'More Comments'.

Chapter 14 Intertextuality and the Making of Mr Shakespeare

1 Can Themba, *Requiem for Sophiatown* (Johannesburg: Penguin, 2006).
2 Themba, *Requiem for Sophiatown*, 127.

3 Charles Dickens, *A Tale of Two Cities* (London: Chapman and Hall, 1859).
4 Interview, Mbulelo Mzamane, 2013.
5 Can Themba, 'They Counsel', *The Fort Harian*, August 1951.
6 Can Themba, *The Will to Die* (Cape Town: David Philip, 1985 [1972]).
7 Themba, *The Will to Die*, 77.
8 Themba, *Requiem for Sophiatown*, 62.
9 Interview, Keorapetse Kgositsile, 2013.
10 Interview, Anne Themba, 2013.
11 Lindy Stiebel and Michael Chapman, eds., *Writing Home: Lewis Nkosi on South African Writing* (Pietermaritzburg: UKZN Press, 2016), 32.
12 Stiebel and Chapman, eds., *Writing Home*, 41.
13 Casey Motsisi, 'Can Remembered', *The Classic* 2, no. 4 (1968): 8–9.
14 Interview, Abdul Bham, 2020.
15 Themba, *Requiem for Sophiatown*, 131.
16 Themba, *Requiem for Sophiatown*, 2.
17 Themba, *Requiem for Sophiatown*, 2.
18 Themba, *Requiem for Sophiatown*, 6.
19 Themba, *Requiem for Sophiatown*, 6.
20 Themba, *Requiem for Sophiatown*, 9.
21 Themba, *Requiem for Sophiatown*, 16.
22 Themba, *Requiem for Sophiatown*, 24.
23 Interview, Don Mattera, 2013.
24 Natasha Distiller, *South Africa, Shakespeare, and Post-Colonial Culture* (New York: Edwin Mellen Press, 2005), 171.
25 Themba, *Requiem for Sophiatown*, 132.
26 Themba, *Requiem for Sophiatown*, 133.
27 Themba, *Requiem for Sophiatown*, 134.
28 Themba, *Requiem for Sophiatown*, 121.
29 Themba, *Requiem for Sophiatown*, 124.
30 William Shakespeare, *Othello* (New York: Spark Publishing, 2003).
31 Themba, *Requiem for Sophiatown*, 41.
32 Scott L. Newstok, '"Why *Macbeth*?" Looking Back on *Umabatha* after Forty Years: An Interview with Welcome Msomi', *Shakespeare in Southern Africa* 21 (2009): 73–80.
33 Ben Okri, *A Way of Being Free* (London: Head of Zeus, 2014 [1997]), 69.
34 Themba, *The Will to Die*, 5.

Chapter 15 The Suit for All Seasons

1 Nathaniel Nakasa, 'Comment', *The Classic* 1, no. 1 (1963): 4.
2 Harold Bloom, *The Anxiety of Influence: A Theory of Poetry* (New York: Oxford University Press, 1973), xxiv.

3 M. G. Andrew, *The Southern African Short Story Review* (Fouriesburg: QACE, 2002).
4 Mbulelo V. Mzamane, ed., *Words Gone Two Soon: A Tribute to Phaswane Mpe and K. Sello Duiker* (Pretoria: Umgangatho Media and Communications, 2005), xiii.
5 Mbulelo V. Mzamane, *My Cousin Comes to Jo'burg and Other Stories* (London: Longman, 1981).
6 Ellis Ayitey Komey and Ezekiel Mphahlele, eds., *Modern African Stories* (London: Faber & Faber, 1964).
7 Can Themba, *The Will to Die* (Cape Town: David Philip, 1985 [1972]), 40.
8 Dorothy Driver, 'The Fabulous Fifties: Short Fiction in English', in *The Cambridge History of South African Literature*, ed. David Attwell and Derek Attridge (Cambridge: Cambridge University Press, 2012), 405.
9 Wanner's article was later published in Siphiwo Mahala, *African Delights* (Johannesburg: Jacana Media, 2011), 30.
10 Bloke Modisane, 'Short Story Writing in Black South Africa', *AMSAC Newsletter*, March 1963, 3.
11 Mahala, *African Delights*.
12 Siphiwo Mahala, *Red Apple Dreams & Other Stories* (Pretoria: Iconic Productions, 2019).
13 Makhosazana Xaba, *Running and Other Stories* (Cape Town: Modjaji Books, 2013), 155.
14 Xaba, *Running*, 4.
15 Xaba, *Running*, 143.
16 This raises the fascinating question of whether fiction is required to reflect historical fact; in this case, although 'The House of Spirits' can be read as an allusion to the liquor consumed, or the ghosts of Sophiatown, the 'error' jars.
17 Michael Chapman, 'The Fiction Maker: The Short Story in Literary Education', Paper presented at the Association of University English Teachers of Southern Africa conference, 1984, Rand Afrikaans University, 4.
18 Siphiwo Mahala, 'The Changing Topography of Short Story Writing in South Africa', *Imbiza Journal for African Writing* 1, no. 1 (2021): 111.
19 Cheryl Stobie, 'Re-Tailoring Can Themba's "The Suit": Queer Temporalities in Two Stories by Makhosazana Xaba', *Current Writing* 29, no. 2 (2017): 79–88; Julia Sertel, 'Power Relations in "The Suit": Stories of Can Themba and Siphiwo Mahala', 2015, https://www.academia.edu/11257092/Power_Relations_in_The_Suit_Stories_of_Can_Themba_and_Siphiwo_Mahala.
20 Raphael d'Abdon, '"All Futures Are Bred in the Bellies of the Past": Siphiwo Mahala's, Zukiswa Wanner's and Makhosazana Xaba's

Intertextual Dialogues with Can Themba's Short Story "The Suit"', *English in Africa* 46, no. 2 (2019): 30.

21 Chapman, 'The Fiction Maker', 15.
22 Sertel, 'Power Relations in "The Suit"', 4.
23 Stobie, 'Re-Tailoring Can Themba's "The Suit"', 80.
24 Chapman, 'The Fiction Maker', 20.
25 D'Abdon, '"All Futures Are Bred in the Bellies of the Past"', 40.
26 Sertel, 'Power Relations in "The Suit"', 15.
27 Chapman, 'The Fiction Maker', 3.

Chapter 16 Re-Membering the Fragments

1 Mbulelo V. Mzamane, *Hungry Flames and Other Black South African Short Stories* (London: Longman, 1986), xviii.
2 Lars Eckstein, *Re-Membering the Black Atlantic: On the Poetics and Politics of Literary Memory* (Amsterdam: Rodopi, 2006), xiv.
3 Don Gifford, *Zones of Re-membering: Time, Memory, and (un)Consciousness* (Amsterdam: Rodopi, 2011), 14.
4 G. D. Trevelyan, 'At Can Themba's Grave', *Contrast* 5, no. 2 (1968): 26–29.
5 Trevelyan, 'At Can Themba's Grave', 28.
6 Interview, Pitika Ntuli, 2013.
7 Lindy Stiebel and Michael Chapman, eds., *Writing Home: Lewis Nkosi on South African Writing* (Pietermaritzburg: UKZN Press, 2016), 205.
8 Anthony Sampson, *Drum: A Venture into the New Africa* (London: Collins, 1956), 17.
9 Trevelyan, 'At Can Themba's Grave'.
10 Interview, Mbulelo Mzamane, 2013.
11 Directorate of Publications to David Philip Publishers, 'Application for a Decision Review', August 1982.
12 Directorate of Publications, 'Application'.
13 Essop Patel, ed., *The World of Can Themba: Selected Writings of the Late Can Themba* (Johannesburg: Ravan Press, 1985).
14 Can Themba, *Requiem for Sophiatown* (Johannesburg: Penguin Books, 2006).
15 David Rabkin, '*Drum* Magazine (1951–1961): And the Works of Black South African Writers Associated with It' (PhD diss., University of Leeds, 1975), 123.
16 Stiebel and Chapman, eds., *Writing Home*, 60.
17 Stiebel and Chapman, eds., *Writing Home*, 208.

18 Rob Gaylard, 'Writing Black: The South African Short Story by Black Writers' (PhD diss., University of Stellenbosch, 2008).
19 Interview, Keorapetse Kgositsile, 2013.
20 Anne Themba, 'The Wife Remembers', in 'The Duze Workshop Ensemble Presents *The Suit*', Johannesburg, 1993.
21 Lewis Nkosi, *The Transplanted Heart: Essays of South Africa* (Benin City: Ethiope Publishing Corporation, 1975).
22 Aggrey Klaaste, '"The Tyranny of Time and Place": The Crisis of Black South African Writing of the 1960s', in *African Studies Forum*, ed. Romaine Hill, Marie Muller and Martin Trump (Pretoria: HSRC, 1991), 105.
23 G. M. Nkondo, 'Reviews: Posthumous Collection: *The Will to Die*', *The Journal of Commonwealth Literature* 8, no. 1 (1973): 116–118.
24 Mzamane, *Hungry Flames*, xi.
25 Rabkin, '*Drum* Magazine (1951–1961)', 120.
26 Morongwa Sereto [Can Themba], 'The Wanton Waif', *Fighting Talk*, Dec. 1961/Jan. 1962, 16.
27 Michael Chapman, 'Can Themba, Storyteller and Journalist of the 1950s: The Text in Context', *English in Africa* 16, no. 2 (1989): 28.
28 Chapman, 'Can Themba', 26.
29 Mbulelo V. Mzamane, ed., *Words Gone Two Soon: A Tribute to Phaswane Mpe and K. Sello Duiker* (Pretoria: Umgangatho Media and Communications, 2005).
30 Interview, Muxe Nkondo, 22 August 2015.

Postscript: The Three Burials of Can Themba

1 Mbulelo V. Mzamane, 'The Impact of Black Consciousness on Culture', in *Bounds of Possibility: The Legacy of Steve Biko and Black Consciousness*, ed. N. Barney Pityana, Mamphela Ramphele, Malusi Mpumlwana and Lindy Wilson (Cape Town: David Philip, 1991), 182.
2 Andries Oliphant, 'A Tribute to the Spirit of the 50s', *New Nation*, August 1989.
3 Canodoise Daniel Themba (1942–1968)', *The Presidency*, 2006, http://www.thepresidency.gov.za/national-orders/recipient/canodoise-daniel-themba-1942-1968.
4 Nadine Gordimer, 'Can Themba', Can Themba Memorial Lecture, Pretoria State Theatre, 21 June 2013.
5 Can Themba Symposium programme, Market Theatre, New Town, Johannesburg, 13 September 2018.

Bibliography

Primary sources

University of Fort Hare Archives, Letter from Can Themba to Mendi Memorial Scholarship Fund, 24 October 1944.

University of Fort Hare Archives, Letter from the Registrar to Can Themba, 15 February 1945.

University of Fort Hare Archives, Syllabus, Bachelor of Arts, 1945.

University of Fort Hare Archives, Annual Calendar of the South African Native College, 1946.

University of Fort Hare Archives, Letter from Can Themba to the Burser, 19 March 1952.

University of Fort Hare Archives, Letter from Can Themba to Professor Dent, 25 June 1952.

University of Fort Hare Archives, Letter from Can Themba to Fort Hare, 3 February 1953.

University of Fort Hare Archives, Letter from Rhodes University to Can Themba, 5 February 1953.

University of Fort Hare Archives, Letter from the Registrar to Can Themba, 18 August 1953.

Directorate of Publications to David Philip Publishers, 'Application for a Decision Review', August 1982.

Interviews

Abdul Bham, 2020.

Mangosuthu Buthelezi, 2015.

Nadine Gordimer, 2013.

Malcolm Hart, 2020.

Ahmed Kathrada, 2015.

Keorapetse Kgositsile, 2013.

Lucas Ledwaba, 2015.

Lindiwe Mabuza, 2019.

Peter Magubane, 2014.

Parks Mangena, 2017.
Don Mattera, 2013.
Juby Mayet, 2015.
Simon Maziya, 2017.
Mothobi Mutloatse, 2013.
Mbulelo Mzamane, 2013.
Njabulo S. Ndebele, 2013.
Muxe Nkondo, 2013, 2015.
Pitika Ntuli, 2013.
Sol Rachilo, 2015.
Jürgen Schadeberg, 2018.
Anne Themba, 2013.
Joe Thloloe, 2013.

Newspapers and magazines

Bikitsha, Doc. 'Let the Township Idiom Ring through Their Writings'. *Rand Daily Mail*, 27 January 1983.

Klaaste, Aggrey. 'Can Themba's Work Lives On'. *Sowetan*, 26 August 1985.

Mashabela, Harry. 'Can Remembered'. *The Classic* 2, no. 4 (1968): 10–12.

Mathe, Sam. 'Theatre: Can Themba: The Man from the House of Truth'. *Jazz Life Magazine*, 5 February 2017.

Mayet, Juby. 'Can Remembered'. *The Classic* 2, no. 4 (1968): 14–15.

Motjuwadi, Stanley. 'Can Remembered'. *The Classic* 2, no. 4 (1968): 12–14.

Motsisi, Casey. 'Can Remembered'. *The Classic* 2, no. 4 (1968): 7–10.

Mphahlele, Es'kia. 'Themba: Rebel Par Excellence'. *Sowetan*, 1985.

Mpulo, Nontsikelelo. 'Celebrating Can Themba'. *Drum*, 4 July 2013.

Nakasa, Nathaniel. 'Comment'. *The Classic* 1, no. 1, 1963, 4.

Oliphant, Andries. 'A Tribute to the Spirit of the 50s'. *New Nation*, August 1989.

Sampson, Anthony. 'Editorial', *Drum*, August 1953.

Sereto, Morongwa [Can Themba]. 'The Wanton Waif', *Fighting Talk*, Dec. 1961/Jan. 1962, 16.

Themba, Can. 'The Ban on Congress'. *Drum* East Africa, May 1958.

Themba, Can. 'Banned to the Bush'. *Drum*, August 1956.

Themba, Can. 'The Ciskeian Maid'. *The Fort Harian*, August 1951.

Themba, Can. 'Dedication'. *The Fort Harian*, 1947.

Themba, Can, 'Dolly and Her Men'. *Drum*, January 1957.

Themba, Can. 'Here It Is at Last'. *Drum*, May 1959.

Themba, Can. 'How Different is the North'. *Drum*, July 1960.

Themba, Can. 'I Am Not a Fascist Either'. *Golden City Post*, 22 May 1955.

Themba, Can. 'The Man Who Took the Lonely Road to Ghana'. *Drum*, June 1960.

Themba, Can. 'Revelation'. *The Fort Harian*, 1947.

Themba, Can. 'The Suit'. *The Classic* 1, no. 1 (1963): 6–16.

Themba, Can. 'They Counsel'. *The Fort Harian*, August 1951.

Themba, Can. 'This is Why I Am Not a Communist'. *Golden City Post*, 15 May 1955.

Themba, Can. 'Treason Arrests'. *Drum*, January 1957.

Themba, Can. 'World's Longest Walk to Work'. *Drum*, March 1957.

Themba, Can. 'Zeerust: The Women's Battle'. *Drum*, May 1958.

Themba, Can and Todd Matshikiza. 'Special Branch Tries to Keep the Lid on Political Change', *Drum*, April 1957.

Zonk. December 1949.

Films

Changing World; 7; South African Essay, Part 1: Fruit of Fear. Documentary, 1965, https://americanarchive.org/catalog/cpb-aacip_15-51vdnrj3.

Come Back, Africa, Produced and directed by Lionel Rogosin. Lionel Rogosin Films, 1959.

Secondary sources

Achebe, Chinua. *The Education of a British-Protected Child*. London: Penguin, 2009.

Achebe, Chinua. *Hopes and Impediments: Selected Essays, 1965–1987*. London: Heinemann, 1988.

Achebe, Chinua. *Morning Yet on Creation Day*. London: Heinemann Educational Books, 1975.

Achebe, Chinua. *Things Fall Apart*. London: Heinemann, 1958.

Andrew, M. G. *The Southern African Short Story Review*. Fouriesburg: QACE, 2002.

Attridge, Derek and Rosemary Jolly. *Writing South Africa*. Cambridge: Cambridge University Press, 1998.

Attwell, David. *Rewriting Modernity: Studies in Black South African Literary History*. Pietermaritzburg: UKZN Press, 2005.

August, Tyrone. *Dennis Brutus: The South African Years*. Cape Town: HSRC Press.

Bailey, J. R. A., ed. *The Beat of the Drum: The Story of a Magazine that Documented the Rise of Africa, Vol. 1*. Johannesburg: Ravan Press, 1982.

Barnett, Ursula A. *A Vision of Order: A Study of Black South African Literature in English (1914–1980)*. Cape Town: Maskew Miller Longman, 1983.

Bloom, Harold. *The Anatomy of Influence: Literature as a Way of Life*. New Haven: Yale University Press, 2011.

Bloom, Harold. *The Anxiety of Influence: A Theory of Poetry*. New York: Oxford University Press, 1973.

Brown, Ryan. *A Native of Nowhere: The Life of Nat Nakasa*. Johannesburg: Jacana Media, 2013.

'Canodoise Daniel Themba (1942–1968)'. *The Presidency*, 2006. http://www.thepresidency.gov.za/national-orders/recipient/canodoise-daniel-themba-1942-1968.

Chapman, Michael. *Art Talk, Politics Talk*. Pietermaritzburg: UKZN Press, 2006.

Chapman, Michael. 'Can Themba, Storyteller and Journalist of the 1950s: The Text in Context'. *English in Africa* 16, no. 2 (1989): 19–29.

Chapman, Michael, ed. *The Drum Decade: Stories from the 1950s*. Pietermaritzburg: University of Natal Press, 2001 [1989].

Chapman, Michael. 'The Fiction Maker: The Short Story in Literary Education'. Paper presented at the Association of University English Teachers of Southern Africa conference, 1984, Rand Afrikaans University.

Coplan, David B. *In Township Tonight: South Africa's Black City Music and Theatre*. Johannesburg: Ravan Press, 1985.

Creary, Nicholas M., ed. *African Intellectuals and Decolonisation*. Athens, OH: Ohio University Press, 2012.

D'Abdon, Raphael. '"All Futures Are Bred in the Bellies of the Past": Siphiwo Mahala's, Zukiswa Wanner's and Makhosazana Xaba's Intertextual Dialogues with Can Themba's Short Story "The Suit"'. *English in Africa* 46, no. 2 (2019): 25–46.

Deleuze, Gilles and Michel Foucault. 'Intellectuals and Power', 1972. https://theanarchistlibrary.org/library/gilles-deleuze-michel-foucault-intellectuals-and-power.

Dhillon, Pradeep, ed. *Multiple Identities: A Phenomenology of Multicultural Communication*. New York: Peter Lang, 1994.

Dhlomo, R. R. R. *An African Tragedy*. Lovedale: Lovedale Institution Press, 1928.

Dickens, Charles. *A Tale of Two Cities*. London: Chapman and Hall, 1859.

Dikobe, Modikwe. *The Marabi Dance*. London: Heinemann, 1984.

Distiller, Natasha. *South Africa, Shakespeare, and Post-Colonial Culture*. New York: Edwin Mellen Press, 2005.

Driver, Dorothy. 'The Fabulous Fifties: Short Fiction in English'. In *The Cambridge History of South African Literature*, edited by David Attwell and Derek Attridge, 381–409. Cambridge: Cambridge University Press, 2012.

Eckstein, Lars. *Re-Membering the Black Atlantic: On the Poetics and Politics of Literary Memory*. Amsterdam: Rodopi, 2006.

Eliot, T. S. *The Sacred Wood: Essays on Poetry and Criticism*. New York: Alfred A. Knopf, 1921.

Evans, Gwynne Blackmore, ed. *Shakespeare: Aspects of Influence*. Cambridge, MA: Harvard University Press, 1976.

Falola, Toyin. *Nationalism and African Intellectuals*. Rochester, NY: University of Rochester Press, 2001.

Gallagher, Catherine and Stephen Greenblatt. *Practicing New Historicism*. Chicago: University of Chicago Press, 2000.

Gaylard, Rob. 'Writing Black: The South African Short Story by Black Writers'. PhD diss., University of Stellenbosch, 2008.

Gealy, S. 'Biographical and Historical Criticism'. Paper on Literary Theory/ Critical Thinking, 2008–2009.

Gevisser, Mark. *Thabo Mbeki: The Dream Deferred*. Johannesburg: Jonathan Ball, 2007.

Gifford, Don. *Zones of Re-membering: Time, Memory, and (un)Consciousness*. Amsterdam: Rodopi, 2011.

Goodley, Dan, Rebecca Lawthom, Peter Clough and Michele Moore, eds. *Researching Life Stories: Method, Theory and Analysis in a Biographical Age*. London: RoutledgeFalmer, 2004.

Gordimer, Nadine. 'Can Themba'. Can Themba Memorial Lecture, Pretoria State Theatre, 21 June 2013.

Gordimer, Nadine. 'The Essential Gesture: Writers and Responsibility'. The Tanner Lectures on Human Values, University of Michigan, 12 October 1984. https://tannerlectures.utah.edu/_resources/documents/a-to-z/g/gordimer85.pdf.

Gordimer, Nadine. *Occasion for Loving*. London: Virago Press, 1963.

Gramsci, Antonio. *Prison Notebooks, Volume 1*. New York: Columbia University Press, 1992.

Gready, Paul. 'Sophiatown Writers of the Fifties: The Unreal Reality of Their World'. *Journal of Southern African Studies* 16, no. 1 (1990): 139–164.

Guerin, Wilfred L. *A Handbook of Critical Approaches to Literature*, 5th ed. Oxford: Oxford University Press, 2005.

Hachten, William A. and C. Anthony Gifford. *The Press and Apartheid: Repression and Propaganda in South Africa*. Madison, WI: University of Wisconsin Press, 1984.

Hart, Malcolm. *A Life of Unintended Consequences*. London: H. H. Dervish, 2019.

'Hendrik Verwoerd: 10 Quotes by Hendrik Verwoerd'. *South African History Online*, 20 September 2016. https://www.sahistory.org.za/archive/hendrik-verwoerd-10-quotes-hendrik-verwoerd-politics-web-20-september-2016.

Herméren, Göran. *Influence in Art and Literature*. Princeton, NJ: Princeton University Press, 1975.

Hopkinson, Tom. *In the Fiery Continent*. London: Victor Gollancz, 1962.

Huddleston, Trevor. *Naught for Your Comfort*. London: Collins Fontana, 1956.

Hughes, Langston. *An African Treasury: Stories, Poems, Articles and Essays by Black Africans*. New York: Outlet, 1960.

Jensma, Wopko. *Sing for Our Execution*. Johannesburg: Ravan Press, 1973.

Johnson, David. *Shakespeare and South Africa*. London: Clarendon, 1996.

Killam, G. D., ed. *African Writers on African Writing*. London: Heinemann, 1973.

Klaaste, Aggrey. 'More Comments about Can Themba'. In 'The Duze Workshop Ensemble Presents *The Suit*'. Johannesburg, 1993.

Klaaste, Aggrey. 'The "Tyranny of Time and Place": The Crisis of Black South African Writing of the 1960s'. In *African Studies Forum*, edited by Romaine Hill, Marie Muller and Martin Trump, 99–107. Pretoria: HSRC, 1991.

Klagsbrun, Samuel. 'Self-Destructive Behavior: Slow Dying'. In *The Will to Live vs. the Will to Die*, edited by Norman Linzer, 235–237. New York: Human Sciences Press, 1984.

Komey, Ellis Ayitey and Ezekiel Mphahlele, eds. *Modern African Stories*. London: Faber & Faber, 1964.

Lange, Matthew. *Comparative-Historical Methods*. Thousand Oaks, CA: Sage, 2013.

Lo Liyong, Taban. 'The Influence of *Drum* Magazine on Me since 1952'. Unpublished paper, 1999.

Mahala, Siphiwo. *African Delights*. Johannesburg: Jacana Media, 2011.

Mahala, Siphiwo. 'The Changing Topography of Short Story Writing in South Africa'. *Imbiza Journal for African Writing* 1, no. 1 (2021): 110–119.

Mahala, Siphiwo. *The House of Truth*. Pretoria: Iconic Productions, 2017.

Mahala, Siphiwo. *Red Apple Dreams & Other Stories*. Pretoria: Iconic Productions, 2019.

Mandela, Nelson. *Long Walk to Freedom*. London: Little, Brown and Company, 1994.

Manganyi, N. Chabani. *Exiles and Homecomings: A Biography of Es'kia Mphahlele*. Johannesburg: Ravan Press, 1983.

Manus, Vicki Briault. *Emerging Traditions: Toward a Postcolonial Stylistics of Black South African Fiction in English*. Lanham, MD: Lexington Books, 2011.

Masemola, Kgomotso. 'Cultural Memory, Discursive Migrancy and the Aporias of the In/Appropriated "Other": The Diphora of Becoming in Anglophone Black South African Biography (1954–1995)'. PhD diss., University of Sheffield, 2006.

Masilela, Ntongela. 'The New African Movement: The Early Years'. http://pzacad.pitzer.edu/NAM/general/Early%20Years-%20Movement.pdf.

Massey, Daniel. *Under Protest: The Rise of Student Resistance at the University of Fort Hare*. Pretoria: UNISA Press, 2010.

Mathebe, Lucky. 'Ideology and the Crisis of Affiliation and Association in the Professional Life and Career of the Drum School Writer, Can Themba (1924–1968)'. *South African Review of Sociology* 47, no. 2 (2016): 78–94. https://doi.org/10.1080/21528586.2016.1147981.

Matshikiza, Todd. *Chocolates for My Wife*. London: Hodder & Stoughton, 1961.

Mbiti, John S. *African Religions and Philosophy*. Nairobi: East African Educational Publishers, 1969.

Mda, Zakes. *The Heart of Redness*. Oxford: Oxford University Press, 2000.

Mehl, Dieter. *Shakespeare's Tragedies: An Introduction*. Cambridge: Cambridge University Press, 1983.

Merril, Barbara and Linden West. *Using Biographical Methods in Social Research*. Thousand Oaks, CA: Sage, 2009.

Modisane, Bloke. *Blame Me on History*. Johannesburg: Ad Donker, 1986 [1963].

Modisane, Bloke. 'Short Story Writing in Black South Africa'. *AMSAC Newsletter*, March 1963.

Mogoboya, Mphoto Johannes. *African Identity in Es'kia Mphahlele's Autobiographical and Fictional Novels: A Literary Investigation*. Polokwane: University of Limpopo, Turfloop, 2011.

Motley, Willard. *Knock on Any Door*. New York: Appleton and Co., 1947.

Mphahlele, Es'kia. *Es'kia*. Cape Town: Kwela Books, 2002.

Mphahlele, Es'kia. 'The Tyranny of Place and Aesthetics'. In *Race and Literature*, edited by Charles Malan. Durban: Owen Burgess, 1987.

Mphahlele, Ezekiel, ed. *African Writing Today*. London: Penguin, 1967.

Mphahlele, Ezekiel. *Down Second Avenue*. London: Faber & Faber, 1959.

Mphahlele, Ezekiel. *The Wanderers*. London: Macmillan, 1971.

Mutloatse, Mothobi, ed. *Casey & Co: Selected Writings of Casey Motsisi*. Johannesburg: Ravan Press, 1980.

Mzamane, Mbulelo V. 'Cultivating a People's Voice in the Criticism of African Literature'. *Research in African Literatures* 22, no. 4 (1991): 117–133.

Mzamane, Mbulelo V. *Hungry Flames and Other Black South African Short Stories*. London: Longman, 1986.

Mzamane, Mbulelo V. 'The Impact of Black Consciousness on Culture'. In *Bounds of Possibility: The Legacy of Steve Biko and Black Consciousness*, edited by N. Barney Pityana, Mamphela Ramphele, Malusi Mpumlwana and Lindy Wilson, 179–193. Cape Town: David Philip, 1991.

Mzamane, Mbulelo V., ed. *My Cousin Comes to Jo'burg and Other Stories*. London: Longman, 1981.

Mzamane, Mbulelo V. 'The Short Story Tradition in Black South Africa'. *Marang: Journal of Language and Literature* 1, no. 1 (1977). https://www.ajol.info/index.php/marang/article/view/111867.

Mzamane, Mbulelo V., ed. *Words Gone Two Soon: A Tribute to Phaswane Mpe and K. Sello Duiker*. Pretoria: Umgangatho Media and Communications, 2005.

Ndebele, S. Njabulo. *Rediscovery of the Ordinary: Essays on South African Literature and Culture*. Pietermaritzburg: UKZN Press, 2006.

Ndletyana, Mcebisi. *African Intellectuals in 19th and Early 20th Century South Africa*. Cape Town: HSRC Press, 2008.

Newstok, Scott L. '"Why *Macbeth*?" Looking Back on *Umabatha* after Forty Years: An Interview with Welcome Msomi'. *Shakespeare in Southern Africa* 21 (2009): 73–80.

Ngũgĩ wa Thiong'o. *Decolonising the Mind: The Politics of Language in African Literature*. Nairobi: East African Educational Publishers, 1981.

Nicol, Mike. *A Good-Looking Corpse*. London: Secker & Warburg, 1991.

Nkondo, G. M. 'Reviews: Posthumous Collection: *The Will to Die*'. *The Journal of Commonwealth Literature* 8, no. 1 (1973): 116–118.

Nkosi, Lewis. 'Bloke Modisane: Blame Me on History'. In *Writing Home: Lewis Nkosi on South African writing*, edited by Lewis Nkosi, Lindy Stiebel and Michael Chapman, 247–263. Pietermaritzburg: UKZN Press, 2016.

Nkosi, Lewis. *Home and Exile and Other Selections*. London: Longman, 1965.

Nkosi, Lewis. 'The Late Can Themba: An Appreciation'. In *Writing Home: Lewis Nkosi on South African writing*. edited by Lewis Nkosi, Lindy Stiebel and Michael Chapman, 205–209. Pietermaritzburg: UKZN Press, 2016.

Nkosi, Lewis. *Mating Birds*. New York: St Martin's Press, 1983.

Nkosi, Lewis. *The Transplanted Heart: Essays of South Africa*. Benin City: Ethiope Publishing Corporation, 1975.

Okri, Ben. *A Way of Being Free*. London: Head of Zeus, 2014 [1997].

Orwell, George. 'Why I Write'. *Gangrel* 4 (Summer 1946). https://www.orwellfoundation.com/the-orwell-foundation/orwell/essays-and-other-works/why-i-write/.

Osofisan, Femi, ed. *Literature and the Pressures of Freedom: Essays, Speeches and Songs*. Ibadan: Opon Ifa Readers, 2001.

Patel, Essop. 'More Comments about Can Themba'. In 'The Duze Workshop Ensemble Presents *The Suit*'. Johannesburg, 1993.

Patel, Essop, ed. *The World of Can Themba: Selected Writings of the Late Can Themba*. Johannesburg: Ravan Press, 1985.

Patel, Essop, ed. *The World of Nat Nakasa: Selected Writings of the Late Nat Nakasa*. Johannesburg: Ravan Press, 1975.

Rabkin, David. '*Drum* Magazine (1951–1961): And the Works of Black South African Writers Associated with It'. PhD diss., University of Leeds, 1975.

Rutherfoord, Peggy. *Darkness and Light: An Anthology of African Writing*. London: Faith Press, 1958.

Sampson, Anthony. *Drum: A Venture into the New Africa*. London: Collins, 1956.

Schadeberg, Jürgen. *The Fifties People of South Africa*. Johannesburg: Bailey's African Photo Archives, 1987.

Schadeberg, Jürgen. *The Way I See It*. Johannesburg: Picador Africa, 2017.

Searle, Clive, Giampietro Gobo, Jaber F. Gubrium and David Silverman, eds. *Qualitative Research Practice*. Thousand Oaks, CA: Sage, 2004.

Sertel, Julia. 'Power Relations in "The Suit": Stories of Can Themba and Siphiwo Mahala'. 2015. https://www.academia.edu/11257092/Power_Relations_in_The_Suit_Stories_of_Can_Themba_and_Siphiwo_Mahala.

Shakespeare, William. *Othello*. New York: Spark Publishing, 2003.

Snyman, Mari. 'Can Themba: The Life of a Shebeen Intellectual'. Master's thesis, University of Johannesburg, 2003.

Stein, Sylvester. *Who Killed Mr Drum?* London: Corvo Books, 2003 [1999].

Stiebel, Lindy and Michael Chapman, eds. *Writing Home: Lewis Nkosi on South African Writing*. Pietermaritzburg: UKZN Press, 2016.

Stiebel, Lindy and Liz Gunner, eds. *Still Beating the Drum: Critical Perspectives on Lewis Nkosi*. Johannesburg: Wits University Press, 2006.

Stobie, Cheryl. 'Re-Tailoring Can Themba's "The Suit": Queer Temporalities in Two Stories by Makhosazana Xaba'. *Current Writing* 29, no. 2 (2017): 79–88.

Themba, Anne. Can Themba Memorial Lecture, pamphlet. Pretoria State Theatre, 21 June 2013.

Themba, Anne. 'The Wife Remembers'. In 'The Duze Workshop Ensemble Presents *The Suit*'. Johannesburg, 1993.

Themba, Can. *Requiem for Sophiatown*. Johannesburg: Penguin, 2006.

Themba, Can. 'Thirst in the Hearts of Men'. *SANC Journal* (Summer 1945).

Themba, Can. *The Will to Die*. Cape Town: David Philip, 1985 [1972].

Themba, Yvonne. 'Daughters Remember'. In 'The Duze Workshop Ensemble Presents *The Suit*'. Johannesburg, 1993.

Trevelyan, G. D. 'At Can Themba's Grave'. *Contrast* 5, no. 2 (1968): 26–29.

Wald, Alan M. *The Responsibility of Intellectuals: Selected Essays on Marxist Traditions in Cultural Commitment*. Atlantic Heights, NJ: Humanities Press, 1972.

Wrenhaven, Kerry L. *Reconstructing the Slave: The Image of the Slave in Ancient Greece*. London: Bloomsbury, 2012.

Xaba, Makhosazana. *Running and Other Stories*. Cape Town: Modjaji Books, 2013.

Index

Entries are related to the subject of Can Themba unless indicated or obviously otherwise. The word 'plate' indicates photographs.

C

D

Printed and bound by CPI Group (UK) Ltd, Croydon, CR0 4YY

09/06/2025

14685819-0005